Java 6™
New Features

A Tutorial

Budi Kurniawan

Table of Contents

Introduction

Welcome to *Java 6 New* Features: *A Tutorial*.

Java 6, code-named Mustang, is the first Java release for which Sun Microsystems has invited outside developers to contribute code and help fix bugs. (See https://mustang.dev.java.net/collaborate.html). True that the company has in the past accepted contributions from non-employees, like the work of Doug Lea on multithreading, but this is the first time Sun has posted an open invitation. The company admits that they have limited resources, and outside contributors help them cross the finish line sooner.

This didn't make Mustang an open source project, though. Not yet, even though Sun has announced its plan to open source Java in the near future. The one reason Sun regularly cited in the past was the fear of incompatibility. Making Java open sourced, Sun argued, could lead to a situation where there were many different and incompatible versions of Java. A well-known case of this is how Microsoft, then a Java licensee, added Windows-specific features to Java, thus undermining the one feature that Java was best known for: portability.

Open-sourced or not, Java SE 6 is here. It is specified in JSR 270, "Java Standard Edition 6 Release Contents" (http://jcp.org/en/jsr/detail?id=270). Unlike other JSRs, however, JSR 270 does not define specific features. Rather, it acts as an "umbrella" JSR that enumerates features in other JSRs. Here are the "member" JSRs.

- JSR 105, XML Digital-Signature APIs
- JSR 173, Streaming API for XML (StAX)
- JSR 181, Web-Services Metadata
- JSR 199, Java Compiler API
- JSR 202, Java Class-File Specification Update
- JSR 221, JDBC 4.0

- JSR 222, Java Architecture for XML Binding (JAXB) 2.0
- JSR 223, Scripting for the Java Platform
- JSR 224, Java API for XML-Based Web Services (JAX-WS) 2.0
- JSR 250, Common Annotations
- JSR 269, Pluggable Annotation-Processing API

As there are a myriad of big and small changes involved, it is not possible to cover all in a single book. Therefore, I could only attempt to include the most important ones. The section "About This Book" later in this introduction provide more details about this book.

This introduction also provides two other important sections, "Java Naming Convention" and "Those New to Java 5." The first talks briefly about Java history, especially with regard to the naming convention. The second is for those who have decided to skip Java 5 entirely. Admittedly, there are several important Java 5 new features that anyone attempting to upgrade to version 6 is strongly recommended to learn. This section provides necessary references. In addition, the appendixes explain the three most important new features in Java 5: enums, generics, and annotations

Java Naming Convention

Sun Microsystems introduced Java in 1995 and Java—even though it had been a general-purpose language right from the start—was soon well known as the language for writing applets, small programs that run inside web browsers and add interactivity to static web sites. The growth of the Internet had much to contribute to the early success of Java.

Having said that, applets were not the only factor that made Java shine. The other most appealing feature of Java was its platform-independence promise, hence the slogan "Write Once, Run Anywhere." What this means is the very same program you write will run on Windows, Unix, Mac, Linux, and other operating systems. This was something no other programming language could do. At that time, C and C++ were the two most commonly used languages for developing serious applications. Java seemed to have stolen their thunder since its first birthday.

That was Java version 1.0.

In 1997, Java 1.1 was released, adding significant features such as a better event model, Java Beans, and internationalization to the original.

Java 1.2 was launched in December 1998. Three days afterwards, the version number was changed to 2, marking the beginning of a huge marketing campaign that started in 1999 to sell Java as the "next generation" technology. Java 2 was sold in four flavors: the Standard Edition (J2SE), the Enterprise Edition (J2EE), the Micro Edition (J2ME), and Java Card (that never adopted "2" in its brand name).

The next version released in 2000 was 1.3, hence J2SE 1.3. 1.4 came two years later to make J2SE 1.4. J2SE version 1.5 was released in 2004. However, the name Java 2 version 1.5 was then changed to Java 5.

The official name for Mustang, the latest version, is Java Platform, Standard Edition 6. Note that 6 is the product version. The developers still often call it version 1.6, which therefore is the developer version.

Note
See http://www.java.com/en/javahistory/ and http://java.sun.com/features/1998/05/birthday.html for more detail on the history of Java. Java naming is also discussed in the article "Building and Strengthening the Java Brand" that can be found at http://java.sun.com/developer/technicalArticles/JavaOne2005/naming.html. For version 6, also see this link: http://java.sun.com/javase/6/webnotes/version-6.html

Those New to Java 5

This book focuses on Mustang's new features. However, Java 5 introduced many language changes that you should be familiar with to understand the new features in Java 6. One of such Java 5 changes is the enhanced **for**. Others are enums, generics, and annotations.

With the enhanced **for**, you can easily iterate over an array or a collection. Use this syntax to iterate over an array:

```
for (Type variable : arrayName)
```

Where *arrayName* is the reference to the array, *Type* is the component type of the array, and *variable* is a variable that references each component of the array.

For example, the following code iterates over an array of **String**s.

```
String[] names = { "John", "Mary", "Paul" };
for (String name : names) {
    System.out.println(name);
}
```

The code prints the following on the console.

```
John
Mary
Paul
```

To iterate over a **Collection** without the need to call the **iterator** method, you can use this syntax.

```
for (Type identifier : expression) {
    statement(s)
}
```

In which *expression* must be an **Iterable**. Since **Collection** extends **Iterable**, you can use enhanced **for** to iterate over any **Collection**. For example, this code shows how to use **for** to iterate over a collection.

```
for (Object object : myList) {
    System.out.println(object);
}
```

Using **for** to iterate over a collection is a shortcut for using **Iterator**. In fact, the code that uses enhanced **for** above is translated into the following by the compiler.

```
for (Iterator iterator = myList.iterator(); iterator.hasNext(); ) {
    String element = (String) iterator.next();
    System.out.println(element);
}
```

As previously mentioned, other important changes in Java 5 include enums, generics, and annotations. Enums are discussed in Appendix A. Generics are covered in Appendix B and are important because many class and method signatures now show the presence of generics. For example, you need to master generics to understand the **<M>** part after the class name in the signature of **javax.swing.RowSorter**, a new class in Mustang.

```
public abstract class RowSorter<M> extends Object
```

Besides enums and generics, Java 5 introduced annotations and provided a small number of default annotation types. Java 6, however, adds dozens more. Naturally, to understand Mustang's new annotations you need to first know what annotations are. Appendix C, "Annotations" can help you.

About This Book

This section presents the overview of each chapter.

Chapter 1, "Core Libraries" explains the new features in the core libraries, including the new **isEmpty** method in **java.lang.String**, the new methods in **java.io.File** for modifying file attributes and enquiring about hard-disk space, array reallocation, the new types in the Collections Framework, enhancements to the floating point, and password prompting using **java.io.Console**.

Chapter 2, "Dynamic Compilation" shows off the reference implementation for JSR 199, Java Compiler API. Also called the Java Compiler Framework, this new API features classes and interfaces in the **javax.tools** package. Chapter 2 introduces this technology and provides a few examples.

JSR 223, Scripting for the Java Platform enables collaboration between Java and scripting languages. Java 6 comes with a reference implementation that supports JavaScript, however other scripting languages are supported through the Scripting project. Chapter 3, "Scripting" presents the API and teaches how to use them.

Chapter 4, "Networking" explains networking-related features Mustang brings to the table. These includes the APIs to work with client-side cookies and a web server to test your web applications and web services. Plus, Mustang also adds types for working with internationalized domain names, internationalized resource identifiers, and interface addresses.

Chapter 5, "Swing Updates" teaches you the many new features in Swing that Mustang brings in. They range from new Windows and GTK look and feels to better support for Drag and Drop to **JTable** sorting and filtering.

Chapter 6, "Abstract Window Toolkit" explains the new features and improvements Java 6 brings to the AWT, including improved dialog modality, splash screens, system tray support, desktop help, GIF writers, and text antialiasing.

Chapter 7, "Internationalization" discusses the internationalization and localization improvements in Mustang. These include the new supported locales, the Locale Sensitive Services SPI, the new methods in **ResourceBundle**, and the new class **ResourceBundle.Control**.

Chapter 8, "Java Database Connectivity 4.0" provides examples of how to use the new features in JDBC 4.0, including automatic driver loading, ease of development features, support for national character sets, the RowId type, and the **SQLXML** interface. Mustang includes the reference implementation for this latest release of JDBC.

Chapter 9, "XML Digital Signature API" deals with the XML Digital Signature API that defines a standard Java API for digitally signing XML documents. Two major tasks you perform using this API are signing documents and validating XML signatures. This chapter provides two examples that explain how to complete these tasks.

Chapter 10, "Streaming API for XML" discusses the new API for accessing and manipulating XML. Unlike SAX that employs a push technology, the Streaming API for XML (StAX) is based on a pull technology. Therefore, the client of the parser controls the parsing process. There are four main interfaces in this API, all of which are members of the **javax.xml.stream** package: **XMLStreamReader**, **XMLEventReader**, **XMLStreamWriter**, and **XMLEventWriter**. The first two interfaces are used for reading XML documents and the last two for creating or writing ones. This chapter presents examples that use these interfaces.

Chapter 11, "Java Architecture for XML Binding" covers JAXB 2.0, which, unlike JAXB 1.0, supports Java-to-schema binding. Like other chapters, this one begins with the necessary background and guides you through the more important classes and interfaces in the API.

Chapter 12, "Web Services" introduces two web services related technologies, Java API for XML-based Web Services (JAX-WS) 2.0 and Web Services Metadata for the Java Platform. These two APIs make developing Java web services much easier than using JAX RPC 1.0.

The JavaBeans Activation Framework (JAF) has been part of many Java programmers' lives for years, without often given much attention to. A required API in many Java mail applications, JAF is now officially a member of a Java SE. Chapter 13, "JavaBeans Activation Framework" reintroduces this technology and explains what it really is and how it can help you with its services.

Chapter 14, "User-Defined MXBeans" discusses the API for Java Management Extensions (JMX) 1.4. New to this version of JMX are user-defined MXBeans, even though standard MXBeans have actually been part of the Java SE since the Tiger era. This chapter teaches you how to write user-defined MXBeans as well as explains the annotation types **MXBean** and **DescriptorKey**. An introduction to JMX and standard MBeans, sisters of MXBeans, are also given at the beginning of this chapter for those new to the technology.

Chapter 15, "Concurrency Updates" talks about new additions to the Concurrency Utilities. Specifically, it explains the **BlockingDeque** interface and provides an example that shows how the Concurrency Utilities spares you from having to deal with low-level concurrency primitives such as the **wait**, **notify**, and **notifyAll** methods in **java.lang.Object** as well as the **synchronized** and **volatile** keywords. In addition, this chapter covers the new methods in the **TimeUnit** enum and the new constructor in **ConcurrentHashMap**.

Appendix A, "Enums" explains the new type introduced in Java 5. You need to be familiar with this data type as many new enums are introduced in Java 6.

Appendix B, "Generics" presents the most important feature in Java 5 that provides stricter type checking at compile time. This is a must-read if you're new to Java 5 as Java 6 contains types that have been parameterized. This appendix teaches you to use and write generic types.

Appendix C, "Annotations" discusses annotations, a new feature in Java 5. Annotations are used to instruct the Java compiler to do something to the annotated program element. Any program element can be annotated, including Java packages, classes, constructors, fields, methods, parameters, and local variables. This Appendix explains the standard annotation types and taught how to create custom annotation types.

Downloading and Installing Java 6

You can download Java 6 SE (The JRE and the JDK) from
http://java.sun.com/javase/6/. Here are the operating systems supported by:

- Solaris SPARC (versions 8, 9, 10, and 11)
- Solaris x86 (versions 8, 9, 10, and 11)
- Solaris AMD Opteron (x64) (versions 10 and 11)
- Microsoft Windows (2000, Server 2003, XP, and Vista)
- Linux (Red Hat 2.1, 3.0, and 4.0; SuSE 9, 9.1, 9.2, 9.3, or 10, Turbo Linux 10 (only Chinese and Japanese locales. No English), Sun Java Desktop System Release 3)
- Linux AMD64/EM64T (SuSE SLES8, SLES 9, SuSE 9.3, Red Hat 3.0 or 4.0)

Mac users can download Java 6 from http://community.java.net/mac/.

Code Download

The program examples accompanying this book can be downloaded from this URL:

```
http://books.brainysoftware.com/download/jdk6Samples.zip
```

Chapter 1
Core Libraries

Let's start with some easy stuff: the changes and the new features in the **java.lang**, **java.io**, and **java.util** packages. Here are the topics in this chapter.

- The new method in **java.lang.String** for empty string checking
- The new methods in **java.io.File** for finding out hard-disk space and changing file attributes
- Array reallocation
- Some new types in the Collections Framework
- Floating point enhancements and the new methods in **java.lang.Math**.
- Password prompting with **java.io.Console**

Empty String Checking

There is more than one way to find out if a string is empty. When I first learned Java, I used the **equals** method like this:

```
if (myString.equals(""))
```

Later on, I figured out that comparing strings was slower than comparing integers, so I started using the **length** method. That's right, the length of an empty string is zero.

```
if (myString.length() == 0))
```

Java 6 adds yet another way, by introducing the **isEmpty** method in **java.lang.String**. Now, you can use this slightly simpler method:

```
if (myString.isEmpty())
```

Listing 1.1 shows how you can use **isEmpty**.

Listing 1.1: Using isEmpty

```
public class StringDemo {
    public static void main(String[] args) {
        String myString = "";
        if (myString.isEmpty()) {
            System.out.println("Empty");
        } else {
            System.out.println("Not empty");
        }
    }
}
```

One may wonder if **isEmpty** internally called **length**, thus making the whole process a bit slower. To my delight, it does not, as you can see in the following fragment of the **String** class definition.

```
private final int count;
public int length() {
    return count;
}

 public boolean isEmpty() {
    return count == 0;
}
```

String uses a **count** variable to store its length. The **length** method returns this variable, meanwhile **isEmpty** compares **count** with zero. Therefore, there is no way **isEmpty** will be slower than **length**.

File Class Enhancements

The **java.io.File** class in Mustang comes with several long-awaited features. For example, it now provides methods for checking hard disk space and the amount used. It also possesses methods for changing file attributes. Here are the new methods:

```
public long getTotalSpace()
```
    Returns the size, in bytes, of the partition referenced by this **File** object.

```
public long getFreeSpace()
```
    Returns the amount of free space, in bytes, in the partition referenced by this **File** object.

```
public long getUsableSpace()
```
Returns the number of bytes available to this virtual machine on the partition referenced by this **File** object. The difference between **getUsableSpace** and **getFreeSpace** is that the former takes into account restrictions imposed by the operating system, such as write permissions. The latter does not.

```
public boolean setWritable(boolean writable, boolean ownerOnly)
```
Sets the owner's or everybody's write permission for the path referenced by this **File** object.

```
public boolean setWritable(boolean writable)
```
Sets the owner's write permission for the path referenced by this **File** object.

```
public boolean setReadable(boolean readable, boolean ownerOnly)
```
Sets the owner's or everybody's read permission for the path referenced by this **File** object.

```
public boolean setReadable(boolean readable)
```
Sets the owner's read permission for the path referenced by this **File** object.

```
public boolean setExecutable(boolean executable, boolean ownerOnly)
```
Sets the owner's or everybody's execute permission for the path referenced by this File object.

```
public boolean setExecutable(boolean executable)
```
Sets the owner's execute permission for the path referenced by this **File** object.

```
public boolean canExecute()
```
Tests if the application has the right to execute the file referenced by this **File** object.

Pre-Mustang the **File** class had the **canRead** and **canWrite** methods. Java 6 adds **canExecute** plus **setReadable**, **setWritable**, and **setExecutable** methods to change a file's attributes.

The code in Listing 1.2 shows how to use the **getFreeSpace** and **getTotalSpace** methods.

Listing 1.2: Using getFreeSpace and getTotalSpace

```
import java.io.File;
```

```java
public class DiskSpaceDemo {

    public static void main(String[] args) {
        // Creates a File object that references the C drive on a
        // Windows machine
        File file = new File("C:");
        long totalSpace = file.getTotalSpace();
        System.out.println("Total space on " + file + " = "
                + totalSpace + " bytes");

        // Check the free space in C:
        long freeSpace = file.getFreeSpace();
        System.out.println("Free space on " + file + " = "
                + freeSpace + " bytes");
    }
}
```

Running the **DiskSpaceDemo** class in Listing 1.2 on my Windows machine gives me the following result on my console.

```
Total space on C: = 57001189376 bytes
Free space on C: = 7864102912 bytes
```

As a second example, the code in Listing 1.3 creates a file and sets it to read-only.

Listing 1.3: Setting file attributes

```java
import java.io.File;
import java.io.IOException;
public class FileAttributesDemo {

    public static void main(String[] args) throws IOException {
        // Create a new file, by default canWrite=true,
      readonly=false
        File file = new File("test.txt");
        if (file.exists()) {
            file.delete();
        }
        file.createNewFile();
        System.out.println("Before. canWrite? " + file.canWrite());

        // set to read-only, atau canWrite = false */
        file.setWritable(false);
        System.out.println("After. canWrite? " + file.canWrite());
    }
}
```

If you run this example, you'll see this on your console.

```
Before. canWrite? true
After. canWrite? false
```

Array Reallocation

Until Java 5, you could not resize an array. You still cannot with Java 6, but you can make a clone of an array and make the new array have a different size. This is attainable thanks to the new **copyOf** method in **java.util.Arrays** , a class that provides methods for manipulating arrays. The **copyOf** method comes with ten overloads, eight for each type of Java primitives and two for objects. Here are their signatures:

```
public static boolean[] copyOf(boolean[] original, int newLength)

public static byte[] copyOf(byte[] original, int newLength)

public static char[] copyOf(char[] original, int newLength)

public static double[] copyOf(double[] original, int newLength)

public static float[] copyOf(float[] original, int newLength)

public static int[] copyOf(int[] original, int newLength)

public static long[] copyOf(long[] original, int newLength)

public static short[] copyOf(short[] original, int newLength)

public static <T> T[] copyOf(T[] original, int newLength)

public static <T,U> T[] copyOf(U[] original, int newLength,
        java.lang.Class<? extends T[]> newType)
```

Each of these overloads can throw a **java.lang.NullPointerException** if *original* is null and a **java.lang.NegativeArraySizeException** if *newLength* is negative.

The *newLength* argument can be smaller, equal to, or larger than the length of the original array. If it is smaller, then only the first *newLength* elements will be included in the copy. If it is larger, the last few elements will have default values, i.e. 0 if it is an array of integers or **null** if it is an array of objects.

Pay attention to the last overload:

```
public static <T,U> T[] copyOf(U[] original, int newLength,
        java.lang.Class<? extends T[]> newType)
```

This method allows you to upcast each element in the original array to a parent type. For example, you can copy an array of **java.io.BufferedOutpuStream** objects into an array of **java.io.FilterOutputStream** instance, because the former is a subclass of the latter.

Another method similar to **copyOf** that is also added to **Arrays** in Java 6 is **copyOfRange**. **copyOfRange** copies a range of elements to a new array. Like **copyOf**, **copyOfRange** also provides overrides for each Java data type. Here are their signatures:

```
public static boolean[] copyOfRange(boolean[] original,
        int from, int to)
```

```
public static byte[] copyOfRange(byte[] original,
        int from, int to)
```

```
public static char[] copyOfRange(char[] original,
        int from, int to)
```

```
public static double[] copyOfRange(double[] original,
        int from, int to)
```

```
public static float[] copyOfRange(float[] original,
        int from, int to)
```

```
public static int[] copyOfRange(int[] original, int from, int to)
```

```
public static long[] copyOfRange(long[] original, int from, int to)
```

```
public static short[] copyOfRange(short[] original, int from,
        int to)
```

```
public static <T> T[] copyOfRange(T[] original, int from, int to)
```

```
public static <T,U> T[] copyOfRange(U[] original, int from,
        int to, java.lang.Class<? extends T[]> newType)
```

Listing 1.4 shows an example of array reallocation. *data1* is an array of five integers. The code shows how you copy the content of *data1* into a new array *data2* that has enough room for six elements. The code also shows how to use **copyOfRange** to copy a range element to a new array **data3**.

Listing 1.4: Array reallocation example

```
import java.util.Arrays;
public class ArrayReallocationDemo {
```

```
    public static void main(String[] args) {
        int[] data1 = {1, 3, 5, 7, 9};
        printArray(data1);
        int[] data2 = Arrays.copyOf(data1, 6);
        data2[5] = 11;
        printArray(data2);

        int[] data3 = Arrays.copyOfRange(data1, 2, 10);
        printArray(data3);
    }

    // print array elements
    private static void printArray(int[] data) {
        StringBuilder stringBuilder = new StringBuilder( "[" );
        for (int i = 0; i < data.length; i++) {
            stringBuilder.append( data[i] );
            if (i < data.length - 1)
                stringBuilder.append( ", " );
        }
        stringBuilder.append("]");
        System.out.println(stringBuilder);
    }
}
```

Here is the result of running the **ArrayReallocationDemo** class:

```
[1, 3, 5, 7, 9]
[1, 3, 5, 7, 9, 11]
[5, 7, 9, 0, 0, 0, 0, 0]
```

Note
StringBuilder was added to Java 5 to complement **StringBuffer**.
Unlike **StringBuffer**, **StringBuilder** is unsynchronized.

The Collections Framework New Types

The Java Collections Framework (in the **java.util** package) gets some new interfaces in Java 6: **Deque**, **BlockingDeque**, **NavigableMap**, and **NavigableSet**. In addition, there are implementation classes for these interfaces.

Each of the new interfaces is explained in the following subsections.

The Deque Interface

Deque [pronounced "deck"] is short for double-ended queue. As you may know, the **java.util.Queue** interface, added to JDK 1.5, extends **java.util.Collection** by adding methods that support the ordering of elements in a first-in-first-out (FIFO) basis. FIFO means that the element first added will be the first you get when you retrieve an element. This is in contrast to a **List,** which lets you pass an index to its **get** method to select an element to retrieve.

Queue adds the following methods.

- **offer**. This method inserts an element just like the **add** method. However, **offer** should be used if adding an element may fail. This method returns **false** upon failing to add an element and does not throw an exception. On the other hand, a failed insertion using **add** throws an exception.
- **remove**. Removes and returns the element at the head of the **Queue**. If the **Queue** is empty, it returns a **java.util.NoSuchElementException.**
- **poll**. This method is like the **remove** method. However, if the **Queue** is empty it returns **null** and does not throw an exception.
- **element**. Returns but does not remove the head of the **Queue**. If the **Queue** is empty, it throws a **java.util.NoSuchElementException.**
- **peek**. Also returns but does not remove the head of the **Queue**. However, **peek** returns **null** if the **Queue** is empty, instead of throwing an exception.

When you call the **add** or **offer** methods on a **Queue**, the element is always added to the tail of the **Queue**. To retrieve an element, you can use the **remove** or **poll** methods. **remove** and **poll** always remove and return the element at the head of the **Queue**.

For example, the following code creates a **LinkedList** (an implementation of **Queue**) to show the FIFO nature of **Queue**.

```
Queue queue = new LinkedList();
queue.add("one");
queue.add("two");
queue.add("three");
System.out.println(queue.remove());
System.out.println(queue.remove());
System.out.println(queue.remove());
```

The code produces this result:

```
one
two
three
```

This demonstrates that **remove** always removes the element at the head of the **Queue**. In other words, you cannot remove "three" (the third element added to the **Queue**) before removing "one" and "two."

Note

By contrast, the **java.util.Stack** class is a **Collection** that behaves in a last-in-first-out (LIFO) manner.

java.util.Deque is a subinterface of **Queue**. A deque is a queue that supports element insertion and removal at both ends. You can also restrict the maximum number of elements in a **Deque**.

On top of the things mentioned, **Deque** can also be used as a stack. Methods are available for adding, removing, and inspecting elements. Here are some of them.

```
public boolean add(E element)
```
Inserts the specified element to the tail of this deque if it's not full. If this deque is capacity-restricted and is currently full, this method throws an **IllegalStateException**. This method is similar to **addLast**.

```
public void addFirst(E element)
```
Inserts the specified element to the front of this deque if it is not full. If the deque is full, calling this method throws an **IllegalStateException**.

```
public void addLast(E element)
```
Inserts the specified element to the end of this deque if it is not full. If the deque is full, calling this method throws an **IllegalStateException**. This method is similar to **add**.

```
public boolean offerFirst(E element)
```
Inserts the specified element to the end of the deque and returns **true** if this deque is not full. Otherwise, it returns **false**.

```
public boolean offerLast(E element)
```
Inserts the specified element to the end of this queue unless it's full. If the deque is full, it returns **false**.

```
public E removeFirst()
```
Removes the first element and returns the element. If the deque is empty, this method throws a **NoSuchElementException**.

```
public E removeLast()
```
Removes the last element and returns it. If the deque is empty, it throws a **NoSuchElementException**.

```
public E pollFirst()
```
Removes the first element and returns it. If the deque is empty, the method returns **null**.

```
public E pollLast()
```
Removes the last element and returns it. If the deque is empty, it returns **null**.

```
public E getFirst()
```
Retrieves, but does not remove, the first element. If the deque is empty, this method throws a **NoSuchElementException**.

```
public E getLast()
```
Retrieves, but does not remove, the last element. If the deque is empty, it throws a **NoSuchElementException**.

```
public E peekFirst()
```
Retrieves, but does not remove, the first element. If the deque is empty, returns **null**.

```
public E peekLast()
```
Retrieves, but does not remove, the last element. If the deque is empty, it returns **null**.

```
public boolean removeFirstOccurrence(java.lang.Object element)
```
Removes the first occurrence of the specified element. If the specified element can be found, it returns **true**. Otherwise, it returns **false**.

```
public boolean removeLastOccurrence(java.lang.Object element)
```
Removes the last occurrence of the specified element. If the specified element can be found, it returns **true**. Otherwise, it returns **false**.

```
public boolean offer(E element)
```
If the deque is not full, inserts the specified element into the end of the deque and returns **true**. If the deque is full, this method returns **false**.

```
public E remove()
```

Removes the first element in the deque and returns the element. If the deque is empty calling this method throws a **NoSuchElementException**.

`public E poll()`

Removes the first element in this deque and returns the element. If the deque is empty, this method returns **null**.

`public E element()`

Retrieves, but does not remove, the first element in the deque. Calling this method on an empty deque throws a **NoSuchElementException**.

`public E peek()`

Retrieves, but does not remove, the first element in this deque. If the deque is empty, it returns **null**.

`public void push(E element)`

Pushes the specified element onto the beginning of this deque. This method is similar to **addFirst**.

`public E pop()`

Removes and returns the first element of this deque. If this deque is empty, throw a **NoSuchElementException**.

`public boolean remove(java.lang.Object object)`

Removes the first occurrence of the specified element and returns **true**. If the specified element is not found, this method returns **false**.

`public boolean contains(java.lang.Object object)`

Returns **true** if this deque contains the specified element. Otherwise, it returns **false**.

`public int size()`

Returns the number of elements in this deque.

`public Iterator<E> iterator()`

Returns an **iterator** over the elements in this deque.

`public Iterator<E> descendingIterator()`

Returns an iterator over elements in this deque in reverse order.

The **ArrayDeque** class is an implementation of **Deque** that does not impose capacity restriction. It always grows as necessary to support new elements.

You can instantiate this class by using one of its constructors below:

```
public ArrayDeque()
public ArrayDeque(Collection<? extends E> collection)
public ArrayDeque(int initialCapacity)
```

Listing 1.5 shows the **IntegerStack** class that uses **Deque** as a stack.

Listing 1.5: Using Deque as a stack

```java
import java.util.ArrayDeque;
import java.util.Deque;

public class IntegerStack {

    // a stack implemented using Deque
    private Deque<Integer> data = new ArrayDeque<Integer>();

    // inserts an element into the head of the deque
    public void push(Integer element) {
        data.addFirst(element);
    }

    // pops the first element
    public Integer pop() {
        return data.removeFirst();
    }

    // peeks the first element
    public Integer peek() {
        return data.peekFirst();
    }

    public String toString() {
        return data.toString();
    }

    public static void main(String[] args) {
        IntegerStack stack = new IntegerStack();
        // push 5 elements
        for (int i = 0; i < 5; i++) {
            stack.push(i);
        }
        System.out.println("After pushing 5 elements: " + stack);

        // pop 1 element
        int m = stack.pop();
        System.out.println("Popped element = " + m);
```

```
        System.out.println("After popping 1 element  : " + stack);

        // peek 1 element
        int n = stack.peek();
        System.out.println("Peeked element = " + n);
        System.out.println("After peeking 1 element : " + stack);
    }
}
```

Here is the result of running the **IntegerStack** class in Listing 1.5:

```
After pushing 5 elements: [4, 3, 2, 1, 0]
Popped element = 4
After popping 1 element  : [3, 2, 1, 0]
Peeked element = 3
After peeking 1 element : [3, 2, 1, 0]
```

Note

A subinterface of **Deque**, **BlockingDeque** is discussed in Chapter 15, "Concurrency Updates."

The NavigableSet Interface

A **Set** represents a mathematical set. It is a **Collection** that, unlike **List**, does not allow duplicates. There must not be two elements in a **Set**, say **e1** and **e2**, such that **e1.equals(e2)**. The **add** method of **Set** returns **false** if you try to add a duplicate element. For example, this code prints "addition failed."

```
Set set = new HashSet();
set.add("Hello");
if (set.add("Hello")) {
    System.out.println("addition successful");
} else {
    System.out.println("addition failed");
}
```

On the first call to **add**, the string "Hello" was added. The second time around it failed because adding another "Hello" would result in duplicates in the **Set**.

Some implementations of **Set** allow at most one **null** element. Some do not allow **null**s. For instance, **HashSet**, the most popular implementation of **Set**, allows at most one **null** element.

A **SortedSet** is a **Set** that provides a total ordering on its elements, which are ordered using their natural ordering or by using a **Comparator**. The **NavigableSet** interface, in turn, is a subinterface of **SortedSet** that provides methods for searching for elements. **java.util.TreeSet** is an implementation of **NavigableSet**.

Here are the methods in **NavigableSet**.

```
public E lower(E element)
```
Returns the greatest element that is less than the specified element. Returns **null** if such an element does not exist.

```
public E floor(E element)
```
Returns the greatest element that is less than or equal to the specified element. It returns **null** if such an element does not exist.

```
public E higher(E element)
```
Returns the least element that is greater than the specified element. Returns **null** if such an element does not exist.

```
public E ceiling(E element)
```
Returns the least element that is greater than or equal to the specified element. It returns **null** if such an element does not exist.

```
public E pollFirst()
```
Returns and removes the lowest element. If the set is empty, this method returns **null**.

```
public E pollLast()
```
Returns and removes the highest element. If the set is empty, this method returns **null**.

```
public Iterator<E> iterator()
```
Returns an iterator over the elements in this set, in ascending order.

```
public Iterator<E> descendingIterator()
```
Returns an iterator over the elements in this set, in descending order.

```
public NavigableSet<E> descendingSet()
```
Returns a reverse order view of this set. Changes to this set will be reflected in the descending set and vice versa.

```
public SortedSet<E> subSet(E fromElement, E toElement)
```
Returns a view of the portion of this set from *fromElement* (inclusive) to *toElement* (inclusive).

```
public NavigableSet<E> subSet(E fromElement, boolean fromInclusive,
```

```
        E toElement, boolean toInclusive)
```
Returns a view of the portion of this set from *fromElement* to *toElement*.

```
public SortedSet<E> headSet(E toElement)
```
Returns a view of the portion of this set whose elements are less than *toElement*.

```
public NavigableSet<E> headSet(E toElement, boolean inclusive)
```
Returns a view of the portion of this set whose elements are less than (or equal to, if *inclusive* is **true**) *toElement*.

```
public SortedSet<E> tailSet(E fromElement)
```
Returns a view of the portion of this set whose elements are greater than *fromElement*.

```
public NavigableSet<E> tailSet(E fromElement, boolean inclusive)
```
Returns a view of the portion of this set whose elements are greater than (or equal to, in *inclusive* is **true**) *fromElement*.

The **NavigableSetDemo** class in Listing 1.6 demonstrates the power of **NavigableSet** and **TreeSet**.

Listing 1.6: Using NavigableSet

```java
import java.util.Arrays;
import java.util.Iterator;
import java.util.List;
import java.util.NavigableSet;
import java.util.TreeSet;

public class NavigableSetDemo {

    public static void main(String[] args) {

        // create a TreeSet containing 5 integers
        // TreeSet will automatically sort the numbers
        List<Integer> list = Arrays.asList(3, 2, 4, 1, 5);
        NavigableSet<Integer> ns = new TreeSet<Integer>(list);
        System.out.println("Ascending order (default): " + ns);

        // Use its descendingIterator
        Iterator<Integer> descendingIterator =
                descendingIterator();
        StringBuilder sb = new StringBuilder("Descending order: ");
        while (descendingIterator.hasNext()) {
            int m = descendingIterator.next();
```

```
            sb.append(m + " ");
        }
        System.out.println(sb);

        int greatest = ns.lower(3);
        System.out.println("Lower of 3 = " + greatest);

        int smallest = ns.higher(3);
        System.out.println("Higher of 3 = " + smallest);
    }
}
```

If you run this class, you will see the following on your console:

```
Ascending order (default): [1, 2, 3, 4, 5]
Descending order: 5 4 3 2 1
Lower of 3 = 2
Higher of 3 = 4
```

The NavigableMap Interface

You must be familiar with the **java.util.Map** interface, which defines a container for key/value pairs. One of the interfaces that derive from **Map** is **java.util.SortedMap**, which provides total ordering of keys. The **java.util.NavigableMap** interface, a new addition to Java 6, inherits **SortedMap** to add navigation methods that allows for key/value pair searching.

Here are some of the methods in **NavigableMap**.

`public Map.Entry<K, V> ceilingEntry(K key)`

Returns the key/value pair whose key is greater than or equal to the specified key. If more than one key/value pair qualifies, the pair with the least key is return. If there is no such a key, the method returns **null**.

`public K ceilingKey(K key)`

Returns the least key that is greater than or equal to the given key, or **null** if there is no such a key.

`public Map.Entry<K, V> floorEntry(K key)`

Returns the key/value pair whose key is less than or equal to the specified key. If more than one key/value pair qualifies, the pair with the greatest key is return. If there is no such a key, the method returns **null**.

```
public K floorKey(K key)
```
Returns the greatest key that is less than or equal to the given key, or **null** if there is no such a key.

```
public NavigableSet<K> descendingKeySet()
```
Returns a reverse order view of the keys contained in this **Map**.

```
public SortedMap<K, V> headMap(K toKey)
```
Returns a view of the portion whose keys are less than *toKey*.

```
public SortedMap<K, V> tailMap(K fromKey)
```
Returns a view of the portion whose keys are greater than or equal to *fromKey*.

The **java.util.TreeMap** class in Java 6 implements **NavigableMap**. In the example in Listing 1.7 we look at **NavigableMap** in action.

Listing 1.7: Using NavigableMap

```java
import java.util.NavigableMap;
import java.util.TreeMap;
import java.util.Map.Entry;

public class NavigableMapDemo {
    public static void main(String[] args) {

        // Create a TreeMap containing key/value pairs
        NavigableMap<Integer, String> map =
                new TreeMap<Integer, String>();
        map.put(2, "two");
        map.put(1, "one");
        map.put(3, "three");
        System.out.println("Original map: " + map + "\n");

        // take and delete the first entry from the map
        Entry firstEntry = map.pollFirstEntry();
        System.out.println("First entry: " + firstEntry);
        System.out.println("After polling the first entry: " + map +
                "\n");

        // take and delete the last entry
        Entry lastEntry = map.pollLastEntry();
        System.out.println("Last entry: " + lastEntry);
        System.out.println("After polling last entry: " + map);
    }
}
```

Running the code in Listing 1.7 produces this output.

```
Original map: {1=one, 2=two, 3=three}

First entry: 1=one
After polling the first entry: {2=two, 3=three}

Last entry: 3=three
After polling last entry: {2=two}
```

Floating Point Enhancements

The floating point in Java now complies with the IEEE 754 standard. The **java.lang.Math** class in Java 6 has also been enhanced with the following new methods:

```
public static int getExponent(float f)
```
Returns the exponent used in the representation of a float. This method has an overload that accepts a double.

```
public static double copySign(double magnitude, double sign)
```
Returns the first floating-point argument with the sign of the second floating-point argument.

```
public static float copySign(float magnitude, float sign)
```
Returns the first floating-point argument with the sign of the second floating-point argument.

```
public static double nextAfter(double start, double direction)
```
Returns the next double after the first argument in the direction of the second argument. If the first argument is equal to the second one, this method returns the latter.

```
public static double nextUp(double d)
```
Returns the next double after the first argument in the direction of positive infinity, equivalent to but faster than **nextAfter(d, Double.POSITIVE_INFINITY)**.

```
public static double scalb(double d, int scaleFactor)
```
Returns $d \times 2^{scaleFactor}$ rounded as if it were performed by a single correctly rounded floating-point multiply to a member of the double value set.

The example in Listing 1.8 highlights some of the new methods in **Math**.

Listing 1.8: Using Math's new methods

```
public class IEEE754Demo {
    public static void main(String[] args) {

        // Returns 12.0 x (2^3)
        double scalbResult = Math.scalb(12.0, 3);
        System.out.println("Math.scalb(12.0, 3) = " + scalbResult);

        // Returns the unbiased exponent value of a double,
        // where 2^exp <= d. In this case, 2^4 <= 17
        int exp = Math.getExponent(17.0);
        System.out.println("Math.getExponent(17.0) = " + exp);

        // Returns the lesser adjacent of a double
        double lesserAdjacent = Math.nextAfter(123.0, 120.0);
        System.out.println("Math.nextAfter(123.0, 120.0) = " +
                lesserAdjacent);

        // Returns the greater adjacent of a double
        double greaterAdjacent = Math.nextUp(123.0);
        System.out.println("Math.nextUp(123.0) = " +
                greaterAdjacent);

        // Returns a copySign of the first argument
        double d = Math.copySign(1234.56, -1);
        System.out.println("Math.copySign(1234.56, -1) = " + d);
    }
}
```

If you run this class, you will see the following result on your console.

```
Math.scalb(12.0, 3) = 96.0
Math.getExponent(17.0) = 4
Math.nextAfter(123.0, 120.0) = 122.99999999999999
Math.nextUp(123.0) = 123.00000000000001
Math.copySign(1234.56, -1) = -1234.56
```

Password Prompting with java.io.Console

There is a need for a password prompting feature if you don't want everybody with a copy of your Java class file to be able to run it. You could use the Swing

JOptionPane class for this, so Windows users do not have to worry. However, since this only works if Java is running with a GUI system, many Linux/UNIX users do not have this luxury. That's why prior to Java 6, people had to invest in extra effort to achieve this. Some wrote shell scripts and some resorted to JNI.

Java 6 comes with **java.io.Console**, a class that supports password prompting. It encapsulates methods that can access the console device from which the virtual machine was invoked. You can obtain the **Console** object by using the **java.lang.System** class's **console** method. Here is the signature.

```
public static java.io.Console console()
```

Note
The **Console** object will not be available if the virtual machine is started automatically via a background job scheduler.

Here are the methods in the **Console** class:

```
public void flush()
```
Forces any buffered output to be written immediately.

```
public Console format(java.lang.String format,
        java.lang.Object... args)
```
Formats the specified **Object** argument(s) using the specified format and writes to this **Console**.

```
public Console printf(java.lang.String format, java.lang.Object...
        args)
```
Writes a formatted string to this console using the specified format and argument(s).

```
public java.io.Reader reader()
```
Returns the **Reader** object associated with this console.

```
public java.lang.String readLine()
```
Reads a single line of user input text from the console.

```
public java.lang.String readLine(java.lang.String format,
        java.lang.Object... args)
```
Reads the user input from the console and formats it using the specified string and arguments.

```
public char[] readPassword()
```
Reads the user password without echoing the typed in characters.

```
public char[] readPassword(java.lang.String format,
```

```
    java.lang.Object... args)
```
Reads the user password without echoing the typed in characters and formats it using the specified format and arguments.

```
public java.io.PrintWriter writer()
```
Returns the **PrintWriter** object associated with this console.

The format and printf Methods

The **format** method in Console work similarly to the ones in **java.lang.String** and **java.io.PrintStream** classes. Here is its signature.

```
public Console format(String formatString, Object... args)
```

The format pattern must follow the rules specified in the **java.util.Formatter** class and you can read them in the JavaDoc for this class. A brief description of these rules are as follows.

To specify an argument, use the notation **$s**, which denotes the next argument in the array. For example, the following is a method call to the **printf** method.

```
String firstName = "John";
String lastName = "Adams";
console.format("First name: %s. Last name: %s",
        firstName, lastName);
```

This prints the following string to the console:
```
First name: John. Last name: Adams
```

The **printf** method is an alias for **format**. The formatting example described here is only the tip of the iceberg. The formatting feature is much more powerful than that and you are encourage to explore it by reading the Javadoc for the **Formatter** class.

As an example, consider the code in Listing 1.9 that shows how the program prompts the user password. The program will only run if the correct password, in this case **mustang**, is entered.

Listing 1.9: Password prompting demo

```java
import java.io.Console;
import java.util.Arrays;
public class PasswordPromptingDemo {

    public static void main(String[] args) {
        // Obtain reference to the Console object
        Console console = System.console();

        // If Console is not available, exit
        if (console == null) {
            System.out.println("Console is not available");
            System.exit(1);
        }

        // password for this application = "mustang"
        char[] password = "mustang".toCharArray();

        // prompt user's password
        char[] passwordEntered = console.readPassword(
                "Enter password: ");

        // compare
        if (Arrays.equals(password, passwordEntered)) {
            // correct password
            System.out.println("\n  Access granted \n");
            Arrays.fill(password, ' ');
            Arrays.fill(passwordEntered, ' ');
            // Run app
            System.out.println("OK ...");
        } else {
            // incorrect password
            System.out.println("Access denied");
            System.exit(1);
        }
    }
}
```

If you run the class in Listing 1.9, you will be prompted to enter a password. The application will print an "OK" if you enter the correct password.

Summary

In this chapter you've learned the new features and changes in the core libraries, including the new **isEmpty** method in **java.lang.String**, the new methods in **java.io.File** for modifying file attributes and finding out hard-disk space, array reallocation, new types in the Collections Framework, enhancements to the floating point, and password prompting using **java.io.Console**

Chapter 2
Dynamic Compilation

One of the JSR implementations included in Java 6 is that of JSR 199, Java Compiler API (http://jcp.org/en/jsr/detail?id=199). This JSR specifies a set of interfaces that allow Java programs to invoke and run a Java compiler programmatically. An implementation of JSR 199 is also called the Java Compiler Framework, which takes the form of the interfaces and classes in the **javax.tools** package.

This chapter introduces this new technology and shows how to use it.

The Compiler Framework

The Compiler Framework centers around **JavaCompilerTool**, an interface that represents a Java compiler that can be invoked from a Java program. **JavaCompilerTool** employs a file manager to manage Java source files and you can obtain the default file manager using the interface's **getStandardFileManager** method, which returns an instance of **StandardJavaFileManager**. A Java source file is represented by a **JavaFileObject** object.

JavaCompilerTool does not have a method for compiling Java source files directly. Instead, it uses the nested class **CompilationTask**. To compile Java source files, you call the **run** method of **CompilationTask**. You can compile one source file or multiple files at the same time.

Compilation can either succeed or fail. The **getResult** method of **CompilationTask** returns **true** only if all source files were successfully compiled. The **getResult** method does not tell you much, however. If you need more information about the errors or warnings during compilation, you need to use two other types of objects, **Diagnostic** and **DiagnosticCollector**. A **Diagnostic** object can tell you the location of failed compilation and allows you to retrieve any error message. The **DiagnosticCollection** class provides an easy way to return a list of **Diagnostic** objects resulting from a compilation task.

By default, all error messages are output to the **System.err** object. However, if these messages are important, you can create a **javax.tools.DiagnosticListener** object and pass it to the **JavaCompilerTool** object to process the compilation diagnostics.

Some of the members of the **javax.tools** package are explained in the following subsections.

The JavaCompilerTool Interface

An implementation of **JavaCompilerTool** is a tool that encapsulates a Java compiler. The easiest way to get an instance of this interface is by calling the **getSystemJavaCompilerTool** static method of the **ToolProvider** class, also in the **javax.tools** package..

Here are the methods defined in the **JavaCompilerTool** interface.

```
StandardJavaFileManager
        getStandardFileManager(DiagnosticListener<?super
        JavaFileObject> diagnosticListener)
```
Returns a standard file manager for managing Java source files.

```
JavaCompilerTool.CompilationTask getTask(java.io.Writer out,
        JavaFileManager fileManager, DiagnosticListener<? super
        JavaFileObject> diagnosticListener,
        java.lang.Iterable<java.lang.String> options,
        java.lang.Iterable<java.lang.String> classes,
        java.lang.Iterable<? extends JavaFileObject>
        compilationUnits)
```
Returns a **CompilationTask** object whose **run** method can be invoked to start a compilation task.

The JavaCompilerTool.CompilationTask Class

An instance of this nested class represents a compilation task. To complete the task, you call its **run** method. To find out if compilation succeeded, invoke the **getResult** method, which will return **true** if it was successful.

Here are the more important methods in this class:

```
public void run()
```
Completes this compilation task. Only the first call to this method will perform the task. Subsequent calls will have no effect.

```
public boolean getResult()
```
Returns **true** if all source files were compiled without errors. A return value of **false** indicates that one or all the compiled files failed.

The JavaFileObject Interface

The **JavaFileObject** interface is an abstraction of Java file objects. Among others, it defines the **JavaFileObject.Kind** enum, which has the following self-explanatory members: **CLASS**, **HTML**, **OTHER**, and **SOURCE**.

JavaFileObject defines two methods, **getKind** and **isNameCompatible**. Here are the signatures of the methods.

```
public JavaFileObject.Kind getKind()
```
Returns the kind of this file object.

```
public boolean isNameCompatible(java.lang.String name,
    JavaFileObject.Kind kind)
```
Verifies that this file object is compatible with the specified name and kind.

The ToolProvider Class

This class is a utility class that provides two static methods:

```
public static JavaCompilerTool getSystemJavaCompilerTool()
```
Returns a Java compiler provided with this Java platform.

```
public static java.lang.ClassLoader getSystemToolClassLoader()
```
Returns the class loader for tools that are provided by this Java platform.

As you can see in the next example, the **getSystemJavaCompilerTool** method provides the default implementation of the **JavaCompilerTool** interface.

The Dagnostic Interface

A **javax.tools.Diagnostic** object provides a report on a specific compilation problem, normally reporting on the position in a source file that is causing the problem. Types of **Diagnostic** are encapsulated by the **Diagnostic.Kind** enum, which has the following values.

- **ERROR**. Problem that prevents the tool from completing the compilation.
- **WARNING**. Problem that does not prevent the tool from completing the compilation process.
- **MANDATORY_WARNING**. A warning that is mandated by the tool's specification.
- **NOTE**. Informative message.
- **OTHER**. Diagnostic that does not fall into any of the first four kinds.

The following are the more important methods of **Diagnostic**.

```
public Diagnostic.Kind getKind()
```
Returns the kind of this **Diagnostic**. The return value is one of the members of the **Diagnostic.Kind** enum.

```
public S getSource()
```
Return the source object associated with this diagnostic.

```
public long getPosition()
```
Returns the character position in the source object that indicates the location of the problem.

```
public long getColumnNumber()
```
Returns the column number of the character position returned by **getPosition()**.

```
public long getLineNumber()
```
Returns the line number of the problem.

```
public String getMessage(java.util.Locale locale)
```
Returns the localized message for the specified locale.

Using JavaCompilerTool

This example shows how you can compile a Java source from inside a Java program. Listing 2.1 shows a Java class named **HelloWorld** that will be compiled from inside the **JavaCompilerDemo** class in Listing 2.2..

Listing 2.1: HelloWorld class

```
import java.util.Date;
public class HelloWorld {
    public static void main(String[] args) {
        Date date = new Date(1234, 11, 12);
        System.out.println("[" + date + "] Hello World !");
    }
}
```

Listing 2.2: JavaCompilerDemo class

```
import java.io.File;
import java.io.IOException;
import java.util.ArrayList;
import java.util.List;
import javax.tools.JavaCompilerTool;
import javax.tools.JavaFileObject;
import javax.tools.StandardJavaFileManager;
import javax.tools.ToolProvider;
import javax.tools.JavaCompilerTool.CompilationTask;

public class JavaCompilerDemo {

    public static void main(String[] args) {
        // specify the source code, change accordingly
        String sourceFile = "c:/temp/HelloWorld.java";
        JavaCompilerTool compiler =
                ToolProvider.getSystemJavaCompilerTool();
        // get the standard JavaFileManager implementation
        // for this tool
        StandardJavaFileManager fileManager =
                compiler.getStandardFileManager(null);

        // prepare the source file(s) to compile
        List<File> sourceFileList = new ArrayList<File>();
        sourceFileList.add(new File(sourceFile));
        Iterable<? extends JavaFileObject> compilationUnits =
```

```
                fileManager.getJavaFileObjectsFromFiles(
                sourceFileList);
        CompilationTask task = compiler.getTask(null,
                fileManager, null, null, null, compilationUnits);
        task.run();
        boolean result = task.getResult();
        if (result) {
            System.out.println("Compilation was successful");
        } else {
            System.out.println("Compilation failed");
        }
        // our task is completed, now close the file manager
        try {
            fileManager.close();
        } catch (IOException e) {
        }
    }
}
```

The **JavaCompilerDemo** class looks for a **HelloWorld.java** file in **C:\temp**. If your platform is Unix/Linux or Macintosh, replace this directory with a directory of your choice. Provided you have created the **HelloWorld.java** file and saved it in the appropriate directory, you will see the following message on your console upon running the **JavaCompilerDemo** class:

```
Note: c:\temp\HelloWorld.java uses or overrides a deprecated API.
Note: Recompile with -Xlint:deprecation for details.
Compilation successful
```

Now, let's tamper with the **HelloWorld** class in Listing 2.1 by removing the semicolon after this line:

```
Date date = new Date(1234, 11, 12);
```

Then, rerun the **JavaCompilerDemo** class. This time you will see a message that tells you that compilation failed.

```
Compilation failed
c:\temp\HelloWorld.java:4: ';' expected
        Date date = new Date(1234, 11, 12)
1 error
```

Note that you can also pass an **Iterable** of **String**s instead of an **Iterable** of **File**s to the **StandardJavaFileManager** object, by calling its **getJavaFileObjectsFromStrings** method. This is good if you have paths to source files. Using this method you don't need to create **File** objects. For instance, the following code snippet creates compilation units from an **Iterable** of strings.

```
List<String> sourceFiles = new ArrayList<String>();
// sourceFile is the path to the source file
sourceFiles.add(sourceFile);
Iterable<? extends JavaFileObject> compilationUnits =
        fileManager.getJavaFileObjectsFromStrings(
        sourceFiles);
```

Using Diagnostics

The second example of dynamic compilation, the **DiagnosticDemo** class in Listing 2.3, shows how you can use a **Diagnostic** object to obtain a more thorough compilation report.

Listing 2.3: Using Diagnostic

```
import java.io.File;
import java.io.IOException;
import java.util.ArrayList;
import java.util.List;
import javax.tools.Diagnostic;
import javax.tools.DiagnosticCollector;
import javax.tools.JavaCompilerTool;
import javax.tools.JavaFileObject;
import javax.tools.StandardJavaFileManager;
import javax.tools.ToolProvider;
import javax.tools.JavaCompilerTool.CompilationTask;

public class DiagnosticDemo {

    public static void main(String[] args) {
        // specify the source code, change accordingly
        String sourceFile = "c:/temp/HelloWorld.java";
        JavaCompilerTool compiler =
                ToolProvider.getSystemJavaCompilerTool();
        DiagnosticCollector<JavaFileObject> diagnostics =
                new DiagnosticCollector<JavaFileObject>();
        // get the standard JavaFileManager implementation
        // for this tool, passing a DiagnosticCollector
        StandardJavaFileManager fileManager =
```

```
        compiler.getStandardFileManager(diagnostics);

    // prepare the source file(s) to compile
    List<File> sourceFileList = new ArrayList<File>();
    sourceFileList.add(new File(sourceFile));
    Iterable<? extends JavaFileObject> compilationUnits =
            fileManager.getJavaFileObjectsFromFiles(
            sourceFileList);
    CompilationTask task = compiler.getTask(null,
            fileManager, null, null, null, compilationUnits);
    task.run();
    // our task is completed, now close the file manager
    try {
        fileManager.close();
    } catch (IOException e) {
    }
    // let's see what's in diagnostics
    List<Diagnostic<? extends JavaFileObject>>
            diagnosticList = diagnostics.getDiagnostics();
    // iterate diagnosticList
    for (Diagnostic<? extends JavaFileObject> diagnostic :
            diagnosticList) {
        // now you can use diagnostic, such as in
        System.out.println("Position:" +
                diagnostic.getStartPosition());
    }

    }
}
```

One thing to point out here is that a **Diagnostic** object requires you to pass a **DiagnosticCollector** object when calling **JavaCompilerTool.getStandardFileManager**.

```
    DiagnosticCollector<JavaFileObject> diagnostics =
            new DiagnosticCollector<JavaFileObject>();
    // get the standard JavaFileManager implementation
    // for this tool, passing a DiagnosticCollector
    StandardJavaFileManager fileManager =
            compiler.getStandardFileManager(diagnostics);
```

Again, the example works with the **HelloWorld.java** class in the preceding example. Check out the last part of the **DiagnosticDemo** class:

```
    // let's see what's in diagnostics
    List<Diagnostic<? extends JavaFileObject>>
```

```
        diagnosticList = diagnostics.getDiagnostics();
   // iterate diagnosticList
   for (Diagnostic<? extends JavaFileObject> diagnostic :
            diagnosticList) {
      // now you can use diagnostic, such as in
      System.out.println("Position:" +
            diagnostic.getStartPosition());
   }
```

For each compilation error the **DiagnosticDemo** class prints the start
position of the error.

Summary

Mustang provides a reference implementation for JSR 199, Java Compiler API,
which specifies a set of interfaces that make up the Java Compiler Framework.
This new technology allows Java programs to invoke and run a Java compiler
programmatically. You've learned how to use the more important classes and
interfaces in this framework in the two examples presented in this chapter.

Chapter 3
Scripting

JSR 223, Scripting for the Java Platform describes various mechanisms for allowing scripting language programs to access information in the Java platform and permitting scripting language pages to be used in a Java server-side application. The concept of enabling communication between scripts and program objects itself is not new. A notable example is how JavaScript, the scripting language supported by most browsers, can access methods in Java applets or Flash programs. A non-Java example: VBScript that can be used to access ActiveX objects inside Microsoft Office applications.

Note

The JSR 223 documentation can be downloaded from
http://jcp.org/en/jsr/detail?id=223

JSR 223 defines a standard on how to do this kind of communication with multiple script languages. Java 6 provides a script engine based on Rhino, an open source implementation of JavaScript. Rhino is written in Java and can be downloaded from http://www.mozilla.org/rhino. Support for other scripting languages can be found in the Scripting project at java.net (https://scripting.dev.java.net). The languages supported so far in this project include Groovy, Java, Jelly, Jexl, JudoScript, OGNL, Pnuts, Python, Ruby, Scheme, Sleep, Tcl, xpath, and XSLT. This chapter concentrates on the JavaScript engine in Java 6.

The Scripting API is defined and implemented as types in the **javax.script** package. This package offers the following areas of functionality.

1. Script execution. This feature allows Java programmers to run scripts written in a scripting language for which an engine is available. For Java 6, only JavaScript scripts are supported.

2. Binding. This unit of functionality enables Java programmers to access Java objects from script programs. Those Java objects must first be bound to variables.
3. Compilation. Before scripts can be executed, the corresponding script engine must first compile the script into intermediate code. This feature allows the storage of such intermediate code so that scripts that are invoked repeatedly need only be compiled once, hence speeding up the whole execution process.
4. Invocation. This feature is related to compilation. However, invocation enables intermediate code to be reused. The difference is very subtle. Compilation allows the whole script to be re-executed and invocation allows individual procedures/functions in the script to be re-executed.
5. Script engine discovery and metadata. For a scripting language to interact with Java, a script engine for that language must be available. The Scripting API allows script engines to be registered and discovered at run time. In addition, you can also query attributes about registered script engines.

The rest of this section takes a look at the core types in the **javax.script** package and provide several examples.

Core Types

The **javax.script** package contains six interfaces, five classes, and one exception. This section explains the more important types in this package.

The ScriptEngineManager Class

When working with the Scripting API, it is almost always the case that you need to first obtain the script engine object for the scripting language you're working with. The **ScriptEngine** interface models script engines, and the **ScriptEngineManager** class provides convenient methods to register and obtain a **ScriptEngine** object.

You can instantiate the **ScriptEngineManager** class by invoking one of its two constructors:

```
public ScriptEngineManager()
```

```
public ScriptEngineManager(java.lang.ClassLoader loader)
```

The first constructor uses the default class loader, which is the one obtained by calling **Thread.currentThread().getContextClassLoader()**. The second constructor allows you to use a different class loader than the default.

To register a script engine, you call the **registerEngineExtension**, **registerEngineMimeType**, or **registerEngineName** methods on a **ScriptEngineManager** object. You do this if you have a script engine implementation of your own that you want to expose. Unless you're developing a script engine, this is something you will very rarely do. Most often, you will use **ScriptEngineManager** to obtain a script engine.

To obtain a script engine, you call the **getEngineByName** method on the **ScriptEngineManager** object. Its signature is as follows.

```
public ScriptEngine getEngineByName(java.lang.String shortName)
```

Since Rhino is the only script engine coming with Java 6, you use the **getEngineByName** method by passing the short name for JavaScript: "js". Therefore,

```
ScriptEngineManager manager = new ScriptEngineManager();
ScriptEngine jsEngine = manager.getEngineByName("js");
```

There is also another interesting method, **getEngineFactories**, that returns a list of **ScriptEngineFactory** objects. Its signature is this.

```
public java.util.List<ScriptEngineFactory> getEngineFactories()
```

The example in the section "Listing All Script Engines" lists all script engines in the current implementation of Java. It will be more interesting when Java includes more engines in the future. For now, be content with Rhino.

The ScriptEngineFactory Interface

A **ScriptEngineFactory** object encapsulates metadata that describes a script engine. Therefore, implementing a script engine also requires writing an implementation of **ScriptEngineFactory**. The following are the more important methods of the **ScriptEngineFactory** interface.

```
public java.lang.String getEngineName()
```

Returns the full name of the script engine.

```
public java.lang.String getEngineVersion()
```
Return the version number of the script engine.

```
public java.lang.String getLanguageName()
```
Returns the name of the supported scripting language.

```
public java.lang.String getLanguageVersion()
```
Returns the version of the supported scripting language.

```
public java.util.List<java.lang.String> getNames()
```
Returns an immutable list of short names that identify the supported script engine.

```
public java.lang.Object getParameter(java.lang.String key)
```
Returns the value of the specified attribute.

```
public ScriptEngine getScriptEngine()
```
Returns an instance of the supported script engine.

The Bindings Interface

I introduce this interface before the **ScriptEngine** interface, which is a much more important interface than **Bindings**, because **ScriptEngine** uses **Bindings**. As such, understanding of **Bindings** is crucial to learning **ScriptEngine**.

Bindings is a subinterface of **java.util.Map** and **Bindings** objects can be used to store key/value pairs that may be useful when executing scripts. For example, you can store a key/value pair in a **Bindings** instance and expose it to scripts. The scripts can then access the key/value pair as if it were a global variable.

Here are the methods defined in the **Bindings** interface:

```
public boolean containsKey(java.lang.Object key)
```
Indicates whether or not this **Bindings** contains the specified key.

```
public java.lang.Object get(java.lang.Object key)
```
Returns the value bound to the specified key.

```
public java.lang.Object put(java.lang.String key,
    java.lang.Object value)
```
Binds the specified key to the specified value. If there is already a key with the specified name, replace the value with the specified value. This

method returns the value previously associated with the specified key. It returns null if no value was previously mapped to the key.

```
public void putAll(java.util.Map<? extends java.lang.String,
    ? extends java.lang.Object> map)
```
Adds the contents of the specified **Map** to this Bindings.

```
public java.lang.Object remove(java.lang.Object key)
```
Removes the key/value pair for the specified key from the **Bindings** and returns the removed value, if any.

The ScriptEngine Interface

An instance of the **ScriptEngine** interface represents a script engine. The most useful methods in this interface can be used to execute scripts and create bindings. The **eval** method, which comes in several overloads, is used to execute scripts. The **put** method can be used to bind keys with values. Here are the signatures of the more important methods.

```
public java.lang.Object eval(java.lang.String script)
    throws ScriptException
```
Executes the specified script. This method returns the value resulting from the execution of the script.

```
public java.lang.Object eval(java.io.Reader reader)
    throws ScriptException
```
Executes the script in *reader* and returns the result of the execution.

```
public java.lang.Object eval(java.lang.String script,
    Bindings bindings)
```
Executes the script and provides a **Bindings** that can be accessed from the script.

```
public java.lang.Object eval(java.io.Reader reader,
    Bindings bindings)
```
Executes the script in *reader* and provides a **Bindings** that can be accessed from the script.

```
public java.lang.Object eval(java.lang.String script,
    ScriptContext context)
```
Executes the script and provides access to the specified **ScriptContext**.

```
public java.lang.Object eval(java.io.Reader reader,
    ScriptContext context)
```

Executes the script in *reader* and provides access to the specified **ScriptContext**.

```
public void put(java.lang.String key, java.lang.Object value)
```
Binds the key with the value.

```
public java.lang.Object get(java.lang.String key)
```
Returns the value bound to the specified key.

```
public ScriptEngineFactory getFactory()
```
Returns the **ScriptEngineFactory** object that encapsulates metadata for this ScriptEngine instance.

Listing All Script Engines

The code in Listing 3.1 shows how to list all script engine factories that come with Java 6.

Listing 3.1: Listing script engine factories

```java
import java.util.List;
import javax.script.ScriptEngineManager;
import javax.script.ScriptEngineFactory;

public class ListEngineFactoryDemo {

    public static void main(String[] args) {
        // create ScriptEngineManager
        ScriptEngineManager manager = new ScriptEngineManager();
        List<ScriptEngineFactory> factoryList =
                manager.getEngineFactories();
        for (ScriptEngineFactory factory : factoryList) {
            System.out.println(factory.getEngineName());
            System.out.println(factory.getLanguageName());
        }
    }
}
```

If you compile and run this class, you will see the following result:

```
Mozilla Rhino
ECMAScript
```

Running Scripts

The code in Listing 3.2 shows how you can run JavaScript code from inside a
Java program.

Listing 3.2: RunScriptDemo class

```
import javax.script.ScriptEngine;
import javax.script.ScriptEngineManager;
import javax.script.ScriptException;

public class RunScriptDemo {

    public static void main(String[] args) {
        // create a ScriptEngineManager object
        ScriptEngineManager manager = new ScriptEngineManager();
        // get the ScriptEngine
        ScriptEngine engine = manager.getEngineByName("js");

        // execute script
        String script = "print('hello')";
        try {
            engine.eval(script);
        } catch (ScriptException e) {
            e.printStackTrace();
        }
    }
}
```

Run the **RunScriptDemo** class and you will see "hello" on your console.

As another example, the code in Listing 3.3 shows the
RunScriptFileDemo class that can be used to execute Javascript script in a
file.

Listing 3.3: RunScriptFileDemo class

```
import java.io.FileReader;
import javax.script.ScriptEngine;
import javax.script.ScriptEngineManager;

public class RunScriptFileDemo {
    public static void main(String[] args) {
        // the first argument must be the path to the script file
```

```
        if (args.length != 1) {
            System.out.println(
                    "Usage: java RunScriptFile [file]");
            System.exit(0);
        }

        // create ScriptEngineManager
        ScriptEngineManager manager = new ScriptEngineManager();

        // get the ScriptEngine for JavaScript (js)
        ScriptEngine engine = manager.getEngineByName("js");

        // open file, and execute the script
        try {
            FileReader reader = new FileReader(args[0]);
            engine.eval(reader);
            reader.close();
        } catch (Exception e) {
            e.printStackTrace();
        }
    }
}
```

Listing 3.4 shows a file named **sample.js** that contains a Javascript function **add** and a script that invokes the function.

Listing 3.4: The sample.js file

```
function add(a, b) {
    print('Adding ' + a + ' with ' + b + ' ...');
    c = a + b;
    return c;
}

result = add(10, 5);
print('Result = ' + result);
```

You can run the **RunScriptFileDemo** class by running this command line command.

```
java RunScriptFileDemo sample.js
```

Note that the **sample.js** file must be located in the same directory as the directory you are invoking the command. Otherwise, you must pass the whole path to the script file.

This is the result from running the Java class:

```
Adding 10 with 5 ...
Result = 15
```

Binding Scripts

As yet another example, Listing 3.5 shows the **BindingDemo** class that illustrates the use of variables that are bound through **ScriptEngine**, so that the variables can be used for the next execution of the script.

Listing 3.5: The BindingDemo class

```java
import javax.script.Bindings;
import javax.script.ScriptContext;
import javax.script.ScriptEngine;
import javax.script.ScriptEngineManager;
import javax.script.ScriptException;

public class BindingDemo {

    public static void main(String[] args) {

        // create ScriptEngineManager
        ScriptEngineManager manager = new ScriptEngineManager();

        // get the ScriptEngine for JavaScript
        ScriptEngine engine = manager.getEngineByName("js");

        // bind a to 10 and b to 5
        engine.put("a", 10);
        engine.put("b", 5);

        // get bound values
        Bindings bindings = engine.getBindings(
                ScriptContext.ENGINE_SCOPE);
        Object a = bindings.get("a");
        Object b = bindings.get("b");
        System.out.println("a = " + a);
        System.out.println("b = " + b);

        // use the bound values in calculations
        try {
```

```
        Object result = engine.eval("c = a + b;");
        System.out.println("a + b = " + result);
    } catch (ScriptException e) {
        e.printStackTrace();
    }
}
}
```

Note that we bound **a** and **b** in these lines of code:

```
engine.put("a", 10);
engine.put("b", 5);
```

And then, we used it in a JavaScript script:

```
Object result = engine.eval("c = a + b;");
```

The output from the **BindingDemo** class is as follows:

```
a = 10
b = 5
a + b = 15.0
```

Using Invocable

Any script that needs executing will first have to be compiled into intermediate code. This compilation takes a relatively large amount of CPU cycles. The same procedure or function that gets called twice will have to be compiled twice too. With the **Invocable** interface you can save time by storing the compiled intermediate code for reuse if the same procedure or function is called the second time.

An implementation of **ScriptEngine** can optionally implement the **Invocable** interface. Since implementing this interface is optional, you need to first perform an **instanceof** check before upcasting a **ScriptEngine** to this interface.

```
if (scriptEngine instanceof Invocable) {
    Invocable invocable = (Invocable) scriptEngine;
    // invoke method/procedure here
}
```

The **Invocable** interface provides the **invoke** methods to invoke a scripting function.

```
public java.lang.Object invoke(java.lang.String functionName,
        Object... args)
        throws ScriptException, java.lang.NoSuchMethodException
```
Invokes the specified top-level function. Note that you can pass any number of arguments.

```
public java.lang.Object invoke(java.lang.Object instance,
        java.lang.String functionName, Object... args)
        throws ScriptException, java.lang.NoSuchMethodException
```
Invokes the specified function on *instance*. Note that you can pass any number of arguments.

In addition, the **Invocable** interface provides two other methods:

```
public <T> T getInterface(java.lang.Class<T> clazz)
```
Returns the implementation of an interface using compiled procedures.

```
public <T> T getInterface(java.lang.Object instance,
        java.lang.Class<T> clazz)
```
Returns the implementation of an interface using compiled procedures. The argument instance refers to the scripting object whose member functions are used to implement the methods of the interface.

As an example, the **InvocableDemo** in Listing 3.6 illustrates the use of **Invocable** through which you can call procedures that have been compiled in subsequent executions of a script. You can call a procedure using one of these methods:

- Use the **invoke** method define in the **Invocable** interface
- Use your own interface, in which case the implementation of this custom interface comes from the **getInterface** method.

In the example, we'll use the custom **Adder** interface in Listing 3.7.

Listing 3.6: The InvocableDemo class

```
import javax.script.Invocable;
import javax.script.ScriptEngine;
import javax.script.ScriptEngineManager;

public class InvocableDemo {
```

```java
public static void main(String[] args) {

    // create ScriptEngineManager
    ScriptEngineManager manager = new ScriptEngineManager();

    // get the ScriptEngine for JavaScript (js)
    ScriptEngine engine = manager.getEngineByName("js");

    try {
        // execute script that contains the add function
        engine.eval("function add(a, b) " +
                "{c = a + b; return c;}");
        Invocable jsInvoke = (Invocable) engine;

        // call the add function, passing 10 and 5
        Object result1 = jsInvoke.invoke("add",
                new Object[] {10, 5});
        System.out.println(result1);

        // call the add function throught the add method
        // in the Adder interface
        Adder adder = jsInvoke.getInterface(Adder.class);
        int result2 = adder.add(10, 5);
        System.out.println(result2);
    } catch (Exception e) {
        e.printStackTrace();
    }
}
}
```

Listing 3.7: The Adder interface

```java
public interface Adder {
    int add(int a, int b);
}
```

Running the **InvocableDemo** class produces the following output on the console:

```
15.0
15
```

Using Compilable

The **Compilable** interface is similar to **Invocable**. However, instead of storing the intermediate code of a specific function/procedure, with **Compilable** you store the intermediate code of an entire script. Like **Invocable**, **Compilable** is an optional interface that is implemented by a **ScriptEngine** implementation, thereby performing an **instanceof** check is necessary before upcasting an instance of **ScriptEngine** to **Compilable**.

```
if (scriptEngine instanceof Compilable) {
    Compilable compilable = (Compilable) scriptEngine
    // invoke script here
}
```

The **Compilable** interface provides two overloads of the **compile** method:

```
public CompiledScript compile(java.lang.String script)
        throws ScriptException
```
      Compiles the script for later execution.

```
public CompiledScript compile(java.io.Reader reader)
        throws ScriptException
```
      Compiles the script in *reader* for later execution.

The return value of the **compile** method is a **CompiledScript** object. You can then execute the script by calling one of the **eval** methods on the **CompiledScript** object. Here are the three overloads of **eval**, which are similar to those defined in the **ScriptEngine** interface:

```
public java.lang.Object eval()
public java.lang.Object eval(Bindings bindings)
public java.lang.Object eval(ScriptContext context)
```

Listing 3.8 shows a class (**CompilableDemo**) that illustrates the use of the **Compilable** interface.

Listing 3.8: The CompilableDemo Class

```
import javax.script.Compilable;
import javax.script.CompiledScript;
import javax.script.ScriptEngine;
import javax.script.ScriptEngineManager;
```

```
public class CompilableDemo {

    public static void main(String[] args) {

        // create ScriptEngineManager
        ScriptEngineManager manager = new ScriptEngineManager();

        // create ScriptEngine for JavaScript (js)
        ScriptEngine engine = manager.getEngineByName("js");

        Compilable jsCompile = (Compilable) engine;
        try {
            CompiledScript script = jsCompile.compile(
                    "function hi() {print('Hello !'); }; hi();");

            for (int i = 0; i < 5; i++) {
                script.eval();
            }
        } catch (Exception e) {
            e.printStackTrace();
        }
    }
}
```

Running the class in Listing 3.8 generates the following message on the console.

```
Hello !
Hello !
Hello !
Hello !
Hello !
```

Summary

JSR 223, Scripting for the Java Platform enables collaboration between Java and scripting languages. Java 6 comes with a reference implementation that supports JavaScript, however other scripting languages are supported through the Scripting project. This chapter presents the API and teaches how to use them.

Chapter 4
Networking

Mustang adds some networking-related features too and in this chapter we'll learn what have been brought to the table. This chapter starts with the new API for working with client-side cookies—that's right, as opposed to cookies manageable by servlets and JSPs, and concludes with the discussion of a brand new HTTP server for testing your web applications and web services. Between the two are topics on internationalized domain names, internationalized resource identifiers, and the **InterfaceAddress** interface.

Client-Side Cookies

HTTP is a network protocol that web servers and browsers use to communicate with each other. An HTTP connection is always initiated by a client browser that sends an HTTP request, to which the web server responds by sending an HTTP response. After this information exchange, the server always closes the connection. If the same client requests another resource from the same server, it must open a new HTTP connection to the server. In addition, the HTTP server is clueless as to whether a client has visited its web site for the 100th time or is a first-time visitor. In geek speak, HTTP is stateless. This amnesia-like symptom forces server application programmers to make extra effort to ensure, say, a user who has successfully logged in will not be required to re-login when requesting a different resource from the same web application. To the rescue server-side technologies provide ways to get around the statelessness of HTTP. One of them is by employing cookies.

A cookie is a small piece of information that is passed back and forth in the HTTP request and response. The cookie sent by the server to the client will be passed back to the server when the client requests another page from the same application. In servlet programming, a cookie is represented by the

javax.servlet.http.Cookie class. You create **Cookie** instances on the server-side from within your servlet.

Java 6 provides new classes for working with cookies on the *client* side. The **java.net.HttpCookie** class, which represents a cookie, is one of such classes. You use **HttpCookie** typically when working with a web client application.

To manage **HttpCookie** objects, you will also use these related objects: **CookieStore**, **CookiePolicy**, and **CookieManager** objects. All these types are members of the **java.net** package, and we'll have a look at these types briefly.

HttpCookie

A **java.net.HttpCookie** object represents a cookie, as specified in the Netscape draft and RFC 2109 and 2965 of the Internet Engineering Task Force (IETF). These RFCs can be found at these locations:

```
http://www.ietf.org/rfc/rfc2109.txt
http://www.ietf.org/rfc/rfc2965.txt
```

A cookie has a name and a value, both of which are always of **String** type. The name can only contain ASCII alphanumeric characters and cannot contain commas, semicolons, or white spaces. It cannot begin with the $ character either. You can create an **HttpCookie** object by passing a name and a value. Here is the **HttpCookie** class's constructor:

```
public HttpCookie(java.lang.String name, java.lang.String value)
```

A cookie may have a domain and a path associated with it as well as the discard and secure attributes. The methods defined in the **HttpCookie** class are mostly for reading and changing the foresaid values. Here are some of them.

```
public java.lang.String getName()
```
    Returns the cookie name, which cannot be changed after the cookie is created. Therefore, there is no **setName** method in this class.

```
public java.lang.String getValue()
```
    Returns the cookie value.

```
public void setValue(java.lang.String newValue)
```
    Assigns the specified value.

```
public java.lang.String getDomain()
```
Returns the domain name associated with this cookie.

```
public void setDomain(java.lang.String pattern)
```
Specifies the domain name that is compliant to RFC 2965.

```
public java.lang.String getPath()
```
Returns the path associated with this cookie.

```
public void setPath(java.lang.String path)
```
Specifies a path for the cookie to which a browser or a web client should return the cookie.

```
public boolean getSecure()
```
Returns **true** if the cookie should only be sent over a secure channel (i.e. HTTPS). Otherwise, it returns **false**.

```
public void setSecure(boolean secure)
```
Specifies whether or not the cookie should only be sent over a secure channel.

```
public long getMaxAge()
```
Returns the maximum age of this cookie in seconds.

```
public void setMaxAge(long age)
```
Sets the maximum age of this cookie in seconds.

```
public boolean hasExpired()
```
Indicates if this cookie has expired.

CookieStore

The **CookieStore** interface represents a repository for **HttpCookie** objects. You can store and remove **HttpCookie** objects in a **CookieStore** as well as retrieve URI-specific cookies. Here are the methods defined in the **CookieStore** interface.

```
void add(URI uri, HttpCookie cookie)
```
Adds a **HttpCookie** to the store. The cookie may or may not be associated with a URI. If it is not associated with a URI, then the cookie's domain and path attributes indicate the domain and path. If it is associated with a URI and the cookie's domain and path attributes are **null**, then the URI will indicate where the cookie comes from.

```
java.util.List<HttpCookie> get(URI uri)
```
Retrieves all cookies associated with the specified URI or whose domain attribute value matches the specified URI. Only cookies that have not expired are returned.

```
java.util.List<HttpCookie> getCookies()
```
Retrieves all cookies that have not expired.

```
java.util.List<URI> getURIs()
```
Returns all URIs associated with the cookies in the store.

```
boolean remove(URI uri, HttpCookie cookie)
```
Removes the specified cookie from the store.

```
boolean removeAll()
```
Removes all cookies in the store.

Currently there is no default implementation for this interface. However, the example in the section "HttpCookie Example" shows how to write one.

CookiePolicy

When working with a **CookieManager**, you need to have a CookiePolicy object that helps the **CookieManager** to determine which cookies should be accepted and which ones should be rejected. The **CookiePolicy** interface defines a method, **shouldAccept**:

```
boolean shouldAccept(URI uri, HttpCookie cookie)
```
This method returns **true** if the cookie should be accepted and **false** otherwise.

It also defines these three static finals.

```
static final CookiePolicy ACCEPT_ALL
```

```
static final CookiePolicy ACCEPT_NONE
```

```
static final CookiePolicy ACCEPT_ORIGINAL_SERVER
```

An example that illustrates how to use **CookiePolicy** is given in the section "HttpCookie Example."

CookieManager

The **java.net.CookieManager** class is an implementation of the **java.net.CookieHandler** interface. You use **CookieManager** for managing client-side cookies. You normally use it along with **CookieStore** and **CookiePolicy**. Here are two constructors in **CookieManager**.

```
public CookieManager()

public CookieManager(CookieStore store, CookiePolicy policy)
```

A **CookieManager** allows you to retrieve all cookies associated with a URI or store them in a cache. Here are the methods in the **CookieHandler** interface:

```
public java.util.Map<java.lang.String,
      java.util.List<java.lang.String>>
      get(URI uri, Map<java.lang.String,
      java.util.List<java.lang.String>> requestHeaders)
         throws java.io.IOException
```
Retrieves all cookies associated with the specified URI in the request header.

```
public void put(URI uri, java.util.Map<java.lang.String,
      java.util.List<java.lang.String>> responseHeaders)
      throws java.io.IOException
```
Sets all the applicable cookies.

```
public void setCookiePolicy(CookiePolicy policy)
```
Sets the cookie policy for this **CookieManager** instance.

```
public CookieStore getCookieStore()
```
Returns the cookie store associated with this **CookieManager**.

HttpCookie Example

The following is a WebClient example on how to use **HttpCookie**, **CookiePolicy**, **CookieStore**, and **CookieManager**. For the application to work, you also need to have a JSP presented in Listing 4.1.

Listing 4.1: The cookieTest.jsp page

```
<%
    Cookie cookie = new Cookie("username", "guest");
```

```
    cookie.setMaxAge(100);
    response.addCookie(cookie);
%>
<html>
<head>
<title>HttpCookie Demo</title>
</head>
<body>
Add cookie. Cookie name = <%=cookie.getName() +
    ". Cookie value = " + cookie.getValue()%>
</body>
</html>
```

You need to deploy this JSP in a servlet/JSP container such as Tomcat. For this example, just copy it to the **webapps/ROOT** directory of Tomcat installation. If you don't already have Tomcat installed, please check out its web site at http://tomcat.apache.org.

The web client application consists of three classes, the **MyCookiePolicy** class in Listing 4.2, the **MyCookieStore** class in Listing 4.3, and the **WebClient** class in Listing 4.4..

Listing 4.2: MyCookiePolicy class

```
package webclient;
import java.net.CookiePolicy;
import java.net.HttpCookie;
import java.net.URI;

public class MyCookiePolicy implements CookiePolicy {
    public boolean shouldAccept(URI uri, HttpCookie cookie) {
        // Only accept cookies from localhost
        String host = uri.getHost();
        return host.equals("localhost");
    }
}
```

MyCookiePolicy implements **CookiePolicy** and is designed to only accept cookies from localhost.

Listing 4.3: MyCookieStore class

```
package webclient;
import java.net.CookieStore;
import java.net.HttpCookie;
import java.net.URI;
```

```java
import java.util.ArrayList;
import java.util.Collection;
import java.util.HashMap;
import java.util.List;
import java.util.Map;
import java.util.Set;
public class MyCookieStore implements CookieStore {
    // Map for storing cookies
    private Map<URI, List<HttpCookie>> map =
            new HashMap<URI, List<HttpCookie>>();
    // Add cookie
    public void add(URI uri, HttpCookie cookie) {
        System.out.println("Add cookie for " + uri + ": "
                + cookie);
        List<HttpCookie> cookies = map.get(uri);
        if (cookies == null) {
            cookies = new ArrayList<HttpCookie>();
            map.put(uri, cookies);
        }
        cookies.add(cookie);
    }
    // get Cookie
    public List<HttpCookie> get(URI uri) {
        List<HttpCookie> cookies = map.get(uri);
        if (cookies == null) {
            cookies = new ArrayList<HttpCookie>();
            map.put(uri, cookies);
        }
        System.out.println("Get cookies for " + uri + ": "
                + cookies);
        return cookies;
    }
    // Get all cookies
    public List<HttpCookie> getCookies() {
        Collection<List<HttpCookie>> values = map.values();
        List<HttpCookie> result = new ArrayList<HttpCookie>();
        for (List<HttpCookie> value : values) {
            result.addAll(value);
        }
        return result;
    }
    // Get all registered URIs
    public List<URI> getURIs() {
        Set<URI> keys = map.keySet();
        return new ArrayList<URI>(keys);
```

```
        }
        // Delete the specified cookie
        public boolean remove(URI uri, HttpCookie cookie) {
            List<HttpCookie> cookies = map.get(uri);
            if (cookies == null) {
                return false;
            }
            return cookies.remove(cookie);
        }
        // Remove all cookies
        public boolean removeAll() {
            map.clear();
            return true;
        }
    }
}
```

The **MyCookieStore** class is an implementation of **CookieStore**. Note that
every time its **add** and **get** methods are called, it will print a **String** on the
console to let you know that a cookie is being added or retrieved.

Listing 4.4: The WebClient class

```
package webclient;
import java.io.BufferedReader;
import java.io.InputStream;
import java.io.InputStreamReader;
import java.net.CookieHandler;
import java.net.CookieManager;
import java.net.CookiePolicy;
import java.net.CookieStore;
import java.net.URL;
import java.net.URLConnection;
public class WebClient {
    public static void main(String[] args) {
        try {
            // Create CookieStore and CookiePolicy
            CookieStore store = new MyCookieStore();
            CookiePolicy policy = new MyCookiePolicy();
            CookieManager handler = new CookieManager(store,
        policy);
            CookieHandler.setDefault(handler);
            // open connection to the cookieTest.jsp page
            URL url = new
        URL("http://localhost:8080/cookieTest.jsp");
            System.out.println("Open URL Connection:");
            URLConnection conn = url.openConnection();
```

```
        // read the HTTP response
        InputStream in = conn.getInputStream();
        BufferedReader reader = new BufferedReader(
                new InputStreamReader(in));
        String input;
        while ((input = reader.readLine()) != null) {
            System.out.println(input);
        }
        // Close connection
        reader.close();
    } catch (Exception e) {
        e.printStackTrace();
    }
    }
}
```

The **WebClient** class is the class that puts everything together. It open a connection to http://localhost:8080/cookieTest.jsp and prints the HTTP response. Along the way, you will see notification that a cookie is added/retrieved.

If you run the **WebClient** class, this is what you'll see on the console:

```
Open URL Connection:
```
Get cookies for http://localhost:8080/cookieTest.jsp: []
Add cookie for http://localhost:8080/cookieTest.jsp: username=guest
Add cookie for http://localhost:8080/cookieTest.jsp: JSESSIONID=
7E5F777D2F60E7F0813D34E2886349C8

```
<html>
<head>
<title>HttpCookie Demo</title>
</head>
<body>
Add cookie. Cookie name = username. Cookie value = guest
</body>
</html>
```

Notice that when the **WebClient** instance connected to the server, it also sent any cookie associated to the server. However, there was currently none, so you saw

```
Get cookies for http://localhost:8080/cookieTest.jsp: []
```

The JSP page sends a cookie, therefore you can see this line:

```
Add cookie for http://localhost:8080/cookieTest.jsp: username=guest
```

The second cookie is a session identifier for the **WebClient** application. You got this because the JSP page participated in the server's session management.

Internationalized Domain Names (IDNs)

The Internet originated in America. No wonder domain names were, and still are, represented in ASCII characters. Inevitably, non-English speaking nations use the Internet and have domain names in their local languages too. The problem is with the current system, domain names must only be in ASCII characters. This is a problem to people who are not familiar with our alphabet. For example, many Chinese people can only read kanji characters and having to read Roman characters would be an great obstacle for them. There is a barrier for people like these to embrace the Internet.

The solution to the problem of not having international domain names is to map them using a widely accepted standard: RFC 3490, Internationalizing Domain Names in Applications (http://www.ietf.org/rfc/rfc3490.txt).

Using browsers that support IDNs, such as Mozilla 1.4, Safari, Netscape 7.1, Opera 7.11 and IE 7.0, non-English speaking people can type in domain names in their original characters directly to the address bar of the browser. In the background, the browser will translate the characters into their ASCII equivalents and serve the contents.

For example, Internet users in Denmark can type in the following URL into the browser address bar:

```
www.brændendekærlighed.com
```

Figure 4.1 shows the web site. Mozilla translates the URL into the ASCII characters. However, if you use IE 6, you will get an HTTP 500 error.

Figure 4.2 shows another example of sites that can be reached using an internationalized domain name. This time around, it's Xinghua University's web site. This university is located in Beijing, China and its web site boasts a Chinese version for local and Chinese-speaking visitors.

Figure 4.1: Using a Danish domain

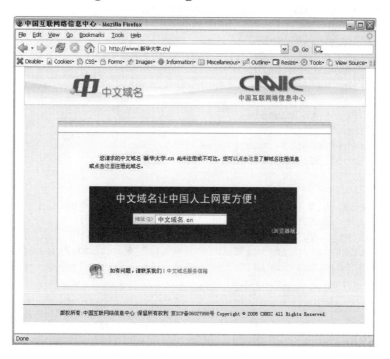

Figure 4.2: A web site that has a Chinese domain name

Java supports the IDN through the **java.net.IDN** class, which is new to JDK 1.6. This class provides methods to convert the representation of an IDN from Unicode to the ASCII Compatible Encoding (ACE) representation and vice-versa. Here are some of the methods in the IDN class for conversion.

```
public static java.lang.String toASCII(java.lang.String input)
```
    Translates the Unicode representation of an IDN to ACE.

```
public static java.lang.String toUnicode(java.lang.String input)
```
    Translates the ACE representation of an IDN to Unicode

The IDNDemo class in Listing 4.5 is an example of how to use these methods.

Listing 4.5: Converting IDN formats

```java
import java.net.IDN;

public class IDNDemo {
    public static void main(String[] args) {
        // An internationalized domain name
        String input = "www.brændendekærlighed.com";
        // Convert to ASCII
        String ascii = IDN.toASCII(input);
        // convert to Unicode
        String unicode = IDN.toUnicode(input);

        // Print to console
        print("Input", input);
        print("toAscii(input)", ascii);
        print("toUnicode(input)", unicode);
    }

    private static void print(String mode, String text) {
        System.out.println("Mode      : " + mode);
        System.out.println("Text      : " + text);
        System.out.println("Code Points: " + getCodePoints(text));
        System.out.println("-----------------------------------
        ");
    }

    // Returns unicode value (in hexadecimal) of each character
    // in the specified String
    private static String getCodePoints(String s) {
        StringBuilder sb = new StringBuilder();
        char[] chars = s.toCharArray();
```

```
        for (int i = 0; i < chars.length; i++) {
            int codePoint = Character.codePointAt(chars, i);
            String hex = Integer.toHexString(codePoint);
            sb.append(hex + " ");
        }
        return sb.toString();
    }
}
```

Here is the result of running the **IDNDemo** class:

```
Mode        : Input
Text        : www.brændendekærlighed.com
Code Points: 77 77 77 2e 62 72 e6 6e 64 65 6e 64 65 6b e6 72 6c 69
67 68 65 64 2e 63 6f 6d
----------------------------------------
Mode        : toAscii(input)
Text        : www.xn--brndendekrlighed-vobh.com
Code Points: 77 77 77 2e 78 6e 2d 2d 62 72 6e 64 65 6e 64 65 6b 72
6c 69 67 68 65 64 2d 76 6f 62 68 2e 63 6f 6d
----------------------------------------
Mode        : toUnicode(input)
Text        : www.brændendekærlighed.com
Code Points: 77 77 77 2e 62 72 e6 6e 64 65 6e 64 65 6b e6 72 6c 69
67 68 65 64 2e 63 6f 6d
```

Internationalized Resource Identifiers

A resource on the Internet is identified using a Uniform Resource Identifier (URI), which is a generalization of the Uniform Resource Locator (URL). URIs and URLs, however, can only cater for names that can be written in ASCII characters. For names that use non-ASCII characters, you need encoded URIs or Internationalized Resource Identifiers (IRIs).s

Java 6 adds support for Internationalized Resource Identifiers (IRIs) through the toIRIString method in the java.net.URI class. This method replaces percent-encoded characters in a URI to Unicode. Here is its signature:

```
public java.lang.String toIRIString()
```

To convert an IRI to a URI, you use the **toASCIIString** method in the same class:

```
public java.lang.String toASCIIString()
```

Note

The IRI is described in RFC 3987 that can be found here:
http://www.ietf.org/rfc/rfc3987.txt and here
http://www.w3.org/International/O-URL-and-ident.html.

The following example shows how you can use the **toIRIString** method to convert a URI to an IRI. All percent-coded characters will be converted into Unicode characters.

Listing 4.6: The IRIDemo class

```java
import java.net.URI;
import java.net.URISyntaxException;

public class IRIDemo {
    public static void main(String[] args)
            throws NullPointerException, URISyntaxException {
        URI uri = new URI("http://r%C3%A9sum%C3%A9.example.org");
        System.out.println("URI      : " + uri);
        System.out.println("Raw Host : " + uri.getRawHost());
        System.out.println("IRI      : " + uri.toIRIString());
    }
}
```

Here is the output from running the **IRIDemo** class:

```
URI      : http://r%C3%A9sum%C3%A9.example.org
Raw Host : r%C3%A9sum%C3%A9.example.org
IRI      : http://résumé.example.org
```

The InterfaceAddress Interface

An **InterfaceAddress** object can represent one of two things:

- an IP address, a subnet mask, and a broadcast address for an IPv4 address
- an IP address and a network prefix length for an IPv6 address.

IPv6, short for Internet Protocol version 6, is often referred to as the Next Generation Internet Protocol (IPng).

Note

For more information on IPv6, see
http://playground.sun.com/ipv6/INET-IPng-Paper.html

The **InterfaceAddress** interface defines the following methods:

`public InetAddress getAddress()`

> Returns an **InetAddress** for this address. The **java.net.InetAddress** class represents an IP address.

`public InetAddress getBroadcast()`

> Returns an **InetAddress** for the broadcast address for this **InterfaceAddress** in the case of IPv4 and **null** in the case of an IPv6 because only IPv4 networks have a broadcast address.

`public short getNetworkPrefixLength()`

> Returns the network prefix length for this address. A network prefix length is the subnet mask for IPv4 addresses (typically 255.0.0.0, 255.255.0.0 or 255.255.255.0).

The following is an example of how to use the **InterfaceAddress** interface to programmatically access network parameters using **NetworkInterface** and **InterfaceAddress**.

Listing 4.7: The NetworkParameterDemo class

```java
package networkparameter;
import java.net.NetworkInterface;
import java.util.Enumeration;

public class NetworkParameterDemo {
    public static void main(String[] args) throws Exception {
        NetworkParameter np = new NetworkParameter();

        // retrieve all NetworkInterfaces from this machine.
        Enumeration<NetworkInterface> en =
                NetworkInterface.getNetworkInterfaces();

        // Display the paramters
        while (en.hasMoreElements()) {
                NetworkInterface ni = en.nextElement();
            np.printParameter(ni);

        System.out.println("==================================");
```

```
            }
        }
}
```

The **NetworkParameter** class in Listing 4.8 is a utility class that prints network parameters.

Listing 4.8: The NetworkParameter class

```
package networkparameter;
import java.net.InterfaceAddress;
import java.net.NetworkInterface;
import java.net.SocketException;
import java.util.Iterator;
import java.util.List;

public class NetworkParameter {

    public void printParameter(NetworkInterface ni)
            throws SocketException {

        // Display the parameters in this network interface
        System.out.println("Network Interface:");
        System.out.println("------------------");
        System.out.println(" Name = " + ni.getName());
        System.out.println(" Display Name = " +
                ni.getDisplayName());
        System.out.println(" Is up = " + ni.isUp());
        System.out.println(" Support multicast = " +
                ni.supportsMulticast());
        System.out.println(" Is loopback = " + ni.isLoopback());
        System.out.println(" Is virtual = " + ni.isVirtual());
        System.out.println(" Is point to point = " +
                ni.isPointToPoint());
        System.out.println(" Hardware address = " +
                ni.getHardwareAddress());
        System.out.println(" MTU = " + ni.getMTU());

        // Get a list of all interface addresses:
        System.out.println("\nList of Interface Addresses:");
        System.out.println("----------------------------");
        List<InterfaceAddress> list = ni.getInterfaceAddresses();
        Iterator<InterfaceAddress> it = list.iterator();

        // iterate
        while (it.hasNext()) {
```

```
            InterfaceAddress ia = it.next();
            System.out.println(" Address = " + ia.getAddress());
            System.out.println(" Broadcast = " + ia.getBroadcast());
            System.out.println(" Network prefix length = "
                    + ia.getNetworkPrefixLength());
            System.out.println("");
        }
    }
}
```

The output when run on my computer is this.

```
Network Interface:
------------------
 Name = lo
 Display Name = MS TCP Loopback interface
 Is up = true
 Support multicast = true
 Is loopback = true
 Is virtual = false
 Is point to point = false
 Hardware address = null
 MTU = 1520

List of Interface Addresses:
----------------------------
 Address = /127.0.0.1
 Broadcast = /127.255.255.255
 Network prefix length = 8


====================================
Network Interface:
------------------
 Name = eth0
 Display Name = Intel(R) PRO/Wireless 2200BG Network Connection -
       Intel Wireless Connection Agent Miniport
 Is up = true
 Support multicast = true
 Is loopback = false
 Is virtual = false
 Is point to point = false
 Hardware address = [B@c17164
 MTU = 1500

List of Interface Addresses:
```

```
---------------------------
Address = /24.16.144.133
Broadcast = /24.16.144.255
Network prefix length = 24


==================================
```

Lightweight HTTP Server

Back in May 2005, a user requested that a web server be included in the JDK. Sun responded by creating a light-weight HTTP server, not yet in the JDK, but as a Sun's class (**com.sun.net.httpserver.HttpServer**). The documentation of this class can be found at:

```
http://download.java.net/jdk6/docs/jre/api/net/httpserver/spec/com/
sun/net/httpserver/HttpServer.html
```

In the same package are several related abstract classes and an interface that can together process HTTP requests. The accompanying classes include **HttpContext, HttpHandler, HttpExchange, Filter,** and **Authenticator**. A web site is represented by the **HttpContext** class, which must be associated with a path and an **HttpHandler**. The **HttpHandler** processes each incoming HTTP request and sends an HTTP response to the client. An **HttpExchange** object encapsulates both the request and response information for each HTTP request call.

The classes previously mentioned are by no means an exhausted list. There are many other classes that are not covered in this chapter but can be found here.

```
http://download.java.net/jdk6/docs/jre/api/net/httpserver/spec/com/
sun/net/httpserver/package-summary.html
```

This section provides an overview of the more important members of the **com.sun.net.httpserver** package and presents an example that illustrates how these classes can be useful for you.

The HttpServer Class

An **HttpServer** object represents a simple Http server that listens for incoming TCP connection at a specified IP address and port number. **HttpServer** is an abstract class and Sun provides a concrete implementation that you can bring to life using the **HttpServer** class's **create** method. There are two overloads of this method:

```
public static HttpServer create() throws java.io.IOException

public static HttpServer(java.net.InetSocketAddress address,
        int backlog) throws java.io.IOException
```

The first overload uses the local address and port (localhost and 80, respectively). The second one allows you to bind any IP address and port and specify the maximum socket backlog. The socket backlog specifies the maximum number of requests allowed in the queue. Requests that arrive when the number of backlog has been achieved will be rejected.

The **getAddress** method returns the **InetSocketAddress** object associated with the **HttpServer**. Here is its signature.

```
public abstract java.net.InetSocketAddress getAddress()
```

An HTTP server can cater for many Web applications, not only one. Each application lives in a separate HTTP context. If you're a Tomcat user, you know that Tomcat can host multiple servlet/JSP applications, each of which can conveniently be deployed as a WAR file or a directory under the **webapps** directory. For example, with Tomcat (or other containers) you prefix your URL with this

```
http://serverName:port/contextName
```

If you have two contexts (**context1** and **context2**) on localhost on port 8080, the prefixes are

```
http://localhost:8080/context1
http://localhost:8080/context2
```

A **HttpContext** is represented by the **HttpContext** class (discussed in the next section) and is associated with a path name. Before you can use an **HttpServer** object, you must first call its **createContext** method:

```
public abstract HttpContext createContext(java.lang.String path,
```

```
        HttpHandler handler)
```

The *path* argument specifies a path. It will be part of the URL of all requests that can be handled by this context. For example, if the path is **myApp**, the context can be invoked by using this URL:

```
http://machineName:port/myApp
```

The second argument to **createContext** is an **HttpHandler** object. An **HttpHandler** handles requests for the HTTP context and the class is explained in the section "The HttpHandler Interface."

To remove a context, you use the **removeContext** method. You can remove a context by passing the context or its associated path to **removeContext**.

```
public abstract void removeContext(HttpContext context)

public abstract void removeContext(java.lang.String path)
```

To start an **HttpServer**, you invoke its **start** method.

```
public abstract void start()
```

This method starts the server in a new background thread that inherits the priority, thread group, and the context class loader of the caller.

To start the server, call the HttpServer's stop method. Here is its signature

```
public abstract void stop(int delay)
```

The *delay* argument specifies the maximum number of seconds to wait until exchanges are finished.

The HttpContext Class

An **HttpContext** object, that you obtain from the **createContext** method of an **HttpServer** instance, represents a web application and maps a path to an **HttpHandler**. As you will see in the section "The HttpHandler Interface," a HttpHandler is the brain that processes HTTP requests that arrive at the **HttpServer** that creates the **HttpContext**. The **getServer** method of the **HttpContext** class returns this server:

```
public abstract HttpServer getServer()
```

The path and **HttpHandler** associated with this **HttpContext** can be obtained by invoking the **getPath** and **getHandler** methods, respectively.

```
public abstract java.lang.String getPath()
public abstract HttpHandler getHandler()
```

The HttpHandler Interface

The **HttpHandler** interface represents a handler for processing HTTP requests that an **HttpServer** receives. You must provide an implementation of this interface in order to use **HttpServer**.

There is only one method in **HttpHandler**, **handle**, that the corresponding **HttpServer** call each time it receives an HTTP request. For each HTTP request, the **HttpServer** instance creates an **HttpExchange** object that encapsulates the request and which the **HttpServer** instance passes to the **handle** method. Here is the signature of the handle method.

```
void handle(HttpExchange exchange) throws java.io.IOException
```

The HttpExchange Class

In the Servlet API, an HTTP request is represented by the **javax.servlet.ServletRequest** interface and an HTTP response by **javax.servlet.ServletResponse**. In Sun's HTTP server package, the **HttpExchange** class encapsulates both the request and the response. **HttpExchange** pales in complexity compared to **ServletRequest** and **ServletResponse**. For example, there's no method in **HttpExchange** for retrieving query parameters.

The following are methods defined in HttpExchange.

```
public abstract HttpContext getHttpContext()
```
Returns the **HttpContext** associated with this **HttpExchange** object.

```
public abstract java.net.InetSocketAddress getLocalAddress()
```
Returns the local address on which the HTTP request arrived.

```
public abstract java.lang.String getProtocol()
```
Returns the protocol of the request in the format protocol/majorVersion.minorVersion. Typically, it is HTTP/1.1

```
public abstract java.net.InetSocketAddress getRemoteAddress()
```
Returns the address of the HTTP client.

```
public abstract java.io.InputStream getRequestBody()
```
Returns an input stream from which the request body can be read.

```
public abstract Headers getRequestHeaders()
```
Returns a **Headers** object containing the request headers. The **Headers** class is an implementation of the **java.util.Map** interface.

```
public abstract java.lang.String getRequestMethod()
```
Obtains the request method, normally either "GET" or "POST."

```
public abstract java.net.URI getRequestURI()
```
Returns the request URI.

```
public abstract java.io.OutputStream getResponseBody()
```
Obtains an OutputStream to which the response is written.

```
public abstract Headers getResponseHeaders()
```
Returns a **Headers** object containing the HTTP response haeders.

An Example of HttpServer

The following application shows how you can use the **HttpServer** and related classes. The **HttpServer** is associated with a context of path header. There are two classes in this application, the main class (**HttpServerDemo** in Listing 4.10) that creates and starts an **HttpServer** instance and the **MyHandler** class, which is an implementation of **HttpHandler** used by the first class.

The **MyHandler** class is presented in Listing 4.9. This class is the handler that will be invoked to process HTTP exchanges.

Listing 4.9: The MyHandler class

```
package httpserver;
import java.io.IOException;
import java.io.OutputStream;
import java.util.Iterator;
import java.util.List;
import java.util.Set;
import com.sun.net.httpserver.Headers;
import com.sun.net.httpserver.HttpExchange;
import com.sun.net.httpserver.HttpHandler;

public class MyHandler implements HttpHandler {
```

```
public void handle(HttpExchange exchange) throws IOException {
    // check the request method and process if it is a GET
    String requestMethod = exchange.getRequestMethod();
    if (requestMethod.equalsIgnoreCase("GET")) {
        // Set response headers
        Headers responseHeaders = exchange.getResponseHeaders();
        responseHeaders.set("Content-Type", "text/plain");
        //* response is OK (200)
        exchange.sendResponseHeaders(200, 0);

        // Get response body
        OutputStream responseBody = exchange.getResponseBody();

        // Print all request headers to HTTP response
        Headers requestHeaders = exchange.getRequestHeaders();
        Set<String> keySet = requestHeaders.keySet();
        Iterator<String> iter = keySet.iterator();
        while (iter.hasNext()) {
            String key = iter.next();
            List values = requestHeaders.get(key);
            String s = key + " = " + values.toString() + "\n";
            responseBody.write(s.getBytes());
        }
        // Close the responseBody
        responseBody.close();
    }
}
}
```

The **HttpServerDemo** class is given in Listing 4.10. This class creates an instance of **HttpServer**, registers a context with the path /header, perform a few settings, and run the **HttpServer** on port 8888.

Listing 4.10: The HttpServerDemo class

```
package httpserver;
import java.io.IOException;
import java.net.InetSocketAddress;
import java.util.concurrent.Executors;
import com.sun.net.httpserver.HttpServer;

public class HttpServerDemo {
    public static void main(String[] args) throws IOException {
        // Create an HttpServer and bind it to port 8888
        int port = 8888;
```

```
InetSocketAddress addr = new InetSocketAddress(port);
HttpServer server = HttpServer.create(addr, 0);

// Create an HttpContext with the /header path,
// and a handler of type MyHandler
server.createContext("/header", new MyHandler());
// Sets an Executor that will handler all HTTP requests
server.setExecutor(Executors.newCachedThreadPool());
// Start the server
server.start();
System.out.println("Server is listening on port " + port);
    }
}
```

After you run the **HttpServerDemo** class, you can use a web browser to test it by directing it to this address:

```
http://localhost:8888/header
```

This is the output I see on my console. Yours may be different.

```
Host = [localhost:8888]
Accept-language = [en-us]
Accept = [image/gif, image/x-xbitmap, image/jpeg, image/pjpeg,
        application/vnd.ms-excel, application/vnd.ms-powerpoint,
        application/msword, application/x-shockwave-flash, */*]
Connection = [Keep-Alive]
Accept-encoding = [gzip, deflate]
User-agent = [Mozilla/4.0 (compatible; MSIE 6.0; Windows NT 5.1)]
```

Summary

To the networking stack, Mustang adds APIs to work with client-side cookies and a web server to test your web applications and web services. These were explained in the first and last sections of this chapter. Plus, it also adds types for working with internationalized domain names, internationalized resource identifiers, and interface addresses. These were also explained in this chapter.

Chapter 5
Swing Updates

Java 6 comes with a number of new features and improvements in Swing, from new Windows and GTK look and feels to better support for drag and drop to JTable sorting and filtering. This chapter explains these changes in detail and provides examples.

Better Windows Look and Feel

Seasoned Swing programmers know that Swing supports multiple look and feels for different operating systems. This is an attempt to make Java GUI applications look more like native applications.

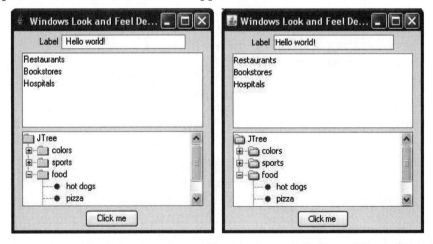

Figure 5.1: Windows Look and Feel in Java 5 (left) and Java 6 (right)

Java 6 brings with it a new look and feel for Windows. Java 6 now uses Microsoft's API for rendering portions of components. As a result, applications written in Mustang look much better than if compiled with

Mustang's predecessors. Figure 5.1 compares the Windows look and feels in Java 5 and Java 6.

As you can see, the Windows look and feel in Java 6 looks more like native Windows applications. Pay special attention to the folder icons of the **JTree** component and the button at the bottom.

I used the code in Listing 5.1 to produce the screenshots.

Listing 5.1: Demonstrating the Windows look and feel in Java 6

```java
import java.awt.Dimension;
import javax.swing.JButton;
import javax.swing.JFrame;
import javax.swing.JLabel;
import javax.swing.JList;
import javax.swing.JPanel;
import javax.swing.JScrollPane;
import javax.swing.JTextField;
import javax.swing.JTree;
import javax.swing.SwingUtilities;
import javax.swing.UIManager;

public class WindowsLookAndFeelDemo {

    private static void constructGUI() {
        JLabel label = new JLabel("Label");
        JTextField field = new JTextField(20);
        field.setText("Hello world!");
        String[] data = new String[] {"Restaurants",
                "Bookstores", "Hospitals"};
        JList list = new JList(data);
        JScrollPane listPane = new JScrollPane(list);
        listPane.setPreferredSize(new Dimension(250, 100));
        JTree tree = new JTree();
        JScrollPane treePane = new JScrollPane(tree);
        treePane.setPreferredSize(new Dimension(250, 100));
        JButton button = new JButton("Click me");
        JPanel cp = new JPanel();
        cp.add(label);
        cp.add(field);
        cp.add(listPane);
        cp.add(treePane);
        cp.add(button);
        JFrame frame = new JFrame();
        frame.setTitle("Windows Look and Feel Demo");
```

```
            frame.setPreferredSize(new Dimension(280, 300));
            frame.setDefaultCloseOperation(JFrame.EXIT_ON_CLOSE);
            frame.setContentPane(cp);
            frame.pack();
            frame.setVisible(true);
        }

    public static void main(String[] args) {
        // Set the look and feel
        try {
            UIManager.setLookAndFeel(
            "com.sun.java.swing.plaf.windows.WindowsLookAndFeel");
        } catch (Exception e) {
            e.printStackTrace();
        }
        SwingUtilities.invokeLater(new Runnable() {
            public void run() {
                constructGUI();
            }
        });
    }
}
```

Better GTK Look and Feel

Similar to the improvement in Windows Look and feel, GTK also gets a new look with Mustang. Figure 5.2 shows a GTK application rendered in Java 6. It looks much better now since the Swing API in Java 6 supports rendering using native calls to GTK engines. As a result, your applications look more like native applications in GTK.

The code in Listing 5.2 is the application I used to get the screenshot in Figure 5.2

Figure 5.2: Improvement on GTK look and feel

Listing 5.2: Demonstrating the new GTK look and feel

```
import java.awt.Dimension;
import javax.swing.JButton;
import javax.swing.JFrame;
import javax.swing.JLabel;
import javax.swing.JList;
import javax.swing.JPanel;
import javax.swing.JScrollPane;
import javax.swing.JTextField;
import javax.swing.JTree;
import javax.swing.SwingUtilities;
import javax.swing.UIManager;

public class WindowsLookAndFeelDemo {

    private static void constructGUI() {
        JLabel label = new JLabel("Label");
        JTextField field = new JTextField(20);
        field.setText("Hello world!");
        String[] data = new String[] {"Restaurants",
                "Bookstores", "Hospitals"};
        JList list = new JList(data);
        JScrollPane listPane = new JScrollPane(list);
        listPane.setPreferredSize(new Dimension(250, 100));
        JTree tree = new JTree();
        JScrollPane treePane = new JScrollPane(tree);
        treePane.setPreferredSize(new Dimension(250, 100));
        JButton button = new JButton("Click me");
```

```
        JPanel cp = new JPanel();
        cp.add(label);
        cp.add(field);
        cp.add(listPane);
        cp.add(treePane);
        cp.add(button);
        JFrame frame = new JFrame();
        frame.setTitle("GTK Look and Feel Demo");
        frame.setPreferredSize(new Dimension(280, 300));
        frame.setDefaultCloseOperation(JFrame.EXIT_ON_CLOSE);
        frame.setContentPane(cp);
        frame.pack();
        frame.setVisible(true);
    }

    public static void main(String[] args) {
        // Set the look and feel
        try {
            UIManager.setLookAndFeel(
                    "com.sun.java.swing.plaf.gtk.GTKLookAndFeel");
        } catch (Exception e) {
            e.printStackTrace();
        }
        SwingUtilities.invokeLater(new Runnable() {
            public void run() {
                constructGUI();
            }
        });
    }
}
```

You can view some other screenshots of GTK look and feel here:

http://ensode.net/java_swing_mustang_screenshots_gtk.html

Improvement to Drag and Drop

Drag and drop (DnD) is a feature that never fails to pique any Swing
beginner's curiosity. This section provides a brief tutorial on the feature as well
as presents the latest enhancement found in Mustang.

There are three sections in this section. The first provides you with a brief
tutorial on DnD in Swing. The second reviews a few classes that you need to

have knowledge of to understand the third subsection, which is a feature on the latest improvement of DnD brought in with Java 6.

DnD Basic

Swing's DnD is surprisingly easy, allowing you to transfer data between two Swing components or between a Swing component and a native application. Many Swing components provide built-in support for DnD, which can be enabled simply by passing **true** to a component's **setDragEnabled** method, such as

```
component.setDragEnabled(true);
```

JTextField, JPasswordField, JFormattedTextField, JTextArea, JTextPane, JTree, JList, JTable, JColorChooser, JEditorPane, and **JFileChooser** have this method, making them DnD ready. Other components, such as **JLabel**, do not, but you can simulate DnD programmatically, even though this topic is beyond the scope of this book.

Listing 5.3 presents an example that demonstrates drag and drop in Swing. Notice how easy it is to achieve this?

Listing 5.3: Simple drag and drop

```
package dnddemo1;
import javax.swing.JFrame;
import javax.swing.JPanel;
import javax.swing.JTextArea;
import javax.swing.JTextField;
import javax.swing.SwingUtilities;

public class DnDDemo {
    private static void constructGUI() {
        //Create and set up the window.
        JFrame frame = new JFrame("Drag and Drop Demo");
        frame.setDefaultCloseOperation(JFrame.EXIT_ON_CLOSE);
        frame.setContentPane(new JPanel());
        JTextField textField = new JTextField(25);
        textField.setText("Let's swing higher");
        frame.add(textField);

        //Create a text area.
        JTextArea textArea = new JTextArea(4, 25);
        textArea.setText("Demonstrating\ndrag and drop");
```

```
        frame.getContentPane().add(textArea);
        textArea.setDragEnabled(true);
        textField.setDragEnabled(true);
        frame.pack();
        frame.setVisible(true);
    }

    public static void main(String[] args) {
        SwingUtilities.invokeLater(new Runnable() {
            public void run() {
                constructGUI();
            }
        });
    }
}
```

Note

Starting from Java 5, you can use the **JFrame** class's **add** method to add a component to it.

If you run the class, you will see something like in Figure 5.3. You can highlight the text in the **JTextArea** and drag it to the **JTextField** to move the highlighted text. Hold the control key while dragging to copy the text instead of moving it.

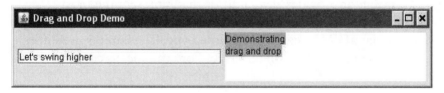

Figure 5.3: Simple drag and drop in Swing

DataFlavor, Transferable, and TransferHandler

Basically, a DnD operation involves packaging some content of a **JComponent** and copy or move it to another component. Behind the scene, a few objects get created and get into action. First off, you need to define the type of the content to be transferred. If the object of a drag operation is a **JTextField**, for example, you need to define what properties of the component you want transferred (the text, foreground, background color, etc).

Afterwards, you need to package it and define how a drop activity impacts the destination component.

An instance of the **java.awt.datatransfer.DataFlavor** class provides the meta information of a component's data that needs to be transferred during a DnD operation. It encapsulates a content type or a MIME type compliant with RFC 2045 (Multipurpose Internet Mail Extensions Part One: Format of Internet Message Bodies) and RFC 2046 (Multipurpose Internet Mail Extensions Part Two: Media Types). Two parts exist in a DataFlavor object, the primary type/subtype part and the representation class. For instance, the MIME type of an image is as follows.

```
image/x-java-image;class=java.awt.Image
```

Here, **image** is the primary type and **x-java-image** is the subtype. **java.awt.Image** is the representation class.

One of the constructors in the **DataFlavor** class expects a MIME type:

```
public DataFlavor(java.lang.String mimeType)
```

To construct a **DataFlavor** that represents a Java image, for instance, you use this line of code:

```
new DataFlavor("image/x-java-image;class=java.awt.Image")
```

In addition, **DataFlavor** provides several fields that represent the most common data flavors. They include **imageFlavor**, **javaFileListFlavor**, **stringFlavor**, and **javaJVMLocalObjectMimeType**. The latter is used if there is no corresponding MIME content type. For example, to construct a **DataFlavor** for a **java.awt.Color** object, use this:

```
new DataFlavor(DataFlavor.javaJVMLocalObjectMimeType +
        ";class=java.awt.Color";
```

A **DataFlavor** instance only represents the meta data of the transferred content. The content itself must be packaged into a transfer object. The class for a transfer object must implement the **java.awt.datatransfer.Transferable** interface. This interface allows you to test if a **DataFlavor** is supported in a transfer object and can return the object associated with the **DataFlavor**. For example, if you wish a DnD operation between two **JTextComponent**s to transfer the text as well as the foreground color of the origin, you must create a **Transferable** implementation that supports two **DataFlavor**s: text and color.

Lastly, any component that supports DnD must employ a **TransferHandler** object. In the previous example, you did not see any because the default **TransferHandler** was used. However, if you want to go beyond basic DnD, you need to create a class that extends the **javax.swing.TransferHandler** class. A **TransferHandler** object determines how to copy the information from the origin **JComponent** to the destination **JComponent**. The term export refers to the act of copying the properties in the source of the data transfer into a **Transferable** object. The term import refers to the copying of the information in a **Transferable** object to the destination of the data transfer.

The following are the minimum methods that you must provide in a **TransferHandler** subclass. Swing invokes some of these methods after a DnD operation is initiated.

```
protected java.awt.datatransfer.Transferable createTransferable(
    JComponent component)
```
> This method gets called after the drag operation is initiated. Swing passes the **JComponent** that is the source of the data transfer. In the method implementation, you need to read the necessary information from the argument **JComponent** and package it to a **Tranferable** object and return the object.

```
public int getSourceActions(JComponent component)
```
> Swing calls this method to enquire what DnD actions are supported. Possible return values are these **TransferHandler** fields: **COPY, COPY_OR_MOVE, LINK, MOVE, NONE**.

```
public boolean importData(JComponent c, Transferable t)
```
> Swing calls this method upon a drop operation, passing the **Transferable** object containing information from the source and the **JComponent** which is the destination of the data transfer. Typically, you override this method so that you can transfer all or part of the information in **Tranferable** to the destination **JComponent**.

```
public boolean canImport(JComponent c, DataFlavor[] flavors)
```
> Swing calls this method to enquire whether or not it should call **importData**. In the overriding method you need to return **true** if the destination **JComponent** can accept one of the MIME types in *flavors*. Return **false** if none of the types in flavors can be handled by the destination component.

As an example, consider the application that consists of three classes (given in Listings 5.4 to 5.6). This example shows how to transfer the text and foreground color of the source component in a DnD operation.

Listing 5.4: The TextColor class

```
package dnddemo2;
import java.awt.Color;
import java.awt.datatransfer.DataFlavor;
import java.awt.datatransfer.Transferable;
import java.awt.datatransfer.UnsupportedFlavorException;
import java.io.IOException;

public class TextColor implements Transferable {

    private String text;
    private Color color;
    private DataFlavor[] flavors;

    public TextColor(String text, Color color) {
        String colorMimeType =
                DataFlavor.javaJVMLocalObjectMimeType +
                ";class=java.awt.Color";
        DataFlavor colorFlavor = null;
        try {
            colorFlavor = new DataFlavor(colorMimeType);
        } catch (ClassNotFoundException e) {
        }
        flavors = new DataFlavor[2];
        flavors[0] = DataFlavor.stringFlavor;
        flavors[1] = colorFlavor;
        this.text = text;
        this.color = color;
    }

    public DataFlavor[] getTransferDataFlavors() {
        return (DataFlavor[])flavors.clone();
    }
    public boolean isDataFlavorSupported(DataFlavor flavor) {
        for (int i = 0; i < flavors.length; i++) {
            if (flavor.equals(flavors[i])) {
                return true;
            }
        }
        return false;
    }
```

```
public Object getTransferData(DataFlavor flavor) throws
    UnsupportedFlavorException, IOException {
  if (flavor.equals(flavors[0])) {
      return text;
  } else if (flavor.equals(flavors[1])) {
      return color;
  } else {
      throw new UnsupportedFlavorException(flavor);
  }
 }
}
```

The **TextColor** class in Listing 5.4 is a **Transferable** implementation that encapsulates two data types, a **String** and a **Color**. When you drag a **JTextComponent**, its text and foreground color will be packaged to a **TextColor** instance. For each data type, you need a **DataFlavor** object that makes an element of the **flavors** array. The elements of flavors are added in the constructor:

```
String colorMimeType =
        DataFlavor.javaJVMLocalObjectMimeType +
        ";class=java.awt.Color";
DataFlavor colorFlavor = null;
try {
    colorFlavor = new DataFlavor(colorMimeType);
} catch (ClassNotFoundException e) {
}
flavors = new DataFlavor[2];
flavors[0] = DataFlavor.stringFlavor;
flavors[1] = colorFlavor;
```

Also, you pass the text and the foreground color of the **JComponent** that is the source of the data transfer to the constructor of **TextColor** and copy them to two class level variables.

```
this.text = text;
this.color = color;
```

The rest of the **TextColor** class body is the implementation methods from **Transferable**. You can obtain a unit of data by passing its data flavor, in this case either a string flavor or a color flavor.

Listing 5.5: The TextColorTransferHandler class

```
package dnddemo2;
```

```java
import java.awt.Color;
import java.awt.datatransfer.DataFlavor;
import java.awt.datatransfer.Transferable;
import javax.swing.JComponent;
import javax.swing.TransferHandler;
import javax.swing.text.JTextComponent;

class TextColorTransferHandler extends TransferHandler {

    public int getSourceActions(JComponent c) {
        return COPY_OR_MOVE;
    }

    protected Transferable createTransferable(
            JComponent component) {
        String text = ((JTextComponent) component).getText();
        Color color = component.getForeground();
        TextColor transferable = new TextColor( text,color );
        return transferable;
    }

    public boolean canImport(JComponent c, DataFlavor[] flavors) {
        return true;
    }

    public boolean importData(JComponent component,
                Transferable transferable) {
        String colorMimeType = DataFlavor.javaJVMLocalObjectMimeType
                + ";class=java.awt.Color";
        JTextComponent textComponent = (JTextComponent) component;
        try {
            DataFlavor colorFlavor = new DataFlavor(colorMimeType);
            Color color = (Color) transferable.getTransferData(
                    colorFlavor );
            String text = (String) transferable
                    .getTransferData( DataFlavor.stringFlavor );
            textComponent.setForeground(color);
            textComponent.setText(text);
        }
        catch( Exception e ) {
            e.printStackTrace();
        }
        return true;
    }
}
```

The **TextColorTransferHandler** class in Listing 5.5 manages the data transfer during a DnD operation in this sample application. It is a subclass of **TransferHandler** and overrides several of its parent's methods. The **getSourceActions** and **createTransferable** methods are invoked during a drag operation. **canImport** and **importData** are called when a drop occurs.

The **getSourceActions** method in **TextColorTransferHandler** indicates that both move and copy actions are supported. The **createTransferable** method creates a **TextColor** object that stores the information about the text and foreground color of the source **JTextComponent**.

The **canImport** method always returns **true** to simplify this application. In real-world applications you may want to test if you can import the **Tranferable** in a **TransferHandler** to the destination component on a drop.

Listing 5.6: The DnDDemo2 class

```java
package dnddemo2;
import java.awt.Color;
import javax.swing.JFrame;
import javax.swing.JPanel;
import javax.swing.JTextArea;
import javax.swing.JTextField;
import javax.swing.SwingUtilities;

public class DnDDemo2 {
    private static void constructGUI() {
        JFrame frame = new JFrame("Drag and Drop Demo 2");
        frame.setDefaultCloseOperation(JFrame.EXIT_ON_CLOSE);
        frame.setContentPane(new JPanel());

        JTextField textField = new JTextField(25);
        textField.setText("Let's swing higher");
        frame.add(textField);

        //Create a text area.
        JTextArea textArea = new JTextArea(4, 25);
        textArea.setText("Demonstrating\ndrag and drop");
        textArea.setForeground(Color.red);
        frame.add(textArea);

        textArea.setDragEnabled(true);
        textField.setDragEnabled(true);
```

```
        TextColorTransferHandler transferHandler =
            new TextColorTransferHandler();
        textArea.setTransferHandler(transferHandler);
        textField.setTransferHandler(transferHandler);
        frame.pack();
        frame.setVisible(true);
    }

    public static void main(String[] args) {
        SwingUtilities.invokeLater(new Runnable() {
            public void run() {
                constructGUI();
            }
        });
    }
}
```

The **DnDDemo2** class is a simple Swing application with two **JTextComponent**s. Note that both components have a **TextColorTransferHandler** instance as their transfer handler.

```
        textArea.setDragEnabled(true);
        textField.setDragEnabled(true);

        TextColorTransferHandler transferHandler =
            new TextColorTransferHandler();
        textArea.setTransferHandler(transferHandler);
        textField.setTransferHandler(transferHandler);
```

You can see the application in Figure 5.4. Note that this time whenever you drag a text component, its text and foreground color will be copied.

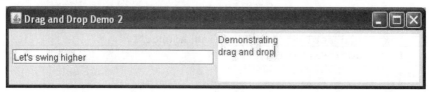

Figure 5.4: Dragging and dropping text as well as color

DnD Improvement in Mustang

Now that you understand how DnD works in Swing, let's look at relevant improvements that Mustang brings. There are two issues addressed by the Drag and Drop feature in Mustang:

1. A component involved in a DnD activity can now determine the drop location.
2. In Java 6 Swing provides all relevant information on a transfer by enquiring the **TransferHandler** if it is acceptable and when telling it to import data.

In term of the first improvement, this takes the form of a new inner class **TransferHandler.DropLocation**. The **getDropPoint** method in this inner class returns a **java.awt.Point** that indicates the mouse's current location within the component. **TransferHandler.DropLocation** have four subclasses: **JList.DropLocation**, **JTable.DropLocation**, **JTextComponent.DropLocation**, and **JTree.DropLocation**.

In addition to the **getDropPoint** method, **JList, JTable, JTree**, and **JTextComponent** all have a new method named **setDropMode** that accepts a **javax.swing.DropMode** enum. This enum is also new in Mustang. Through this enum **setDropMode** bring benefits.

Pre-Mustang, dropping on a **JTextComponent** inserts content to the caret position. Dropping on **JList, JTable**, and **JTree** inserts it on the selection (the element being selected). There were some issues with this approach, however. Swing might ignore selection events that were fired during the DnD operation and a consistent API for fetching the drop location at drop time was not available.

With the addition of **setDropMode** to **JList, JTree, JTable**, and **JTextComponent**, you can now choose the insertion point for these components as drop locations. The **setDropMode** method accepts one of the values defined in the **DropMode** enum: **INSERT, INSERT_COLS, INSERT_ROWS, ON, ON_OR_INSERT, ON_OR_INSERT_COLS, ON_OR_INSERT_ROWS**, and **USE_SELECTION**. The value passed to **setDropMode** lets the component choose the exact location a drop element should be added.

The second enhancement to Swing DnD takes the form of the new inner class of **TransferHandler**, **TransferSupport**, and new method overloads of the **canImport** and **importData** methods in **TransferHandler**:

```
public boolean canImport(TransferHandler.TransferSupport support)
public boolean importData(TransferHandler.TransferSupport support)
```

Both new methods accepts a **TransferHandler.TransferSupport**. It is important that you understand the **TranferSupport** inner class as the two methods are preferred over the old **canImport** and **importData** methods.

The **TransferSupport** inner class defines the following methods.

```
public java.awt.Component getComponent()
```
Returns the transfer's target component.

```
public Transfer.DropLocation getDropLocation()
```
Returns the current drop location.

```
public void setShowDropLocation(boolean show)
```
Specifies if the drop location should be visually indicated for the transfer. By default, the drop location is shown if the TransferHandler has indicated it can accept the transfer content.

```
public void setDropAction(int dropAction)
```
Specifies the drop action for the transfer. The value of *dropAction* must be one these values: **TransferHandler.COPY**, **TransferHandler.COPY_OR_MOVE**, or **TransferHandler.MOVE**.

```
public int getDropAction()
```
Returns the drop action.

```
public int getUserDropAction()
```
Returns the user drop action.

```
public int getSourceDropActions()
```
Returns the drag source's supported drop actions.

```
public java.awt.datatransfer.DataFlavor[] getDataFlavors()
```
Returns the data flavors for this transfer.

```
public boolean isDataFlavorSupported(
        java.awt.datatransfer.DataFlavor df)
```
Indicates if the specified DataFlavor is supported

```
public java.awt.datatransfer.Transferable getTransferable()
```
Returns the **Transferable** associated with this transfer.

The following is an example that shows how you use the new DnD-related types in Java 6 to drop elements in a **JList**. You can choose one of several drop modes to see the difference.

The code is given in Listing 5.7.

Listing 5.7: Enhancement to DnD in Java 6

```java
package dnddemo3;
import java.awt.BorderLayout;
import java.awt.Rectangle;
import java.awt.datatransfer.DataFlavor;
import java.awt.datatransfer.Transferable;
import java.awt.event.ItemEvent;
import java.awt.event.ItemListener;
import javax.swing.DefaultListModel;
import javax.swing.DropMode;
import javax.swing.JComboBox;
import javax.swing.JFrame;
import javax.swing.JLabel;
import javax.swing.JList;
import javax.swing.JPanel;
import javax.swing.JScrollPane;
import javax.swing.JTextField;
import javax.swing.SwingUtilities;
import javax.swing.TransferHandler;

public class DnDDemo3 {

    private static void constructGUI() {

        // The first panel, containing a JTextField
        JPanel north = new JPanel();
        north.add(new JLabel("Drag from here:"));
        JTextField field = new JTextField(10);
        field.setDragEnabled(true);      // enabled drag and drop
        north.add(field);

        // The second panel in the middle, containing
        // list that will become a drop target
        final DefaultListModel listModel = new DefaultListModel();
        listModel.addElement("first");
        listModel.addElement("second");
        final JList list = new JList(listModel);
        list.setDragEnabled(true);       // enabled drag and drop
```

```java
// Set customized transfer handler
list.setTransferHandler(new TransferHandler() {
    public boolean canImport(TransferHandler.TransferSupport
            support) {
        // Return false if string DataFlavor is not
        // supported
        if (! support.isDataFlavorSupported(
                DataFlavor.stringFlavor)) {
            return false;
        }
        JList.DropLocation dl = (JList.DropLocation)
                support.getDropLocation();
        if (dl.getIndex() == -1) {
            return false;
        } else {
            return true;
        }
    }

    public boolean importData(
            TransferHandler.TransferSupport support) {
        if (! canImport(support)) {
            return false;
        }

        // get Transferable
        Transferable transferable =
                support.getTransferable();
        String data;
        try {
            data = (String) transferable.getTransferData(
                    DataFlavor.stringFlavor);
        } catch (Exception e) {
            return false;
        }

        JList.DropLocation dl = (JList.DropLocation)
                support.getDropLocation();
        int index = dl.getIndex();
        if (dl.isInsert()) {
            listModel.add(index, data);
        } else {
            listModel.set(index, data);
        }
```

```
            // Scroll to display the element that was dropped
            Rectangle r = list.getCellBounds(index, index);
            list.scrollRectToVisible(r);
            return true;
        }
    });
    JScrollPane center = new JScrollPane();
    center.setViewportView(list);

    // the third panel containing a combobox to change the
    // JList's drop mode
    DropMode[] modes = new DropMode[] {DropMode.USE_SELECTION,
            DropMode.ON, DropMode.INSERT,
            DropMode.ON_OR_INSERT};
    final JComboBox combo = new JComboBox(modes);
    combo.addItemListener(new ItemListener() {
        public void itemStateChanged(ItemEvent e) {
            DropMode mode = (DropMode) combo.getSelectedItem();
            list.setDropMode(mode);
        }
    });
    JPanel south = new JPanel();
    south.add(new JLabel("Drop mode:"));
    south.add(combo);

    JPanel cp = new JPanel();
    cp.setLayout(new BorderLayout());
    cp.add(north, BorderLayout.NORTH);
    cp.add(south, BorderLayout.SOUTH);
    cp.add(center, BorderLayout.CENTER);
    JFrame frame = new JFrame();
    frame.setDefaultCloseOperation(JFrame.EXIT_ON_CLOSE);
    frame.setTitle("JList's Drag & Drop");
    frame.setContentPane(cp);
    frame.pack();
    frame.setVisible(true);
}

public static void main(String[] args) {
    SwingUtilities.invokeLater(new Runnable() {
        public void run() {
            constructGUI();
        }
    });
}
```

}

If you run the application, you'll see a JFrame that looks like that in Figure 5.5.

Figure 5.5: Testing DnD in Java 6

Type a word in the text field and drag and drop it to the **JList**. Change the value of the drop mode to experiment with various drop modes.

True Double Buffering

If you've been working with GUI-based applications for a while, you already know that repainting GUI components takes time. In most computers with decent CPU speed, this still translates into flickering, tearing, and perceivable delay that reduce the coolness of your application. This is because the monitor constantly refreshes the screen at the rate of about 70 times a second. If your application is not able to finish a drawing or repainting operation in less than $1/70^{th}$ second, then flickering may occur.

One standard solution to this problem is double buffering, in which the repainting or drawing of a screen area is performed to an invisible video page in memory. When the drawing/repainting is complete, the whole page is copied into the video RAM in one operation, normally by also synchronizing the copying with the monitor refresh cycle, so that the copy operation is ahead of the monitor raster beam. Double buffering effectively reduces or even eliminates the annoying slowness.

Prior to Java 6, Swing supported double buffering on an application basis. While this did improve performance, it would be better if double buffering had been on a per window basis. The Swing API in Java 6 provides true double buffering, first on the Windows platform (at the time of this writing) but later on all other platforms.

JTable Sorting

Pre-Mustang, sorting a JTable column was an involved task. In Java 6, happily, this important task is much easier to achieve, thanks to the new abstract class **javax.swing.RowSorter**. To make lives even easier, Mustang provides a subclass of **RowSorter**, **javax.swing.DefaultRowSorter**, which is also an abstract class. A concrete implementation of **DefaultRowSorter**, the **javax.swing.TableRowSorter** class, is readily available.

A **RowSorter** essentially provides a mapping between the view coordinate system of a **JTable** and its data model's coordinate system. You won't believe how easy it is to add sorting capability to a JTable until you try it. All you need to do is instantiate the **TableRowSorter** class and pass a reference to a **TableModel** to its constructor. Like this.

```
TableRowSorter<TableModel> sorter =
    new TableRowSorter<TableModel>(tableModel);
```

Then, you need to pass the sorter to the **JTable**'s **setRowSorter** method, which is a new addition to Mustang.

```
table.setRowSorter(sorter);
```

As an example, the class in Listing 5.8 presents a small Swing application that demonstrates the sorting capability in Java 6 **JTable**.

Listing 5.8: Sorting JTable

```
package jtable;
import javax.swing.JFrame;
import javax.swing.JScrollPane;
import javax.swing.JTable;
import javax.swing.SwingUtilities;
import javax.swing.table.DefaultTableModel;
import javax.swing.table.TableModel;
```

```java
import javax.swing.table.TableRowSorter;

public class JTableSortDemo {

    private static void constructGUI() {

        // Table content with 2 columns and 4 rows
        Object[][] data = {
                {"United States"   ,   297200005},
                {"China"           ,  1306313812},
                {"Brazil"          ,   186112794},
                {"India"           ,  1080264388}
        };
        String columnNames[] = {"Country", "Population"};
        TableModel model = new
                DefaultTableModel(data, columnNames) {
            public Class<?> getColumnClass(int column) {
                return getValueAt(0, column).getClass();
            }
        };
        JTable table = new JTable(model);

        // Appry RowSorter to JTable
        TableRowSorter<TableModel> sorter =
                new TableRowSorter<TableModel>(model);
        table.setRowSorter(sorter);

        JScrollPane scrollPane = new JScrollPane(table);
        JFrame frame = new JFrame("Sorting Table");
        frame.setDefaultCloseOperation(JFrame.EXIT_ON_CLOSE);
        frame.add(scrollPane);
        frame.setSize(300, 200);
        frame.setVisible(true);
    }

    public static void main(String[] args) {
        SwingUtilities.invokeLater(new Runnable() {
            public void run() {
                constructGUI();
            }
        });
    }
}
```

Running the **JTableSortDemo** class gives you a JFrame like the one in Figure 5.6

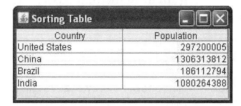

Figure 5.6: Before sorting JTable

If you click one of the columns in the **JTable**, the data will be sorted based on the content of the clicked column. Figure 5.7 shows the table after sorting by country.

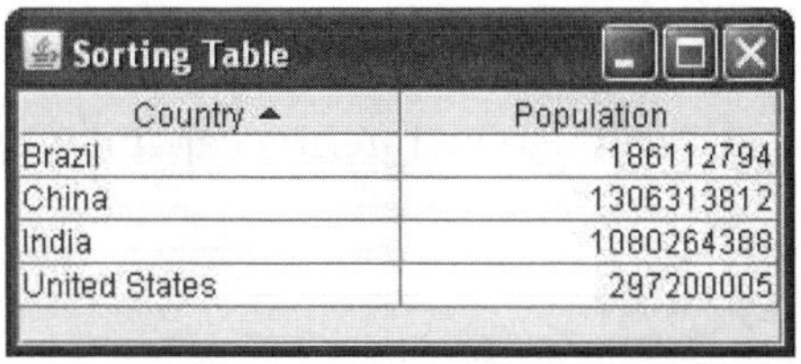

Figure 5.7: After sorting

Note that after sorting there is an arrow on the header of the column that defines the sort order.

JTable Filtering

In addition to sorting, Java 6 provides filtering capability to **JTable**. The backbone of this feature is the **javax.swing.RowFilter** abstract class. In a subclass, you need to provide the implementation for its **include** method. Here is the signature of **include**. You write the filtering rule here.

```
public abstract boolean include(RowFilter.Entry<? extends M,
    ? extends I> entry)
```

A **RowFilter.Entry** represents an element that may or may not be filtered out. You return **true** if you want the entry to be displayed in the JTable and return **false** otherwise.

For instance, the following **include** method passes the entry of type Integer if the value is more than one billion.

```
public boolean include(Entry entry) {
    // Filter the JTable based on the content of the
    // second column
    Integer population = (Integer) entry.getValue(1);
    return population.intValue() > 1000000000;
}
```

Unfortunately, there is no **setRowFilter** method in **JTable**, so you cannot directly apply a filter to a **JTable**. Instead, you pass the **RowFilter** to a **RowSorter** and pass the **RowSorter** to the **JTable**.

```
sorter.setRowFilter(filter);
table.setRowSorter(sorter);
```

The following example shows the new filtering capability in **JTable**. The code is given in Listing 5.10.

Listing 5.10: Filtering JTable

```
package jtable;
import javax.swing.JFrame;
import javax.swing.JScrollPane;
import javax.swing.JTable;
import javax.swing.RowFilter;
import javax.swing.SwingUtilities;
import javax.swing.table.DefaultTableModel;
import javax.swing.table.TableModel;
import javax.swing.table.TableRowSorter;

public class JTableFilterDemo {

    private static void constructGUI() {

        // Table content
        Object data[][] = {
                {"China"           , 1306313812},
                {"India"           , 1080264388},
                {"United States"   ,  297200005},
                {"Brazil"          ,  186112794}
        };
        String columnNames[] = {"Country", "Population"};
        TableModel model = new
                DefaultTableModel(data, columnNames) {
```

```
        public Class<?> getColumnClass(int column) {
            return getValueAt(0, column).getClass();
        }
    };
    JTable table = new JTable(model);

    // Apply row filter to JTable
    RowFilter<Object, Object> filter =
            new RowFilter<Object, Object>() {
        public boolean include(Entry entry) {
            // Filter the JTable based on the content of the
            // second column
            Integer population = (Integer) entry.getValue(1);
            return population.intValue() > 1000000000;
        }
    };

    TableRowSorter<TableModel> sorter =
            new TableRowSorter<TableModel>(model);
    sorter.setRowFilter(filter);
    table.setRowSorter(sorter);

    JScrollPane scrollPane = new JScrollPane(table);
    JFrame frame = new JFrame("Filtering Table");
    frame.setDefaultCloseOperation(JFrame.EXIT_ON_CLOSE);
    frame.add(scrollPane);
    frame.setSize(300, 200);
    frame.setVisible(true);
}

public static void main(String[] args) {
    SwingUtilities.invokeLater(new Runnable() {
        public void run() {
            constructGUI();
        }
    });
}
}
```

If you run the class in Listing 5.10, you'll see something similar to Figure 5.8.
Note that the **JTable** has been filtered so that it only displays countries with a
population of over a billion.

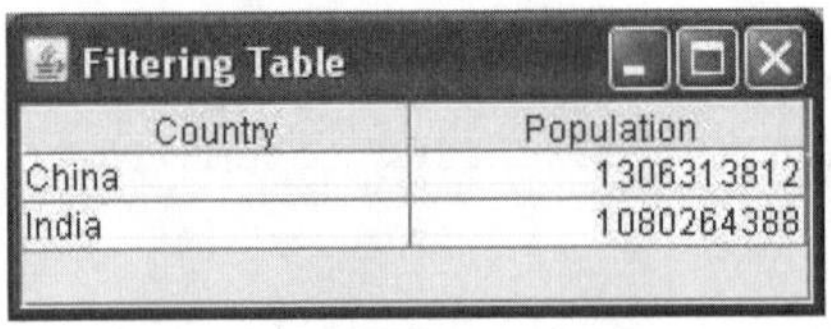

Figure 5.8: Filtered JTable

Swing Worker

In any Swing application, a single thread is responsible for painting the GUI and handling events. This thread is called the event-dispatching thread (EDT). The use of the same thread for both tasks guarantees that each event handler finishes executing before the next one executes and that GUI painting will not be interrupted by events. If an event handler must perform a lengthy task, the task needs to run in a separate thread, or else your application will become unresponsive during the execution of the event handler. On the other hand, Swing components should be accessed on the EDT only, and, unfortunately, communication between the EDT and another thread could be tricky. Therefore, if you need to access Swing components from another thread, you need to be extra-careful.

The **javax.swing.SwingWorker** abstract class, new in Mustang, is a utility class that helps you with time-consuming tasks in a Swing application. After you instantiate a subclass of **SwingWorker**, you can call its **execute** method to start the worker. Calling **execute** will in turn invoke the **doInBackground** method on a different thread. You should write your code in this method. From within **doInBackground** you can call the **publish** method to publish intermediate data that will be received by the **process** method. **SwingWorker** invokes the **process** method each time the **publish** method is called on the EDT. Therefore, this is your chance to update any Swing component. For example, you can send intermediate results to the **publish** method from **doInBackground** and let **process** prints the results in a **JLabel**. Finally, when **doInBackground** finishes executing, **SwingWorker** will invoke the **done** method. In addition, there are also a **cancel** method to cancel a running **SwingWorker** and a **isCancelled** method that indicates if the worker has been cancelled.

The following example shows a Swing application with a **SwingWorker** subclass named **CounterTask**. The task takes 10 seconds to complete and during its execution all other Swing components must still be responsive. For example, you can click a **Cancel** button to cancel the task. During execution, it will also repeatedly send the status that will be displayed in a **JTextArea** in the application. The **CounterTask** class is given in Listing 5.11. The main Swing application that instantiates **CounterTask** and provides a handler to call the **CounterTask**'s **execute** method is named **SwingWorkerDemo** and is presented in Listing 5.12.

Listing 5.11: The CounterTask class

```java
package swingworker;
import javax.swing.JTextArea;
import javax.swing.SwingWorker;

public class CounterTask extends SwingWorker<Integer, Integer> {
    private static final int DELAY = 1000;
    private JTextArea textArea;

    // A calling application must pass a JTextArea
    public CounterTask(JTextArea textArea) {
        this.textArea = textArea;
    }

    @Override
    protected Integer doInBackground() throws Exception {
        int i = 0;
        int count = 10;
        while (! isCancelled() && i < count) {
            i++;
            publish(new Integer[] {i});
            setProgress(count * i / count);
            Thread.sleep(DELAY);
        }

        return count;
    }

    @Override
    protected void process(Integer... chunks) {
        for (int i : chunks)
            textArea.append(i + "\n");
    }
```

```
    @Override
    protected void done() {
        if (isCancelled())
            textArea.append("Cancelled !");
        else
            textArea.append("Done !");
    }
}
```

Listing 5.12: The SwingWorkerDemo class

```
package swingworker;
import java.awt.LayoutManager;
import java.awt.event.ActionEvent;
import java.awt.event.ActionListener;
import java.beans.PropertyChangeEvent;
import java.beans.PropertyChangeListener;
import javax.swing.BoxLayout;
import javax.swing.JButton;
import javax.swing.JFrame;
import javax.swing.JPanel;
import javax.swing.JProgressBar;
import javax.swing.JScrollPane;
import javax.swing.JTextArea;
import javax.swing.SwingUtilities;

public class SwingWorkerDemo {
    private static void constructGUI() {
        // Text area that displays results
        JTextArea textArea = new JTextArea(10, 20);

        // Progress bar displaying the progress of the
        // time-consuming task
        final JProgressBar progressBar = new JProgressBar(0, 10);

        final CounterTask task = new CounterTask(textArea);
        task.addPropertyChangeListener(new PropertyChangeListener()
        {
            public void propertyChange(PropertyChangeEvent evt) {
                if ("progress".equals(evt.getPropertyName())) {

                    progressBar.setValue((Integer)evt.getNewValue());
                }
            }
        });
```

```
        // Start button
        JButton startButton = new JButton("Start");
        startButton.addActionListener(new ActionListener() {
            public void actionPerformed(ActionEvent e) {
                task.execute();
            }
        });

        // Cancel button
        JButton cancelButton = new JButton("Cancel");
        cancelButton.addActionListener(new ActionListener() {
            public void actionPerformed(ActionEvent e) {
                task.cancel(true);
            }
        });

        JPanel buttonPanel = new JPanel();
        buttonPanel.add(startButton);
        buttonPanel.add(cancelButton);

        JPanel cp = new JPanel();
        LayoutManager layout = new BoxLayout(cp, BoxLayout.Y_AXIS);
        cp.setLayout(layout);
        cp.add(buttonPanel);
        cp.add(new JScrollPane(textArea));
        cp.add(progressBar);

        JFrame frame = new JFrame("SwingWorker Demo");
        frame.setDefaultCloseOperation(JFrame.EXIT_ON_CLOSE);
        frame.setContentPane(cp);
        frame.pack();
        frame.setVisible(true);
    }

    public static void main(String[] args) {
        SwingUtilities.invokeLater(new Runnable() {
            public void run() {
                constructGUI();
            }
        });
    }
}
```

If you run the application, you can see a Swing application with two buttons like the one in Figure 5.9. Click the **Start** button to start the process. Notice

that the **Cancel** button is still responsive during the **SwingWorker** execution
and can be clicked to cancel the execution.

Figure 5.9: SwingWorker demo

Text Component Printing

The **javax.swing.text.JTextComponent** class has been blessed with three
print methods to print the content of the text component easily. Each of these
print methods displays the **print** dialog and blocks until printing is done. The
first and easiest **print** method to use has this signature:

```
public boolean print() throws java.awt.print.PrinterException
```

This method is, needless to say, very easy to use. No further explanation
needed except to add that the method always returns true **unless** the print job
is cancelled.

The second **print** method is as follows.

```
public boolean print(java.text.MessageFormat header,
        java.text.MessageFormat footer) throws
        java.awt.print.PrinterException
```

This is slightly complex than the first but is still easy to use. It presents to you
the opportunity to pass a header and a footer to the printed page. The
MessageFormat class is an old face in Swing and I don't intend to explain it
except to say that you can construct a **MessageFormat** simply by passing a
string to its constructor:

```
new MessageFormat(string)
```

The third **print** method in **JTextComponent** accepts more parameters, as you can witness in its signature.

```
public boolean print(java.text.MessageFormat header,
        java.text.MessageFormat footer, boolean showPrintDialog,
        javax.print.PrintService service,
        javax.print.attributes.PrintRequestAttributeSet attributes,
        boolean interactive) throws java.awt.print.PrinterException
```

The extra arguments are:

- *showPrintDialog*. Pass **true** to display the print dialog or **false** to bypass the dialog, in which case the text component content will be sent to the default printer.
- *service*. Representing a **PrintService**, which describes the features of a printer.
- *attributes*. Representing a **PrintRequestAttributeSet** that specifies the interface for a set of print request attributes.

The example in Listing 5.13 shows the new printing capability of **JTextComponent**.

Listing 5.13: Testing JTextComponent print capability

```
import java.awt.BorderLayout;
import java.awt.event.ActionEvent;
import java.awt.event.ActionListener;
import java.text.MessageFormat;
import javax.swing.JFrame;
import javax.swing.JMenu;
import javax.swing.JMenuBar;
import javax.swing.JMenuItem;
import javax.swing.JPanel;
import javax.swing.JScrollPane;
import javax.swing.JTextArea;
import javax.swing.SwingUtilities;

public class TextComponentDemo {

    private static void constructGUI() {

        // The text are whose content will be printed
```

```java
        final JTextArea textArea = new JTextArea();
        textArea.setText("To print the content of this text area, "
                + " select File -> Print ");
        JScrollPane jScrollPane = new JScrollPane(textArea);
        // Header and footer on the printed page
        final MessageFormat header = new MessageFormat("My Header");
        final MessageFormat footer = new MessageFormat("My Footer");

        JMenu menu = new JMenu("File");
        JMenuItem printItem = new JMenuItem("Print");
        printItem.addActionListener(new ActionListener() {
            public void actionPerformed(ActionEvent e) {
                try {
                    textArea.print(header, footer, true, null,
                            null, true);
                } catch (Exception ex) {
                    ex.printStackTrace();
                }
            }
        });
        menu.add(printItem);

        JMenuBar menuBar = new JMenuBar();
        menuBar.add(menu);

        JPanel contentPane = new JPanel();
        contentPane.setLayout(new BorderLayout());
        contentPane.add(jScrollPane, BorderLayout.CENTER);

        JFrame frame = new JFrame();
        frame.setTitle("Text-component Printing Demo");
        frame.setSize(400, 200);
        frame.setDefaultCloseOperation(JFrame.EXIT_ON_CLOSE);
        frame.setJMenuBar(menuBar);          // set menu bar
        frame.setContentPane(contentPane);   // set content pane
        frame.setVisible(true);
    }

    public static void main(String[] args) {
        SwingUtilities.invokeLater(new Runnable() {
            public void run() {
                constructGUI();
            }
        });
    }
}
```

If you run the class in Listing 5.13 you will see a JFrame like that in Figure 5.10.

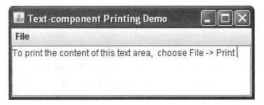

Figure 5.10: Text-component printing demo

If you click the **Print** menu from **File**, you can will see the print dialog like the one in Figure 5.11.

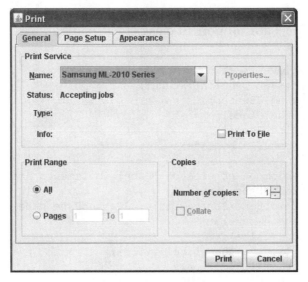

Figure 5.11: The print dialog

Clicking **Print** will print the content of the **JTextArea** to the printer.

New Methods in the JTabPane Component

The **javax.swing.JTabbedPane** class has three new methods in Mustang:

```
public void setTabComponentAt(int index, java.awt.Component c)
```
Sets the component that will be displayed at the title portion of the tab at the specified index.

```
public java.awt.Component getTabComponentAt(int index)
```
Returns the tab component at the specified index.

```
public int indexOfTabComponent(java.awt.Component tabComponent)
```
Returns the index for the argument tab component or -1 if the argument does not match any of the tab components in the **JTabbedPane**.

The following example teaches you how to use these new methods. There are two classes in the example. The first one, **TabComponent**, in Listing 5.14, is a tab component for each tab. The second class, **TabComponentDemo** in Listing 5.15, is the main class that creates a **JFrame** and adds a **JTabbedPane** to it.

Listing 5.14: The TabComponent class

```java
package tab;
import java.awt.event.ActionEvent;
import java.awt.event.ActionListener;
import javax.swing.JButton;
import javax.swing.JLabel;
import javax.swing.JPanel;
import javax.swing.JTabbedPane;

public class TabComponent extends JPanel implements ActionListener {
    private JTabbedPane pane;
    public TabComponent(String title, JTabbedPane pane) {
        this.pane = pane;
        setOpaque(false);
        JLabel label = new JLabel(title);
        add(label);
        JButton button = new JButton("Close");
        button.addActionListener(this);
        add(button);
    }

    public void actionPerformed(ActionEvent e) {
        int i = pane.indexOfTabComponent(this);
        if (i != -1)
            pane.remove(i);
    }
}
```

The **TabComponent** class encapsulates a **JLabel** and a **JButton**. The **JButton** can be clicked to remove the pane.

Listing 5.15: The TabComponentDemo class

```
package tab;
import javax.swing.JFrame;
import javax.swing.JLabel;
import javax.swing.JTabbedPane;
import javax.swing.SwingUtilities;

public class TabComponentDemo {
    private static void constructGUI() {

        JTabbedPane pane = new JTabbedPane();
        // Initialize the JTabbedPane, adding 3 panes, with
        // a title and a JLabel on each pane
        for (int i = 0; i < 3; i++) {
            String title = "Tab " + i;
            pane.add(title, new JLabel(title));
            pane.setTabComponentAt(i, new TabComponent(title,
        pane));
        }

        JFrame frame = new JFrame("Tab Component Demo");
        frame.setDefaultCloseOperation(JFrame.EXIT_ON_CLOSE);
        frame.add(pane);
        frame.setSize(500, 200);
        frame.setVisible(true);
    }

    public static void main(String[] args) {
        SwingUtilities.invokeLater(new Runnable() {
            public void run() {
                constructGUI();
            }
        });
    }
}
```

Figure 5.12 shows the JTabbedPane with three tab components.

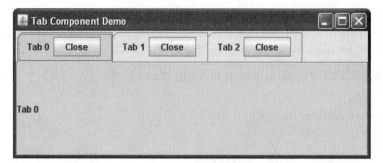

Figure 5.12: Using JTabbedPane class's new methods

Summary

In this chapter you've learned many new features in Swing that Mustang brings in. They include new Windows and GTK look and feels, better support for drag and drop, and **JTable** sorting and filtering.

Chapter 6
Abstract Window Toolkit

Improved dialog modality, splash screens, system tray support, desktop help, and text antialiasing are among the things that Mustang 6 brings to the Abstract Window Toolkit (AWT). We look at each of them in this chapter.

Improved Dialog Modality

In JDK 1.5 and earlier there were only two types of modality for a **java.awt.Dialog**, either modal or modeless. A modeless dialog does not block any other windows in the same application from getting focus. On the other hand, a modal one, when shown, makes all other windows in the same application inaccessible, except if the windows has the showing modal dialog as their owner.

When working with a modal dialog, however, you may want to interact with other components in the application, such as opening the Help window to get assistance on how to fill in the form in the modal dialog. Prior to Mustang, this was not possible . This case is demonstrated in the code in Listing 6.1.

Listing 6.1: A modal dialog in pre Mustang JDKs

```
package modality;
import java.awt.Dialog;
import java.awt.FlowLayout;
import java.awt.event.ActionEvent;
import java.awt.event.ActionListener;
import javax.swing.JButton;
import javax.swing.JDialog;
import javax.swing.JFrame;
import javax.swing.SwingUtilities;

public class PreMustangModalDialogDemo {
```

```java
    private static void constructGUI() {
        final JFrame parent = new JFrame("Main");
        parent.setLayout(new FlowLayout());
        parent.setDefaultCloseOperation(JFrame.EXIT_ON_CLOSE);

        JButton showButton = new JButton("Show Modal Dialog");
        showButton.addActionListener(new ActionListener() {
            public void actionPerformed(ActionEvent e) {
                JDialog modalDialog = new JDialog(parent);
                modalDialog.setModal(true);
                modalDialog.setTitle("Modal Dialog");
                modalDialog.setBounds(300, 200, 300, 200);
                modalDialog.setVisible(true);
            }
        });
        parent.add(showButton);

        JButton helpButton = new JButton("Help");
        helpButton.addActionListener(new ActionListener() {
            public void actionPerformed(ActionEvent e) {
                JDialog dialog = new JDialog(parent);
                dialog.setTitle("Help");
                dialog.setBounds(400, 200, 300, 200);
                dialog.setVisible(true);
            }
        });
        parent.add(helpButton);
        parent.setBounds(100, 100, 300, 200);
        parent.setVisible(true);
    }

    public static void main(String[] args) {
        SwingUtilities.invokeLater(new Runnable() {
            public void run() {
                constructGUI();
            }
        });
    }
}
```

By default a **Dialog** is modeless. To make it modal, you pass **true** to its **setModal** method:

```java
modalDialog.setModal(true);
```

Figure 6.1 shows the main **JFrame** and the modal dialog that result from running the code in Listing 6.1. Note that once the modal dialog is shown, you cannot click the Help button.

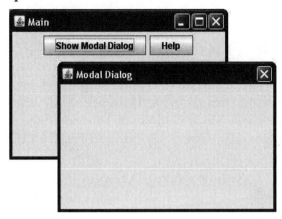

Figure 6.1: Limitation of modality in previous releases of Java

Mustang introduces different types of modality, in which you no longer use **setModal** but the new method **setModalityType** in the Dialog class to make a dialog modal.

```
public void setModalityType(Dialog.ModalityType type)
```

Dialog.ModalityType is an enum in the **java.awt** package. Its values are as follows:

- **APPLICATION_MODAL**. Blocks all windows in the same application except those with the modal dialog as their owner.
- **DOCUMENT_MODAL**. Makes all windows from the same document inaccessible, except those from the modal dialog's child hierarchy.
- **MODELESS**. Does not block any other windows.
- **TOOLKIT_MODAL**. Makes all windows from the same toolkit inaccessible, except those from the modal dialog's child hierarchy.

As you can guess, the **MODELESS** option is the same as the default dialog in pre-Mustang JDKs. **APPLICATION_MODAL**, **DOCUMENT_MODAL**, and **TOOLKIT_MODAL** are similar but differ in scopes.

The alternative to calling **setModalityType** to set the modality of a dialog is by passing a **Dialog.ModalityType** value to the constructor **JDialog** class's constructor:

```
JDialog(Window owner, String title, Dialog.ModalityType type)
```

Using APPLICATION_MODAL

APPLICATION_MODAL produces a **Dialog** that is similar in modality to a modal dialog in pre-Mustang releases. However, as you will learn later in this section, you can exclude other windows that are not in the modal dialog's child hierarchy. The example in Listing 6.2 shows **APPLICATION_MODAL** in action.

Listing 6.2: Using APPLICATION_MODAL

```java
package modality;
import java.awt.Dialog;
import java.awt.FlowLayout;
import java.awt.event.ActionEvent;
import java.awt.event.ActionListener;
import javax.swing.JButton;
import javax.swing.JDialog;
import javax.swing.JFrame;
import javax.swing.SwingUtilities;

public class ApplicationModalDialogDemo {

    private static void constructGUI() {
        final JFrame parent1 = new JFrame("Parent Frame 1");
        parent1.setLayout(new FlowLayout());
        parent1.setDefaultCloseOperation(JFrame.EXIT_ON_CLOSE);

        JButton button = new JButton("Application modal dialog");
        button.addActionListener(new ActionListener() {
            public void actionPerformed(ActionEvent e) {
                JDialog dialog = new JDialog(parent1,
                        "Application-Modal Dialog",
                        Dialog.ModalityType.APPLICATION_MODAL);
                dialog.setBounds(200, 150, 200, 150);
                dialog.setVisible(true);
            }
        });
        parent1.add(button);
```

```
        parent1.setBounds(100, 100, 200, 150);
        parent1.setVisible(true);

        // Another frame in the same application
        JFrame parent2 = new JFrame("Parent Frame 2");
        parent2.setBounds(500, 100, 200, 150);
        parent2.setVisible(true);
    }

    public static void main(String[] args) {
        SwingUtilities.invokeLater(new Runnable() {
            public void run() {
                constructGUI();
            }
        });
    }
}
```

There are two **JFrame**s produced by the class in Listing 6.2, and the modality type of the **JDialog** in the first **JFrame** is set to **APPLICATION_MODAL**, which means it will prevent other windows not in its child hierarchy from being accessed. This is shown in Figure 6.2.

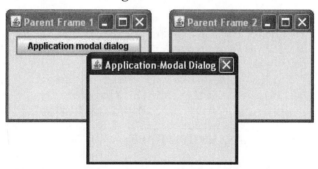

**Figure 6.2: A modal dialog with modality type
APPLICATION_MODAL**

Note that once the dialog is shown, you cannot access the second **JFrame** despite it being another parent container in the application.

Using DOCUMENT_MODAL

The **DOCUMENT_MODAL** option has a smaller scope than
APPLICATION_MODAL. a document-modal dialog does not block
windows from other parents. This is demonstrated by the code in Listing 6.3.

Listing 6.3: Using DOCUMENT_MODAL

```
package modality;
import java.awt.Dialog;
import java.awt.FlowLayout;
import java.awt.event.ActionEvent;
import java.awt.event.ActionListener;
import javax.swing.JButton;
import javax.swing.JDialog;
import javax.swing.JFrame;
import javax.swing.SwingUtilities;

public class DocumentModalDialogDemo {
    private static void constructGUI() {
        final JFrame parent = new JFrame("Parent Frame");
        parent.setLayout(new FlowLayout());
        parent.setDefaultCloseOperation(JFrame.EXIT_ON_CLOSE);

        JButton button = new JButton("Document modal dialog");
        button.addActionListener(new ActionListener() {
            public void actionPerformed(ActionEvent e) {

                // modeless dialog, child of parent
                JDialog dialog1 = new JDialog(parent,
                        "Dialog1 - Modeless Dialog");
                dialog1.setBounds(200, 200, 300, 200);
                dialog1.setVisible(true);

                // document-modal dialog, child of parent
                JDialog dialog2 = new JDialog(parent,
                        "Dialog2 - Document-Modal Dialog",
                        Dialog.ModalityType.DOCUMENT_MODAL);
                dialog2.setBounds(300, 300, 300, 200);

                // modeless dialog, child of dialog2,
                // not affected by the modality of dialog2
                JDialog dialog3 = new JDialog(dialog2,
                        "Dialog3 - Modeless Dialog");
                dialog3.setBounds(400, 400, 300, 200);
                dialog3.setVisible(true);
```

```
                // display dialog2 after dialog3 is shown so that
                // dialog 3 won't be blocked by dialog2
                dialog2.setVisible(true);
            }
        });
        parent.add(button);
        parent.setBounds(100, 100, 300, 200);
        parent.setVisible(true);
    }

    public static void main(String[] args) {
        SwingUtilities.invokeLater(new Runnable() {
            public void run() {
                constructGUI();
            }
        });
    }
}
```

Run the **DocumentModalDialogDemo** class and you will see windows similar to those in Figure 6.3.

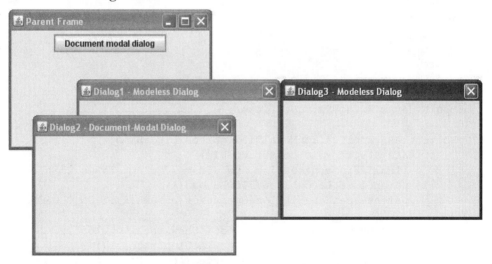

Figure 6.3: Using DOCUMENT_MODAL

Notice that event though **dialog2** is a modal dialog, you can still access **dialog3** because the latter comes from a different parent.

Modality Exclusion

In addition to **setModalityType**, the **Dialog** class has another new modality-related method, **setModalExclusionType**, that allows you to exclude windows from the modality rule of a modal dialog. Here is its signature.

```
public void setModalExclusionType(Dialog.ModalExclusionType type)
```

The **Dialog.ModalExclusionType** is an enum with these values:

- **APPLICATION_EXCLUDE**. Indicates that a window will not be blocked by any application-modal dialog.
- **NO_EXCLUDE**. No modal exclusion.
- **TOOLKIT_EXCLUDE**. Indicates that a window will not be blocked by any toolkit-modal dialog.

As an example, the class in Listing 6.4 uses **APPLICATION_EXCLUDE** to exclude a frame from being blocked when a modal dialog is being displayed.

Listing 6.4: Using modality exclusion

```java
package modality;
import java.awt.Dialog;
import java.awt.FlowLayout;
import java.awt.event.ActionEvent;
import java.awt.event.ActionListener;
import javax.swing.JButton;
import javax.swing.JDialog;
import javax.swing.JFrame;
import javax.swing.SwingUtilities;

public class ApplicationModalDialogWithExcludeDemo {
    private static void constructGUI() {
        final JFrame parent1 = new JFrame("Parent Frame 1");
        parent1.setLayout(new FlowLayout());
        parent1.setDefaultCloseOperation(JFrame.EXIT_ON_CLOSE);

        JButton button = new JButton("Show modal dialog");
        button.addActionListener(new ActionListener() {
            public void actionPerformed(ActionEvent e) {
                JDialog dialog = new JDialog(parent1,
                        "Application-Modal Dialog",
                        Dialog.ModalityType.APPLICATION_MODAL);
                dialog.setBounds(300, 200, 300, 150);
                dialog.setVisible(true);
```

```
            }
        });
        parent1.add(button);
        parent1.setBounds(100, 100, 200, 150);
        parent1.setVisible(true);

        // the second frame, affected by the modality of dialog
        JFrame parent2 = new JFrame("Parent Frame 2");
        parent2.setBounds(500, 100, 300, 150);
        parent2.setVisible(true);

        // the third frame, excluded from the modality of dialog
        JFrame parent3 = new JFrame("Parent Frame 3 - Excluded");
        parent3.setBounds(300, 400, 300, 150);
        parent3.setModalExclusionType(
                Dialog.ModalExclusionType.APPLICATION_EXCLUDE);
        parent3.setVisible(true);
    }
    public static void main(String[] args) {
        SwingUtilities.invokeLater(new Runnable() {
            public void run() {
                constructGUI();
            }
        });
    }
}
```

If you run the **ApplicationModalDialogWithExcludeDemo** class in Listing 6.4, you'll see windows like those in Figure 6.4.

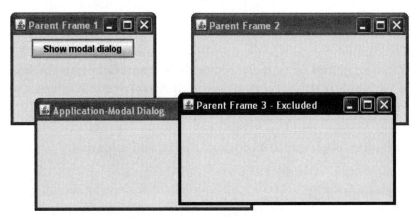

Figure 6.4: Modality exclusion

As you can see in Figure 6.4, after the modal dialog is shown, you can still access **frame3** because it is excluded. However, you cannot access **frame2** when the modal dialog is active because **frame2** is not excluded.

Fast Splash Screens

Mustang adds the **java.awt.SplashScreen** class, which can be used to display a splash screen before the JVM starts. The splash screen is a window that contains an image and is centered in the screen. The GIF, PNG, and JPG formats are supported, and so are transparency in GIF and PNG and animation in GIF. The splash screen is shown until the first Swing/AWT window is displayed.

To use a splash screen, include the new **splash** option in **java** when you invoke your application. For example, the following uses the **myImage.jpg** file as the splash screen.

```
java -splash:myImage.jpg MyClass
```

To use a splash screen in an application packaged in a JAR file, you must use the **SplashScreenImage** option in a manifest file and include the image file in the JAR. You must also specify the path to the image without a leading slash. For instance, the following **manifest.mf** file indicates that the **myImage.jpg** file should be used as the splash screen.

```
Manifest-Version: 1.0
Main-Class: MyClass
SplashScreen-Image: myImage.jpg
```

The **SplashScreen** class is a singleton whose instance can be obtained by calling the static **getSplashScreen** method. The **createGraphics** method returns a **Graphics2D** object that allows you to draw over the splash screen. Here is the complete list of methods in **SplashScreen**.

```
public void close() throws IllegalStateException
```
Closes the splash screen and releases all related resources.

```
public Graphics2D createGraphics()
```
Returns a **Graphics2D** object as a context for drawing on the splash screen.

```
public Rectangle getBounds()
```

Returns the bounds of the splash screen window.

```
public java.net.URL getImageURL()
```
Returns the URL of the current splash screen.

```
public Dimension getSize()
```
Returns the size of the splash screen.

```
public static SplashScreen getSplashScreen()
```
Returns the instance of **SplashScreen**.

```
public boolean isVisible()
```
Indicates whether the splash screen is visible

```
public void setImageURL(java.net.URL imageURL)
```
Specifies a new image for the splash screen.

```
public void update()
```
Updates the splash screen with current contents of the overlay image.

The SplashScreenDemo class in Listing 6.5 demonstrates the power of **SplashScreen** class.

Listing 6.5: The splash screen

```
import java.awt.AlphaComposite;
import java.awt.Color;
import java.awt.Graphics2D;
import java.awt.SplashScreen;
import javax.swing.JFrame;
import javax.swing.SwingUtilities;

public class SplashScreenDemo {
    private static void constructGUI() {
        SplashScreen splash = SplashScreen.getSplashScreen();
        if (splash != null) {
            Graphics2D g = (Graphics2D) splash.createGraphics();

            // Simulate lengthy loading
            for (int i = 0; i < 10; i++) {
                String message = "Process " + i + " of 10 ...";
                g.setComposite(AlphaComposite.Clear);
                g.fillRect(130, 350, 280, 40);
                g.setPaintMode();
                g.setColor(Color.RED);
                g.drawString(message, 130, 360);
                g.fillRect(130, 370, i * 30, 20);
```

```
                splash.update();
                try {
                    Thread.sleep(500);
                } catch (InterruptedException e) {
                    e.printStackTrace();
                }
            }
        }

        JFrame frame = new JFrame("Splash Screen Demo");
        frame.setDefaultCloseOperation(JFrame.EXIT_ON_CLOSE);
        frame.setSize(300, 200);
        frame.setLocationRelativeTo(null);
        frame.setVisible(true);
    }

    public static void main(String[] args) {
        SwingUtilities.invokeLater(new Runnable() {
            public void run() {
                constructGUI();
            }
        });
    }
}
```

You need to run the class from the location of the **SplashScreenDemo.class** file and make sure the **splash.jpg** is in the same directory. To run the application, type this:

```
java -splash:splash.jpg SplashScreenDemo
```

The code itself is nothing more than a blank frame. However, before it is uploaded, the user will see a splash screen like that in Figure 6.5

Figure 6.5: Splash screen

System Tray Support

Thinking about learning C++ to create GUI applications that can be added to the system tray? Maybe it's no longer necessary because Mustang can now access the operating system's system tray through the **SystemTray** class.

Like **SplashScreen**, **SystemTray** is a singleton, so there is only one instance per application. You can get the instance by calling the **SystemTray** class's **getSystemTray** method:

```
public static SystemTray getSystemTray()
```

Because you normally use Java to write programs that run in various operating systems, a word of caution here. **SystemTray** works on many platforms, including Windows, KDE, and Gnome, but some systems may not be supported. Therefore, you may want to check if **SystemTray** is supported using the **isSupported** method:

```
public static boolean isSupported()
```

The **SystemTray** class represents the tray bar, each icon on it is represented by the **TrayIcon** class. You can add a **TrayIcon** to the **SystemTray** by invoking **SystemTray.add**:

```
public void add(TrayIcon trayIcon) throws AWTException
```

And, to remove a **TrayIcon**, use its **remove** method:

```
public void remove(TrayIcon trayIcon)
```

In addition, all the **TrayIcon**s in the **SystemTray** can be retrieved by using **getTrayIcons**.

```
public TrayIcon[] getTrayIcons()
```

Now, let's take a look at the **TrayIcon** class. An instance of this class resembles a tray icon in a native application. It can have a tooltip, an image, and a popup menu. You can create a **TrayIcon** using one of its three constructors:

```
public TrayIcon(Image image)
public TrayIcon(Image image, java.lang.String tooltip)
public TrayIcon(Image image, java.lang.String tooltip,
        PopupMenu popup)
```

The **SystemTrayDemo** class in Listing 6.6 uses **SystemTray** and **TrayIcon**. The application adds a **TrayIcon** with an image, a tooltip, and a **PopupMenu**.

Listing 6.6: Using system tray

```
import java.awt.AWTException;
import java.awt.Image;
import java.awt.MenuItem;
import java.awt.PopupMenu;
import java.awt.SystemTray;
import java.awt.Toolkit;
import java.awt.TrayIcon;
import java.awt.event.ActionEvent;
import java.awt.event.ActionListener;
import javax.swing.JOptionPane;
import javax.swing.SwingUtilities;
```

```java
public class SystemTrayDemo {
    private static void constructGUI() {
        if (! SystemTray.isSupported()) {
            System.out.println("SystemTray is not supported");
            return;
        }

        SystemTray tray = SystemTray.getSystemTray();
        Toolkit toolkit = Toolkit.getDefaultToolkit();
        Image image = toolkit.getImage("trayIcon.jpg");

        PopupMenu menu = new PopupMenu();
        // Menu item to show the message
        MenuItem messageItem = new MenuItem("Show Message");
        messageItem.addActionListener(new ActionListener() {
            public void actionPerformed(ActionEvent e) {
                JOptionPane.showMessageDialog(null,
                        "Java 6 - Mustang");
            }
        });
        menu.add(messageItem);

        // create menu item to close the application
        MenuItem closeItem = new MenuItem("Close");
        closeItem.addActionListener(new ActionListener() {
            public void actionPerformed(ActionEvent e) {
                System.exit(0);
            }
        });
        menu.add(closeItem);
        TrayIcon icon = new TrayIcon(image, "SystemTray Demo",
                menu);
        icon.setImageAutoSize(true);

        try {
            tray.add(icon);
        } catch (AWTException e) {
            System.err.println(
                    "Could not add tray icon to system tray");
        }
    }

    public static void main(String[] args) {
        SwingUtilities.invokeLater(new Runnable() {
```

```
        public void run() {
            constructGUI();
        }
    });
}
}
```

Upon running the class, an icon will be added to the system tray. If you right-click on it, the menu will be shown. (See Figure 6.6)

Figure 6.6: Java 6 system tray

Desktop Help Applications

If you are a Windows user, you must know how handy Windows Explorer is. Not only does it allow you to navigate through your file system, it also lets you double-click on a document file to open the file with the default application and right-click on it to print it. Now you can do the same in Java thanks to the **java.awt.Desktop** class. In addition to launching the default application to open, edit, or print, Desktop also allows you to open the default browser and direct it to a URL as well as launch the user's default email client.

Desktop is a singleton class and you get the instance by using the static **getDesktop** method:

```
public static Desktop getDesktop()
```

Once you have the instance, it is recommended that you check if **Desktop** is supported on the running platform using the **isDesktopSupported** method, before calling other methods of **Desktop**. Here is the signature of **isDesktopSupported**.

```
public static boolean isDesktopSupported()
```

The **open**, **edit**, and **print** methods allow you to pass a **java.io.File** to open, edit, or print the file.

```
public void open(java.io.File file) throws java.io.IOException
```

```
public void edit(java.io.File file) throws java.io.IOException
public void print(java.io.File file) throws java.io.IOException
```

Each of these method can throw an **IOException** if the extension of the specified file has no associated application that can handle it. For example, an **IOException** will be thrown if you try to open a PDF file and your computer does not have Adobe Reader or Adobe Acrobat installed.

The **browse** method launches the default browser and direct the browser to the specified URL. Here is its signature.

```
public void browse(java.net.URI uri) throws java.io.IOException
```

browse throws an **IOException** if the default browser cannot be found or fails to launch.

Also, the **mail** methods launches the Compose window of the default email client application.

```
public void mail() throws java.io.IOException
public void mail(java.netURI mailtoURI) throws java.io.IOException
```

The mail methods throw an **IOException** if the user default mail client is not found or if it fails to launch.

Now, how do you prevent an embarrassing **IOException** when trying to perform a **Desktop** action? By using **isSupported** method:

```
public void boolean isSupported(Desktop.Action action)
```

The **Desktop.Action** enum has these values: **BROWSE**, **EDIT**, **MAIL**, **OPEN**, and **PRINT**. You should always test if an action is supported before calling the action.

The **DesktopDemo** class in Listing 6.7 shows how convenient and powerful the **Desktop** class can be.

Listing 6.7: Using the Desktop class

```
import java.awt.Desktop;
import java.awt.event.ActionEvent;
import java.awt.event.ActionListener;
import java.io.File;
import java.net.URI;
import java.net.URISyntaxException;
```

```java
import java.net.URL;
import javax.swing.JFileChooser;
import javax.swing.JFrame;
import javax.swing.JMenu;
import javax.swing.JMenuBar;
import javax.swing.JMenuItem;
import javax.swing.SwingUtilities;

public class DesktopDemo {
    private static Desktop desktop;

    private static void constructGUI() {
        JMenuItem openItem;
        JMenuItem editItem;
        JMenuItem printItem;
        JMenuItem browseToItem;
        JMenuItem mailToItem;
        JMenu fileMenu = new JMenu("File");
        JMenu mailMenu = new JMenu("Email");
        JMenu browseMenu = new JMenu("Browser");

        openItem = new JMenuItem("Open");
        openItem.addActionListener(new ActionListener() {
            public void actionPerformed(ActionEvent e) {
                JFileChooser chooser = new JFileChooser();
                if(chooser.showOpenDialog(null) ==
                        JFileChooser.APPROVE_OPTION) {
                    try {
                        desktop.open(chooser.getSelectedFile().
                                getAbsoluteFile());
                    } catch (Exception ex) {
                        ex.printStackTrace();
                    }
                }
            }
        });
        fileMenu.add(openItem);

        editItem = new JMenuItem("Edit");
        editItem.addActionListener(new ActionListener() {
            public void actionPerformed(ActionEvent e) {
                JFileChooser chooser = new JFileChooser();
                if(chooser.showOpenDialog(null) ==
                        JFileChooser.APPROVE_OPTION) {
                    try {
```

```
                    desktop.edit(chooser.getSelectedFile()
                            .getAbsoluteFile());
            } catch (Exception ex) {
                ex.printStackTrace();
            }
        }
    }
});
fileMenu.add(editItem);

printItem = new JMenuItem("Print");
printItem.addActionListener(new ActionListener() {
    public void actionPerformed(ActionEvent e) {
        JFileChooser chooser = new JFileChooser();
        if(chooser.showOpenDialog(null) ==
                JFileChooser.APPROVE_OPTION) {
            try {
                desktop.print(chooser.getSelectedFile().
                    getAbsoluteFile());
            } catch (Exception ex) {
                ex.printStackTrace();
            }
        }
    }
});
fileMenu.add(printItem);

browseToItem = new JMenuItem("Go to www.yahoo.com");
browseToItem.addActionListener(new ActionListener() {
    public void actionPerformed(ActionEvent e) {
        try {
            URI browseURI = new URI("www.yahoo.com");
            desktop.browse(browseURI);
        } catch (Exception ex) {
            System.out.println(ex.getMessage());
        }
    }
});
browseMenu.add(browseToItem);

mailToItem = new JMenuItem("Email to sun@sun.com");
mailToItem.addActionListener(new ActionListener() {
    public void actionPerformed(ActionEvent e) {
        try {
                URI mailURI = new
```

```
                            URI("mailto:support@mycompany.com");
                        desktop.mail(mailURI);
                    } catch (Exception ex) {
                        System.out.println(ex.getMessage());
                    }
                }
            });
        mailMenu.add(mailToItem);

        JMenuBar jMenuBar = new JMenuBar();
        jMenuBar.add(fileMenu);
        jMenuBar.add(browseMenu);
        jMenuBar.add(mailMenu);

        JFrame frame = new JFrame();
        frame.setTitle("Desktop Helper Applications");
        frame.setSize(300, 100);
        frame.setDefaultCloseOperation(JFrame.EXIT_ON_CLOSE);
        frame.setJMenuBar(jMenuBar);
        frame.setVisible(true);
    }


    public static void main(String[] args) {
        if (Desktop.isDesktopSupported()) {
            desktop = Desktop.getDesktop();
        } else {
            System.out.println("Desktop class is not supported");
            System.exit(1);
        }
        SwingUtilities.invokeLater(new Runnable() {
            public void run() {
                constructGUI();
            }
        });
    }
}
```

If you run the class in Listing 6.7, you'll see something similar to Figure 6.7. You can select a file from the File menu and open, edit, and print the file. Alternatively, you can go to Yahoo.com or send an email.

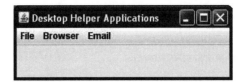

Figure 6.7: Java Desktop

GIF Writer

There are three graphic file formats that can be rendered by GUI web browsers: JPEG, GIF, and PNG. GIF, short for Graphics Interchange Format, is sometimes referred to as GIFF (Graphics Interchange File Format) and was introduced by CompuServe in 1987. It supports lossless compression but can only render 256 colors. In web pages, GIF images are used for simple images such as logos and screen widgets (buttons, labels, and the likes) while JPEG supports more complex graphics such as photos. JPEG employs lossy compression techniques, so images compressed into JPEG cannot be restored to their original form. Unisys owned the patent for the Lempel-Ziv-Welch (LZW) compression algorithm used to compress GIF images, so any software that uses that algorithm, practically any commercial software that supports GIF graphic creation, must pay royalties. This lead to the development of the PNG (Portable Network Graphics) format. PNG is considered more superior to GIF, however support for PNG is not as full and widespread as GIF. For one, IE 6, still the most popular browser on this planet, does not provide PNG alpha channel support natively. This partly explains why people were reluctant to abandon GIF and switch to PNG completely. This is why you are still seeing GIF everywhere on the World Wide Web.

The patent on the LZW algorithm expired on June 20, 2003 in the United States and similar patents expired on June 18 and June 20, 2004 in Europe and Japan, respectively. This means, anyone using the algorithm does not have to pay Unisys anything any longer. Java 6 introduces a class for creating GIF images. The **ImageConverter** class in Listing 6.8 converts a BMP to a GIF.

Listing 6.8: GIF converter

```
import java.awt.image.BufferedImage;
import java.io.File;
```

```java
import java.io.IOException;
import java.util.StringTokenizer;
import javax.imageio.ImageIO;

public class ImageConverter {
    public static void main(String[] args) {
        String imageFilePath = "C:/myBmp.bmp";
        String gifFilePath = "C:/myPic.gif";
        ImageConverter converter = new ImageConverter();
        try {
            File inputFile = new File(imageFilePath);
            BufferedImage image = ImageIO.read(inputFile);
            File outputFile = new File(gifFilePath);
            ImageIO.write(image, "GIF", outputFile);
        } catch (IOException e) {
            e.printStackTrace();
        }
    }
}
```

Text Antialiasing

Antialiasing reduces the jagged-ness of lines drawn as monitor pixels. Jagged-ness can be perceived especially on monitors with lower resolution. For example, the upper part of Figure 6.8 is text that has not been smoothed out, while the lower part is antialiased.

Figure 6.8: Normal text (top) and anti-aliased text (below)

Various operating systems have long been supporting anti-aliasing, but Swing has its own renderer so it cannot enjoy the anti-aliasing rendering facility offered natively by the operating system. Swing has provided this capability since before Mustang, and now Mustang supports subpixel text which optimizes for LCD displays using the subpixel striping to increase the text resolution. Well, the word subpixel appears twice in the last sentence alone. If you're not familiar with this term, here is some explanation.

Each pixel on an LCD screen is composed of three color elements: red, green, and blue. Each color element of a pixel is called a subpixel. Subpixel rendering is based on the phenomenon that changing the intensities of subpixels can cause the location of the pixel to shift, without changing the color. This way subpixel rendering can reduce the jagged-ness of text on LCD, hence producing anti-aliased text rendering.

Java 6 lets you tap into this facility through the five new fields in **java.awt.RenderingHints** class:

- **VALUE_TEXT_ANTIALIAS_LCD_HRGB**
- **VALUE_TEXT_ANTIALIAS_LCD_HBGR**
- **VALUE_TEXT_ANTIALIAS_LCD_VRGB**
- **VALUE_TEXT_ANTIALIAS_LCD_VBGR**
- **VALUE_TEXT_ANTIALIAS_GASP**

You use each of these values when using the **setRenderingHint** method of the **Graphics2D** object to set the key text antialiasing value:

```
g2.setRenderingHint(RenderingHints.KEY_TEXT_ANTIALIASING,
      RenderingHints.VALUE_TEXT_ANTIALIAS_LCD_HBGR);
```

The **TextQualityDemo** class in Listing 6.9 shows how to use all the new field values. It declares an **antialiasHintValues Object** array that consists of seven elements, five of which are the new fields in **RenderingHints**. It then creates seven **JPanels** of type **MyPanel** in Listing 6.10, passing an element in **antialiasHintValues**. The **MyPanel** class takes the antialias hint value and uses it to render the text.

Listing 6.9: The TextQualityDemo class

```
package antialiasing;
import java.awt.Dimension;
import java.awt.RenderingHints;
import javax.swing.JFrame;
import javax.swing.JPanel;
import javax.swing.SwingUtilities;

public class TextQualityDemo {
```

```
    private static Object[] antialiasHintValues = {
        RenderingHints.VALUE_TEXT_ANTIALIAS_OFF,
        RenderingHints.VALUE_TEXT_ANTIALIAS_GASP,      // new to 1.6
        RenderingHints.VALUE_TEXT_ANTIALIAS_LCD_HBGR,// new to 1.6
        RenderingHints.VALUE_TEXT_ANTIALIAS_LCD_HRGB,// new to 1.6
        RenderingHints.VALUE_TEXT_ANTIALIAS_LCD_VBGR,// new to 1.6
        RenderingHints.VALUE_TEXT_ANTIALIAS_LCD_VRGB,// new to 1.6
        RenderingHints.VALUE_TEXT_ANTIALIAS_ON
    };
    private static void constructGUI() {

        JPanel cp = new JPanel();
        for (int i = 0; i < antialiasHintValues.length; i++) {
            MyPanel p = new MyPanel(antialiasHintValues[i]);
            cp.add(p);
        }

        JFrame frame = new JFrame("LCD Text Demo");
        frame.setDefaultCloseOperation(JFrame.EXIT_ON_CLOSE);
        frame.setPreferredSize(new Dimension(630, 460));
        frame.setContentPane(cp);
        frame.pack();
        frame.setVisible(true);
    }

    public static void main(String[] args) {
        SwingUtilities.invokeLater(new Runnable() {
            public void run() {
                constructGUI();
            }
        });
    }
}
```

Listing 6.10: The MyPanel class

```
package antialiasing;
import java.awt.Color;
import java.awt.Dimension;
import java.awt.Graphics;
import java.awt.Graphics2D;
import java.awt.RenderingHints;
import java.awt.image.BufferedImage;
import javax.swing.JPanel;
import javax.swing.border.Border;
import javax.swing.border.TitledBorder;
```

```java
public class MyPanel extends JPanel {
    private Object hintValue;

    public MyPanel(Object hintValue) {
        this.hintValue = hintValue;
        this.setPreferredSize(new Dimension(300, 100));
        String title = hintValue.toString();
        Border border = new TitledBorder(title);
        this.setBorder(border);
    }

    public void paintComponent(Graphics g) {
        Dimension d = this.getSize();

        // Create buffer where we will draw boxes and text
        BufferedImage backBuffer = (BufferedImage)
                this.createImage(d.width, d.height);
        Graphics2D g2 = backBuffer.createGraphics();

        // Fill with white
        g2.setColor(Color.WHITE);
        g2.fillRect(0, 0, d.width, d.height);

        // Set pen color and antialiasing type
        g2.setColor(Color.BLACK);
        g2.setRenderingHint(RenderingHints.KEY_TEXT_ANTIALIASING,
                hintValue);

        // Draw black border
        g2.drawRect(0, 0, d.width - 1, d.height - 1);

        // Draw strings
        g2.drawString("abcdefghijklmnopqrstuvwxyz", 20, 40);
        g2.drawString("ABCDEFGHIJKLMNOPQRSTUVWXYZ", 20, 60);
        g2.drawString("1234567890-=!@#$%^&*()_+,./<>?", 20, 80);

        // Draw image
        g.drawImage(backBuffer, 0, 0, this);
    }
}
```

If you run the application, you'll see something similar to Figure 6.9.

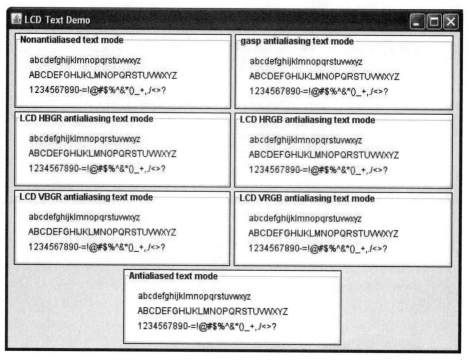

Figure 6.9: Utilizing anti-aliasing

Summary

There are several new features in AWT brought by Mustang, including new types for dialog modality, splash screens, system tray support, and desktop help. In addition, an enhancement to text antialiasing technique was also introduced. Each of these improvements was discussed in this chapter.

Chapter 7
Internationalization

Today it is often a requirement that an application be able to "speak" many languages. A technique for developing applications that support multiple languages and data formats without having to rewrite the programming logic is called *internationalization*. Internationalization is abbreviated **i18n** because the word starts with an *i* and ends with an *n*, and there are 18 characters between the first *i* and the last *n*. In addition, localization is the technique of adapting an internationalized application to support a specific locale. A locale is a specific geographical, political, or cultural region. An operation that takes a locale into consideration is said to be *locale-sensitive*. For example, displaying a date is locale-sensitive because the date must be in the format used by the country or region of the user. The 15th day of November 2006 is written as 11/15/2006 in the US, but written as 15/11/2006 in Australia. Localization is abbreviated **l10n** because the word starts with an *l* and ends with an *n* and there are 10 letters between the *l* and the *n*.

In this chapter we look at new i18n and l10n features in Java 6.

New Supported Locales

Java 6 ships with ten new locales. They are listed in Table 7.1.

As an example, consider the code in Listing 7.1 that uses the new locale Japanese calendar.

Language	Country	Locale Identifier
Chinese (Simplified)	Singapore	zh_SG
English	Malta	en_MT
English	Philippines	en_PH
English	Singapore	en_SG
Greek	Cyprus	el_CY
Indonesian	Indonesia	in_ID
Japanese (Japanese calendar)	Japan	ja_JP_JP
Malay	Malaysia	ms_MY
Maltese	Malta	mt_MT
Spanish	US	es_US

Table 7.1: New locales in Java 6

Listing 7.1: Japanese calendar testing

```
import java.text.DateFormat;
import java.util.Calendar;
import java.util.Locale;
import javax.swing.JOptionPane;

public class JapaneseCalendar {

    public static void main(String[] args) {

        // Create Japanese locale
        Locale japanese = new Locale("ja", "JP", "JP");

        Calendar cal = Calendar.getInstance(japanese);
        System.out.println(cal);

        // Format time
        DateFormat df = DateFormat.getDateTimeInstance(
                DateFormat.FULL, DateFormat.FULL, japanese);
        String str = df.format(cal.getTime());

        // Display the string in JOptionPane
        JOptionPane.showMessageDialog(null, str);
    }
}
```

If you run the JapaneseCalendar class in Listing 7.1, you'll see a **JOptionPane** similar to that in Figure 7.1. The JOptionPane contains a date and time in the new Japanese locale.

Figure 7.1: Using the new Japanese locale

Locale Sensitive Services SPI

Most Java programmers must have used the **java.text.DateFormat** class, an abstract class for formatting and parsing dates. What is interesting is that you can format dates according to your locale of choice, by passing a **Locale** object to its **getDateInstance**, **getTimeInstance**, or **getDateTimeInstance** methods:

```
public static DateTime getDateInstance(int dateStyle,
        java.util.Locale locale)
public static DateTime getTimeInstance(int timeStyle,
        java.util.Locale locale)
public static DateTime getDateTimeInstance(int dateStyle,
        int timeStyle, java.util.Locale locale)
```

For example, to obtain a **DateTime** for the France locale, you call this method:

```
DateFormat.getDateInstance(DateFormat.LONG, Locale.FRANCE);
```

However, what if the JRE does not have a **DateFormat** for the locale you wish to use? With Mustang, this should not be a problem because it now has the Locale Sensitive Services SPI, where SPI stands for service provider interface. What it means is now you can write your own implementations for most locale sensitive classes in the **java.text** and **java.util** packages for locales that are not (yet) supported by the JRE. You create an implementation by subclassing corresponding the abstract provider class in the **java.util.spi** and **java.text.spi** packages. To be precise, with the new Java 6 feature, you can provide locale-sensitive implementations for the following entities.

- Language and country names for the **java.util.Locale** class

- Time zone names for the **java.util.TimeZone** class
- Symbols for the **java.util.Currency** class
- **java.text.BreakIterator**
- **java.text.Collator**
- **java.text.DateFormat**
- **java.text.NumberFormat**
- **java.text.DateFormatSymbols**
- **java.text.DecimalFormatSymbol**

A locale-specific implementation must return the list of all supported locales through its **getAvailableLocales** methods. The return value of this method will be added to the list returned by the **getAvailableLocales** method of the corresponding class, after the implementation is registered through the Java extension mechanism, which was introduced as a new feature in JDK 1.2. If you're not familiar with the extension mechanism, read this tutorial at Sun's Web site:

```
http://java.sun.com/docs/books/tutorial/ext/
```

The following example shows how to implement a new **DateFormat** provider for the Antarctica locale. Antarctica, as you may suspect, is a fictitious country whose people speak Antarctican English. A date and a date/time in Antarctica are written in this format:

```
year~month~date
```

```
year~month~date hour.minute.second
```

Notice that a tilde (~) is used to separate the year and the month as well as the month and the date. Therefore, the sixteenth day of April 2008 is written as 2008~4~16.

What a country!

To implement a **DateFormat** provider, you need to subclass the corresponding **DateFormatProvider** class from the **java.text.spi** package. Our class is given in Listing 7.2 and named **DateFormatProviderImpl**.

Listing 7.2: DateFormatProviderImpl class

```
package spi;
import java.text.DateFormat;
import java.text.SimpleDateFormat;
import java.text.spi.DateFormatProvider;
```

```java
import java.util.Locale;

public class DateFormatProviderImpl extends DateFormatProvider {
    // Antarctica locale
    private Locale antarctica = new Locale("en", "AQ");

    public Locale[] getAvailableLocales() {
        return new Locale[] {antarctica};
    }

    // All styles return the same format: HH.mm.ss
    public DateFormat getTimeInstance(int style, Locale locale) {
        if (locale.equals(antarctica)) {
            return new SimpleDateFormat("HH.mm.ss");
        }
        return null;
    }

    // All styles return the same format: yyyy~MM~dd
    public DateFormat getDateInstance(int style, Locale locale) {
        if (locale.equals(antarctica)) {
            return new SimpleDateFormat("yyyy~MM~dd");
        }
        return null;
    }
    // All styles return the same format: yyyy~MM~dd HH.mm.ss
    public DateFormat getDateTimeInstance(int dateStyle,
            int timeStyle, Locale locale) {
        if (locale.equals(antarctica)) {
            return new SimpleDateFormat("yyyy~MM~dd HH.mm.ss");
        }
        return null;
    }
}
```

Now, to make **spi.DateFormatProviderImpl** usable, you need to 'plug' it into the JRE. You first need to create a file that describes the new class, build a directory structure that contains the class, and package it. Then, take the JAR file and copy it to the lib/ext directory under your JRE installation.

The descriptor for the DateFormatProviderImpl class must be named according to the fully-qualified name of the class that **DateFormatProviderImpl** extends, in this case java.text.sip.DateFormatProvider. This file is a simple text file containing the fully-qualified name of DateFormatProviderImpl. Listing 7.3 shows the content of the java.text.spi.DateFormatProvider file.

Listing 7.3: The descriptor file (java.text.spi.DateFormatProvider)

```
spi.DateFormatProviderImpl
```

The java.text.spi.DateFormatProvider file contains a single line.

Now, you need to package both the **DateFormatProviderImpl.class** and **java.text.spi.DateFormatProvider** files in a structure compliant with the Java Extension Mechanism. In our example, it would be like the one depicted in Figure 7.2.

Figure 7.2: The directory structure for creating a Java extension

The **package** directory is our working directory, it should not be part of the JAR file itself. There are two things that need to be under **package**:

- the META-INF directory containing any descriptor
- the class or classes that make up the Java extension

To create a JAR file out of this directory structure, change directory to the **package** directory and type

```
jar -cf AntarcticaDateFormatProvider.jar *.*
```

An **AntarcticaDateFormatProvider.jar** file will be created in the **package** directory. Now, copy the jar file to lib/ext directory under your JRE. You can now use the provider you just implemented.

You can use the AntarcticaLocaleDemo class in Listing 7.3 to test your plug-in.

Listing 7.3: The AntarcticaLocaleDemo class

```
package spi;
import java.text.DateFormat;
import java.util.Date;
```

```
import java.util.Locale;

public class AntarcticaLocaleDemo {

    public static void main(String[] args) {
        // Display all available locales,
        // note there is a new locale named en_AQ
        System.out.println("Available locales:");
        Locale[] locales = Locale.getAvailableLocales();
        for (Locale locale : locales) {
            System.out.println(" xx " + locale);
        }
        System.out.println("");

        // Current time
        Date now = new Date();

        // Display using the default locale format
        DateFormat defaultFormat = DateFormat.getDateTimeInstance();
        String defaultString = defaultFormat.format(now);
        System.out.println("Default   : " + defaultString);

        // Display using the Antarctica locale format
        DateFormat antarcticaFormat =
                DateFormat.getDateTimeInstance(
                DateFormat.FULL, DateFormat.FULL,
                new Locale("en", "AQ"));

        String antarcticaString = antarcticaFormat.format(now);
        System.out.println("Antarctica: " + antarcticaString);
    }
}
```

If you run the **AntarcticaLocaleDemo** class, you will see the list of available locales, one of which is **en_AQ**. After the list comes the current date in two formats, your computer default format and one in Antarctica format. In my computer it looks like this:

```
Default   : Dec 4, 2006 10:52:19 PM
Antarctica: 2006~12~04 22.52.19
```

Resource Bundle Enhancement

There are several new methods added to the **java.util.ResourceBundle** class in Mustang. First and foremost, you can now pass a **ResourceBundle.Control** object to the **getBundle** method that returns an instance of **ResourceBundle**. Recall that **ResourceBundle** itself is an abstract class. I'll explain about the **ResourceBundle.Control** class in a later section.

To retrieve a value from a resource bundle, you can use the **ResourceBundle** class's **getString** method:

```
public final java.lang.String getString(java.lang.String key)
```

This method throws a **MissingResourceException** if the specified key does not exist, and there was no way you could check if a key existed prior-to Mustang. Fortunately, there's now a **containsKey** method for this purpose:

```
public boolean containsKey(java.lang.String key)
```

In Mustang you can even retrieve all the keys as a **Set** using one of these two methods, **keySet** and **handleKeySet**:

```
public Set<java.lang.String> keySet()
```

```
protected Set<java.lang.String> handleKeySet()
```

The difference between the two methods is **keySet** returns all keys in this **ResourceBundle** and its parent bundles whereas **handleKeySet** returns the keys in this **ResourceBundle** only.

For improved performance, **ResourceBundle** also caches bundles that have been loaded. Mustang programmers can clear these caches using one of these methods:

```
public static void clearCache()
```
  Removes all resource bundles from the cache loaded using the caller's class loader.

```
public static void clearCache(java.lang.ClassLoader loader)
```
  Removes bundles from the cache loaded using the specified class loader.

The following example create a resource bundle and then prints all the keys in the resource bundle. There are two properties files used, the default one (in Listing 7.4) and the German version (Listing 7.5).

Listing 7.4: The MyResources.properties file

```
okKey = OK
cancelKey = Cancel
submitKey = Submit
```

Listing 7.5: The MyResources_de.properties file

```
cancelKey = Abbrechen
```

Notice that there are three key/value pairs in the default properties file, but only one in the second file. Therefore, if the German locale is used and a certain key is not found in the **MyResources_de.properties** file, the **ResourceBundle** will try the default.

The **RBPropDemo** class in Listing 7.6 creates a bundle using the German locale and calls the new methods in Java 6.

Listing 7.6: Using the latest ResourceBundle class

```
package rbprop;
import java.util.Locale;
import java.util.ResourceBundle;
import java.util.Set;
import java.util.ResourceBundle.Control;

public class RBPropDemo {
    public static void main(String[] args){

        // Removes all bundles from the cache
        ResourceBundle.clearCache();
        String bundleName = "rbprop.MyResources";

        // Create resource bundle
        ResourceBundle myResources = ResourceBundle.getBundle(
                bundleName, Locale.GERMAN);

        // Print the key's value
        System.out.println("Key's values:");
        System.out.println(myResources.getString("okKey"));
        System.out.println(myResources.getString("cancelKey"));
        System.out.println(myResources.getString("submitKey"));
```

```
            System.out.println("\nChecking okKey in resource bundle:");
            if (myResources.containsKey("okKey")) {
                System.out.println("okKey exists! "
                    + " Value = " + myResources.getString("okKey"));
            } else {
                System.out.println("The key Doesn't Exist");
            }

            // Returns all keys in this resource bundle and
            // its parent bundles
            System.out.println("\nGet a set of keys:");
            Set<String> keySet = myResources.keySet();
            Object[] keys = keySet.toArray();
            for (int i = 0; i < keys.length; i++) {
                System.out.println("Key " + (i + 1) + " = " + keys[i]);
            }
        }
    }
}
```

If you run the RBPropDemo class, here is what you get:

```
Key's values:
OK
Abbrechen
Submit

Checking okKey in resource bundle:
okKey exists!  Value = OK

Get a set of keys:
Key 1 = okKey
Key 2 = submitKey
Key 3 = cancelKey
```

ResourceBundle.Control

As you know, ResourceBundle is an abstract class and you create an instance
of it by calling one of its static **getBundle** methods. These methods return an
instance of a subclass and tere are two subclasses of **ResourceBundle** that
have been present in the **java.util** package since JDK 1.1:
ListResourceBundle and **PropertyResourceBundle**. **ListResourceBundle**
is an abstract class that you extend if you want to provide key/value pairs in

Java classes. Alternatively, **PropertyResourceBundle** is chosen if you wish to use files to store key/value pairs. Pre-Mustang, when you called **getBundle** with a specific locale, it would first check if an appropriately named Java class that extends **ListResourceBundle** can be found. If so, it would instantiate this subclass and retrieve key/value pairs from the instance. If no such class was present, getBundle would try to find an appropriate .properties file.

Mustang provides a way for you to control how **getBundle** works by adding new overloads that accept a **ResourceBundle.Control** object. Here are the new **getBundle** methods:

```
public static final ResourceBundle getBundle(java.lang.String
    baseName, Locale targetLocale, ResourceBundle.Control control)

public static final ResourceBundle getBundle(java.lang.String
    baseName, Locale targetLocale, java.lang.ClassLoader loader,
    ResourceBundle.Control control)
```

The first overload uses the caller's class loader to load the bundle, the second overload uses the specified class loader.

Without a **ResourceBundle.Control** argument, the **getBundle** method always tries to find a Java class first before attempting to load a properties file if an appropriate class cannot be located. With the new **getBundle** methods, you can instruct **getBundle** to only attempt to locate a Java class only or a properties file only. If you want the **getBundle** method to locate a Java class only, create your **ResourceBundle.Control** by passing **ResourceBundle.Control.FORMAT_CLASS**, like this:

```
ResourceBundle.Control.getControl(
    ResourceBundle.Control.FORMAT_CLASS)
```

For example, this code creates a **ResourceBundle** that looks for Java classes only:

```
ResourceBundle.Control control = ResourceBundle.Control.getControl(
        ResourceBundle.Control.FORMAT_CLASS);
ResourceBundle rb = ResourceBundle.getBundle(bundleName, locale,
        control);
```

To instruct **getBundle** to look for properties files only, pass the **FORMAT_PROPERTIES** field to **getControl**.

```
ResourceBundle.Control.getControl(
```

```
ResourceBundle.Control.FORMAT_PROPERTIES)
```

Alternatively, to tell **getBundle** to behave in the default way, i.e. look for Java class first and then properties files, use this:

```
ResourceBundle.Control.getControl(
    ResourceBundle.Control.FORMAT_DEFAULT)
```

However, the most powerful feature offered by **ResourceBundle.Control** is that now you can subclass **ResourceBundle.Control** and write your own mechanism for loading key/value pairs. If you decide to do so, you need to override the **getFormats** and **newBundle** methods. The **getFormats** method should return a list of formats supported by the **ResourceBundle.Control**. The **newBundle** method returns your own instance of **ResourceBundle**.

The following example shows a **ResourceBundle** that gets its key/value pairs from XML documents, with the help of a **ResourceBundle.Control** subclass. First of all, note that we use the two XML files in Listings 7.7 and 7.8.

Listing 7.7: The MyResources.xml file

```xml
<?xml version="1.0" encoding="UTF-8"?>
<properties >
    <entry key="okKey">Ok</entry>
    <entry key="cancelKey">Cancel</entry>
    <entry key="submitKey">Submit</entry>
</properties>
```

Listing 7.8: The MyResources_de.xml file

```xml
<?xml version="1.0" encoding="UTF-8"?>
<properties >
    <entry key="cancelKey">Abbrechen</entry>
</properties>
```

This sample application consists of three classes. The first one is a **ResourceBundle.Control** subclass named **RBCXml**, short for resource bundle control for XML. This subclass is designed to provide a **ResourceBundle** that works with XML documents. The **newBundle** method of **RBCXml** returns an instance of **XmlResourceBundle**, the second class in this application. **XmlResourceBundle** retrieves key/pair values from XML documents. The last class is **RBXmlDemo**, the test class that puts everything together.

The **RBCXml** class is given in Listing 7.9.

Listing 7.9: The RBCXml class

```java
package rbxml;
import java.io.BufferedInputStream;
import java.io.IOException;
import java.io.InputStream;
import java.net.URL;
import java.net.URLConnection;
import java.util.Arrays;
import java.util.List;
import java.util.Locale;
import java.util.ResourceBundle;

public class RBCXml extends ResourceBundle.Control {

    // Indicates that only "xml" is supported
    public List<String> getFormats(String baseName) {
        if (baseName == null) {
            throw new NullPointerException();
        }
        return Arrays.asList("xml");
    }

    // Create ResourceBundle
    public ResourceBundle newBundle(String baseName, Locale locale,
            String format, ClassLoader loader, boolean reload)
        throws IllegalAccessException, InstantiationException,
                IOException {

        if (baseName == null || locale == null || format == null
                || loader == null)
            throw new NullPointerException();

        ResourceBundle bundle = null;
        if (format.equals("xml")) {
            String bundleName = toBundleName(baseName, locale);
            String resourceName = toResourceName(bundleName,
                    format);
            InputStream stream = null;
            if (reload) {
                URL url = loader.getResource(resourceName);
                if (url != null) {
                    URLConnection connection = url.openConnection();
```

```
                    if (connection != null) {
                        // Disable caching
                        connection.setUseCaches(false);
                        stream = connection.getInputStream();
                    }
                }
            } else {
                stream = loader.getResourceAsStream(resourceName);
            }

            // Create XMLResourceBundle
            if (stream != null) {
                BufferedInputStream bis =
                        new BufferedInputStream(stream);
                bundle = new XMLResourceBundle(bis);
                bis.close();
            }
        }
        return bundle;
    }
}
```

As I mentioned previously, a child class of **ResourceBundle.Control** must override the **newBundle** method that returns an instance of **ResourceBundle**. As you can see in Listing 7.9, the **newBundle** method returns an instance of the **XMLResourceBundle** class, which is presented in Listing 7.10.

Listing 7.10: The XmlResourceBundle class

```
package rbxml;
import java.io.IOException;
import java.io.InputStream;
import java.util.Enumeration;
import java.util.Properties;
import java.util.ResourceBundle;
import java.util.Vector;

public class XMLResourceBundle extends ResourceBundle {
    private Properties props;

    public XMLResourceBundle(InputStream stream) throws IOException
      {
        props = new Properties();
        props.loadFromXML(stream);
    }
```

```
protected Object handleGetObject(String key) {
    return props.getProperty(key);
}

public Enumeration<String> getKeys() {
    Vector<String> vString = new Vector<String>();
    Enumeration en = props.keys();
    while (en.hasMoreElements()) {
        vString.add((String) en.nextElement());
    }
    return vString.elements();
}
}
```

The **XMLResourceBundle** class uses the **loadFromXML** method of
java.util.Properties to convert XML stream into key/value pairs. It also
overrides two methods, **handleGetObject** and **getKeys**. **handleGetObjects**
returns the value of the specified key from the internal **Properties** object.
getKeys returns an enumeration of keys.

The last class, the **RBXmlDemo** class in Listing 7.11, demonstrates the
power of this new feature.

Listing 7.11: The RBXmlDemo class

```
package rbxml;
import java.util.Locale;
import java.util.ResourceBundle;
import java.util.ResourceBundle.Control;

public class RBXmlDemo {

    public static void main(String[] args) {

        String baseName = "rbxml.MyResources";
        Locale locale = Locale.GERMAN;
        ClassLoader loader = RBXmlDemo.class.getClassLoader();
        Control control = new RBCXml();

        ResourceBundle rb = ResourceBundle.getBundle(
                baseName, locale, loader, control);

        System.out.println(rb.getString("okKey"));
        System.out.println(rb.getString("cancelKey"));
```

```
            System.out.println(rb.getString("submitKey"));
    }
}
```

Running the **RBXmlDemo** class produces the following output:

```
Ok
Abbrechen
Submit
```

Summary

Internationalization is a very important issue nowadays. This chapter presented the improvements Mustang brings that help you work with internationalization and localization.

Chapter 8
Java Database Connectivity 4.0

Java 6 includes Java Database Connectivity (JDBC) 4.0, which is defined in JSR 221 (http://jcp.org/en/jsr/detail?id=221). In this chapter we look at the new features in this latest release of JDBC, which include automatic driver loading, ease of development features, support for national character sets, the RowId type, and the **SQLXML** interface.

Driver Loading

Prior to JDBC 4.0, a call to **Class.forName** always preceded the **getConnection** method invocation. In other words, you needed to explicitly load the JDBC driver before you could create a Connection object. This is described in these two lines of code.

```
Class.forName(jdbcDriver);
Connection connection = DriverManager.getConnection(dbUrk, user,
        password)
```

Note
The exception was when you were getting the connection through a **javax.sql.DataSource**, which was almost always the case in an enterprise application.

JDBC 4.0 eliminates the need for invoking **Class.forName** to load the JDBC driver. You can now simply write:

```
Connection connection = DriverManager.getConnection(dbUrl, user,
        password)
```

It's because JDBC 4.0 compliant **DriverManager** now searches for JDBC drivers in the classpath and call the **forName** method in the background.

There is more advantage than simply removing one line of code. Since the programmer does not need to hard code the JDBC driver class name, upgrading a driver involves only replacing the old JAR with a new one, the new class name does not need to match the old one.

Ease of Development Features

If you've been involved in enterprise application development, you must be familiar with the Data Access Object (DAO) pattern and/or products that implement it, such as Hibernate. The DAO pattern is useful for mapping objects to relational database data as well as hiding the complexity of database access and data manipulation code from the rest of the application. JDBC 4.0 brings something similar to the DAO pattern, the **Query** interface. It is part of what is called the "Ease of Development" features in JSR 221. Also, note that page 183 of the JSR mentions that the JDBC Ease of Development features are not intended to be used as an Object-Relational Mapping (ORM) Technology and advises the use of the Java Persistence API. However, I can't help noticing the similarity between the DAO pattern and the Query interface. Read on.

The Query Interface

First of all, note that there is no **java.sql.Query** type in Java, so this is not something you write an implementation for. Rather, the Query interface refers to a user-defined interface that exposes a set of methods decorated with JDBC annotations (more about these later). An implementation will be generated for you and an instance of the implementation will be created for you as well, through the **createQueryObject** method of **java.sql.Connection.** Here is the signature of **createQueryObject**:

```
<T extends BaseQuery> T createQueryObject(java.lang.Class<T> class)
        throws SQLException
```

One thing to note when writing a Query interface is that it must extend the **java.sql.BaseQuery** interface, which defines methods for closing any Query object.

Here is a simplistic example of a Query interface named MyQueries.

```
public interface MyQueries extends BaseQuery {
}
```

Why the plural? Because a Query interface normally contains multiple methods for querying the database, multiple queries.

Listing 8.1 shows a Query interface called **UserQueries** that looks more like what you will find in a real-world application.

Listing 8.1: The UserQueries interface

```
import java.sql.BaseQuery;
import java.sql.DataSet;
import java.sql.Select;
public interface UserQueries extends BaseQuery {

    // Select all users
    @Select(sql = "SELECT userId, firstName, lastName FROM Users",
            readOnly=false, connected=false, tableName="Users")
    DataSet<User> getAllUsers();

    // Select user by name */
    @Select(sql = "SELECT userId, firstName, lastName FROM Users "
            + "WHERE userName=?", readOnly=false, connected=false,
            tableName = "Users")
    DataSet<User> getUserByName(String userName);

    // Delete user
    @Update("DELETE Users WHERE firstName={firstName} " +
            "AND lastName={lastName}")
    int deleteUser(String firstName, String lastName);
}
```

The **getAllUsers, getUserByName**, and **deleteUser** methods are annotated. The **@Select** and **@Update** annotations may look foreign to you. However, fear not as these will be discussed in the section "JDBC Annotations." The **DataSet** interface will be explained in the section "The DataSet Interface."

As you can see, **UserQueries** really looks and feels like a DAO class, only easier. In addition, you don't need to provide an implementation for a Query interface since one will be generated for you. I provide an example at the end of this section.

JDBC Annotations

You use JDBC annotations to decorate methods in a Query interface. There are four of them in JDBC 4.0: **Select**, **Update**, **AutoGeneratedKeys**, and **ResultColumn**. The discussion of each of these annotations can be found next.

Select

The **Select** annotation is used to adorn a Query interface method to indicate to the JDBC driver that the decorated method specifies an SQL select statement. You specify the SQL statement for this query in the **sql** element of the annotation.

Table 8.1 lists the **Select** annotation elements.

Element	Type	Accessibility
sql or value	String	The SQL statement to be executed
tableName	String	The name of the table that will be updated when the DataSet.sync method is called
readOnly	boolean	Indicates the returned DataSet is read-only
connected	boolean	Indicates if the DataSet is connected to the data source
allColumnsMapped	boolean	Indicates if there is a one-to-one mapping between the column names in the SQL statement and the fields in the returned DataSet
scrollable	boolean	Indicates if the returned DataSet is scrollable. This element only takes effect only when in connected mode.

Table 8.1: Select annotation elements

For example, the following **Select** annotation decorates the **getAllUsers** method in a Query interface.

```
@Select(sql = "SELECT userId, firstName, lastName FROM Users",
            readOnly=false, connected=false, tableName="Users")
DataSet<User> getAllUsers();
```

If the only element that appears in a **Select** annotation is **sql**, you can replace it with **value**, in which case the annotation element can be omitted:

```
@Select("SELECT userId, firstName, lastName FROM Users")
```

```
DataSet<User> getAllUsers();
```

Update

The **Update** annotation is used to decorate a Query interface method to indicate to the JDBC driver that the method specifies an SQL update statement. You specify the SQL statement for this query in the **sql** element of the annotation. The method's return value can be an **int** or **void**. Only if the return value type is **int** will the update count be returned.

Table 8.2 presents the elements that can appear in an Update annotation.

Element	Type	Accessibility
sql or value	String	The SQL statement to be executed
keys	GeneratedKeys	Indicates if autogenerated keys are returned. The default value is GeneratedKeys.NO_KEYS_RETURNED

Table 8.2: Update annotation elements

For instance, the following **Update** annotation decorates the **deleteUser** method in a Query interface.

```
@Update("DELETE Users WHERE firstName={firstName} " +
        "AND lastName={lastName}")
int deleteUser(String firstName, String lastName);
```

AutoGeneratedKeys

This annotation is used to decorate a method to indicate that the DataSet returned by the method is used to hold auto-generated keys.

For example, the UserKeys class in Listing 8.2 is decorated with **@AutoGeneratedKeys**.

Listing 8.2: Using AutoGeneratedKeys

```
public class UserKeys {
    public String firstName;
    public String lastName;
}
```

ResultColumn

A Query interface method decorated with **@Select** returns a **DataSet** of data transfer objects (DTOs). The properties or fields in these objects normally match the fields in the queried table. If this is not the case, you can use **@ResultColumn** to decorate a field in a DTO class to indicate that a particular table column should be mapped to the field.

Another use of **@ResultColumn** is to specify that a **DataSet** field will be used as the unique key when the **DataSet** is not connected to the data source.

Table 8.3 shows the elements in the **ResultColumn** elements.

Element	Type	Accessibility
name or value	String	The name of the column in the SQL statement to be mapped to the decorated field.
uniqueIdentifier	boolean	Indicates if field will be used as a unique key when modifying a row when the DataSet is not connected to the data source.

Table 8.3: ResultColumn annotation elements

For example, the **name** field in the **User** class in Listing 8.3 will be mapped to the **userName** column in the queried database table.

Listing 8.3: Using ResultColumn

```
public class User {
    @ResultColumn(name="userName") public String name;
    public String firstName;
    public String lastName;
}
```

The DataSet Interface

JDBC 4.0 introduces the **java.sql.DataSet** interface, a subinterface of **java.util.List**, that provides a type safe collection of data retrieved through a method decorated by **@Select** in a Query interface. A **DataSet** operates in one of two modes, connected and disconnected. In connected mode, it is like a **ResultSet**. In disconnected mode, it acts like a **CachedRowSet**.

Suppose you have the following **getUsers** method in a Query interface.

```
public interface MyQueries extends BaseQuery {
```

```
@Select(sql = "SELECT userId, firstName, lastName FROM Users",
        readOnly=false, connected=false, tableName="Users")
DataSet<User> getUsers();
}
```

If you call the **createQueryObject** method of the **Connection** object used to connect to the database, you will get an instance of the Query interface **MyQueries**:

```
MyQueries queries = connection.createQueryObject(MyQueries.class);
```

You can then call any method in the Query interface. For example, you can use this code to call **getUsers**:

```
DataSet<User> dataSet = queries.getUsers();
```

Because **DataSet** is a subinterface of **java.util.Iterable**, you can use the enhanced **for** to iterate over it:

```
for (User user : dataSet) {
    System.out.println(user.getFirstName());
}
```

Just like a database table, you can insert, update, and delete a row in a DataSet. To insert a row, you call its **insert** method.

```
User newUser = new User("Tom", "Jerry");
dataSet.insert(newUser);
```

For update and delete, you need to first find the row you want to modify, normally by iterating over the **DataSet**. For instance, the following code updates the first name of each row whose value is "Tom."

```
for (User user : dataSet) {
    if (user.getFirstName().equals("Tom")) {
        user.setFirstName("Tommy");
        dataSet.modify() ;
    }
}
```

The following snippet deletes the row whose last name is Jerry.

```
for (User user : dataSet) {
    if (user.getLastName().equals("Jerry")) {
        dataSet.delete() ;
    }
```

```
}
```

Query Interface Example

The following example shows how to use the Ease of Development features in JDBC 4.0. The Microsoft SQL Server JDBC 4.0 driver from Merlia (http://www.inetsoftware.de/products/jdbc/mssql/merlia/) is used for this example, as at the time of this writing not many companies have updated their drivers to comply with JDBC 4.0.

The example shows how to connect to an **Adaptor** database and retrieve data from the **M_ROLE** table and return the data as a **DataSet** containing **Role** objects. The **Role** class is a DTO class for roles.

The script for creating the M_ROLE table is given in Listing 8.4.

Listing 8.4: The SQL script for creating the M_ROLE Table

```
CREATE TABLE [M_ROLE] (
    [ROLE_ID] [int] NOT NULL,
    [NAME] [varchar] (50) NOT NULL,
    [DESCRIPTION] [varchar] (250) NOT NULL
)
GO
```

Listing 8.5 shows the **Role** class.

Listing 8.5: The Role class

```
package query;
public class Role {
    public int roleId;
    public String name;
    public String description;

    public String toString() {
        StringBuilder buf = new StringBuilder();
        buf.append("\n\tRole ID     = ").append(roleId);
        buf.append("\n\tName        = ").append(name);
        buf.append("\n\tDescription = ").append(description);
        return buf.toString();
    }
}
```

And, Listing 8.6 shows the Query interface for manipulating roles.

Listing 8.6: The RoleQueries interface

```java
package query;
import java.sql.BaseQuery;
import java.sql.DataSet;
import java.sql.Select;

public interface RoleQueries extends BaseQuery {
    // Select all roles
    @Select(sql = "SELECT ROLE_ID, NAME, DESCRIPTION FROM M_ROLE",
            readOnly=false, connected=false)
    DataSet<Role> getAllRoles();

    // Select role by name
    @Select("SELECT ROLE_ID, NAME, DESCRIPTION FROM M_ROLE"
            + " where NAME = ?")
    DataSet<Role> getRoleByName(String name);
}
```

Finally, the **QueryDemo** class in Listing 8.7 connects to the database and retrieves **Role** objects.

Listing 8.7: The QueryDemo class

```java
package query;
import java.sql.Connection;
import java.sql.DataSet;
import java.sql.DriverManager;
import java.sql.SQLException;
public class QueryDemo {

    public static void main(String[] args) {

        Connection connection = null;
        try {
            String url = "jdbc:inetdae7:localhost:1433?"
                    + "database=Adaptor";
            String login = "sa";
            String password = "admin";
            connection = DriverManager.getConnection(url, login,
                    password);

            // Create Query object
            RoleQueries qo = connection
                    .createQueryObject(RoleQueries.class);
```

```java
        // Get all roles
        DataSet<Role> rows = qo.getAllRoles();
        for (Role role : rows) {
            System.out.println(role);
        }

        // Create new Role object
        if (! rows.isReadOnly()) {
            System.out.println("\nCreate new role");
            Role r = new Role();
            r.role_id = 12345;
            r.name = "Supervisor";
            r.description = "Do monitoring job";

            boolean insertResult = rows.insert(r);
            rows.sync(connection);
            System.out.println("\tInserted: " + insertResult);
        }

        // Retrieve Role by name
        System.out.println("\nGet role by name:");
        DataSet<Role> rows2 = qo.getRoleByName("Supervisor");
        Role role = rows2.get(0);
        System.out.println(role);

        if (role != null) {
            // Modify Role
            System.out.println("\nModify current role:");
            role.description = "Do supervising job";
            boolean modifyResult = rows2.modify(role);
            rows2.sync(connection);
            System.out.println("\tModified: " + modifyResult);
        }
    } catch (SQLException e) {

        for (Throwable t : e) {
            t.printStackTrace();
        }
    } finally {

        // Close connection
        try {
            connection.close();
        } catch (SQLException e) {
            e.printStackTrace();
        }
```

```
              }
         }
    }
```

Support for National Character Sets

In order to support different character sets, the JDBC API has added these types: **NCHAR, NVARCHAR, LONGNVARCHAR**, and **NCLOB**, which correspond to the existing types **CHAR, VARCHAR, LONGVARCHAR**, and **CLOB**, respectively. The new types are encoded using the national character set, as opposed to UTF-16, which is the encoding scheme for Java types. Strings are used to represent **NCHAR, NVARCHAR**, and **LONGNVARCHAR** data and conversion between the Java character set and the national character set happens automatically.

Support for the new types are reflected in the methods **setNString**, **setNCharacterStream**, and **setNClob** of the **PreparedStatement** interface and the methods **getNClob, getNString**, and **getNCharacterStream** in the **ResultSet** and **CallableStatement** interfaces.

Here are the signatures of the new methods in **PreparedStatement**:

```
void setNCharacterStream(int parameterIndex, java.io.Reader value)
       throws SQLException

void setNCharacterStream(int parameterIndex, java.io.Reader value,
       long length) throws SQLException

void setNClob(int parameterIndex, NClob value) throws SQLException

void setNClob(int parameterIndex, java.io.Reader value) throws
       SQLException

void setNClob(int parameterIndex, java.io.Reader value, long length)
       throws SQLException

void setNString(int parameterIndex, java.lang.String value)
```

And, here are the signatures of the new methods in **ResultSet**:

```
NClob getNClob(int columnIndex)

NClob getNClob(java.lang.String columnLabel)
```

```
java.lang.String getNString(int columnIndex)

java.lang.String getNString(java.lang.String columnLabel)

java.io.Reader getNCharacterStream(int columnIndex)

java.io.Reader getNCharacterStream(java.lang.String columnLabel)
```

Iterable SQLException

In JDBC 4.0 the **SQLException** class implements **java.lang.Iterable**. What this means is now you can easily navigate all **Throwable**s in an **SQLException**, like this:

```
try {
    // do some data manipulation here
} catch (SQLException e) {
    for (Throwable t : e) {
        System.out.println("Error: " + t);
    }
}
```

In addition, the **SQLException** class now has four new constructors:

```
public SQLException(java.lang.Throwable cause)

public SQLException(java.lang.String reason,
        java.lang.Throwable cause)

public SQLException(java.lang.String reason,
        java.lang.String sqlState, java.lang.Throwable cause)

public SQLException(java.lang.String reason, java.lang.String
        sqlState, int vendorCode, java.lang.Throwable cause)
```

RowId Type

The new **java.sql.RowId** interface represents a unique identifier for a row in a result set. You can verify if a data source supports **RowID** and check the lifetime validity of **RowId** by calling the **getRowIdLifetime** method on the **DatabaseMetaData** object retrieved from **Connection.getMetaData()**. Here is the signature of **getRowIdLifetime**:

```
RowIdLifetime getRowIdLifetime() throws SQLException
```

RowIdLifetime is an enum with the following members:

- **ROWID_UNSUPPORTED**. Indicates that the RowId type is not supported by this data source
- **ROWID_VALID_FOREVER**. Indicates that the RowId from this data source is valid indefinitely.
- **ROWID_VALID_OTHER**. Indicates that the lifetime of the RowId from this data source cannot be determined.
- **ROWID_VALID_SESSION**. Indicates that the RowId from this data source is valid at least during the containing session.
- **ROWID_VALID_TRANSACTION**. Indicates that the RowId from this data source is valid at least until the containing transaction terminates.

The **ResultSet** interface adds two **getRowId** methods:

```
RowId getRowId(int columnIndex)
RowId getRowId(java.lang.String columnLabel)
```

You use these to retrieve a RowId from the data source. The use of these methods is similar to other **get** methods, such as **getString** and **getShort**. For example, if you have a **ResultSet** from executing this SQL statement:

```
SELECT ROWID, userName, firstName, lastName FROM Users
```

you can retrieve the ROWID from the first column. For example, to iterate the **ResultSet**, you use this code:

```
while (resultSet.next()) {
    System.out.println("Row Id: " + resultSet.getRowId(1));
    System.out.println("userName: " + resultSet.getString(2));
}
```

SQLXML Interface

An instance of **java.sql.SQLXML** represents an XML content. This interface is added to support storing XML values in a table column. It provides methods that allow you to access the value as a **String**, a **Reader**, a **Writer**, or a **Stream**. There is no default implementation for **SQLXML** in the **java.sql** package, you create an instance of it by invoking the **createSQLXML** method on a **Connection** object. Note though that the instance is always an empty object. You can assign a value by calling its **setString** method:

```
SQLXML sqlXml = connection.createSQLXML();
sqlXml.setString(xml);
```

To store it into the database, you use the **setSQLXML** method on a **PreparedStatement**, just as you would with **setString** or **setInt**:

```
void setSQLXML(int parameterIndex, SQLXML xmlObject) throws
    SQLException
```

To retrieve **SQLXML** objects from the database, use the new method **getSQLXML** on a **ResultSet** instance.

```
SQLXML getSQLXML(int columnIndex) throws SQLException
SQLXML getSQLXML(java.lang.String columnLabel) throws SQLException
```

Once you retrieve a SQLXML object, you can use its various methods to get its value:

```
java.io.InputStream getBinaryStream() throws SQLException
java.io.Reader getCharacterStream() throws SQLException
java.lang.String getString() throws SQLException
```

Summary

Mustang includes the latest version of JDBC, JDBC 4.0. This chapter provides examples of how to use the new features in JDBC 4.0, including automatic driver loading, ease of development features, support for national character sets, the RowId type, and the **SQLXML** interface.

Chapter 9
XML Digital Signature API

XML is an open standard for data exchange as well as the format used in web services SOAP messages. As a format for data exchange often used to carry sensitive data, there needs to be a way of securing XML messages, and securing SOAP messages involves signing them. JSR 105, XML Digital Signature API, defines a standard Java API for digitally signing XML documents. The API is particularly useful for digitally signing XML documents and validating XML signatures. In addition, if you or your company is in the business of making software for making software, you need to understand the JSR so that you can write an implementation for it. Mustang includes the reference implementation for JSR 105.

The primary focus of this chapter is the packages created along with JSR 105, namely the **javax.xml.crypto** package and its subpackages. To smooth your learning experience, this tutorial starts with a general discussion of Java cryptography, in particular these four types: **KeyPair**, **KeyPairGenerator**, **PrivateKey**, and **PublicKey**. They are all but new to Mustang, but you will invariably use them when writing code that uses the new cryptography packages. In addition, the following site may be useful to refresh your memory about Java security:

```
http://java.sun.com/javase/6/docs/technotes/guides/security/
```

Java Cryptography

Java specifies security services such as for creating message digests, encrypting and decrypting messages, signing documents, etc. Each activity involves different algorithms that can sometimes be very complex. The Java security API specifies interfaces for these services. Any person or company can create an implementation of these interfaces to provide security algorithms. Such a person or company, you guessed it right, is called a JCA provider or simply a provider. JCA, by the way, stands for Java Cryptography Architecture.

Sun Microsystems is one of such providers. The JRE from Sun includes cryptographic methods you can use. Another example is Bouncy Castle (http://www.bouncycastle.org/). You can easily install a provider to make use of the services it provides. You can find the instructions to install and register a provider here:

```
http://java.sun.com/javase/6/docs/technotes/guides/security/crypto/
CryptoSpec.html#ProviderInstalling
```

The rest of this section deals with several activities you perform when using Java Cryptography services.

Key Generation

Before you can sign or encrypt anything, you need to have a pair of public and private keys. The KeyTool program is a utility to create and maintain public and private keys as well as digital certificates. It comes with the JDK and is located in the **bin** directory of the JDK. Keytool is a command-line program.

Note
More information on Keytool can be found here:
http://java.sun.com/j2se/1.5.0/docs/tooldocs/windows/keytool.html

However, this section will teach you to achieve this programmatically. Four types are discussed. They are **KeyPairGenerator**, **KeyPair**, **PrivateKey**, and **PublicKey**.

The KeyPairGenerator Class

You use the **java.security.KeyPairGenerator** class to generate a public/private key pair. The generation process utilizes a specific algorithm (e.g. DSA) and you have to specify the algorithm when creating an instance of **KeyPairGenerator**. The **KeyPairGenerator** class does not have a public constructor, so you use one of its **getInstance** methods to construct an instance:

```
public static KeyPairGenerator getInstance(
        java.lang.String algorithm)
```

```
public static KeyPairGenerator getInstance(
        java.lang.String algorithm, java.lang.String provider)
```

The first **getInstance** method creates an instance using the default provider (the one provided by Sun Microsystems, if you are using Sun's JRE). The second overload lets you specify a provider. The **getInstance** methods throw a **NoSuchAlgorithmException** if the specified algorithm cannot be found in the registered providers.

The minute you have a **KeyPairGenerator**, you can use its **initialize** and **generateKeyPair** methods to initialize the key pair generator and generate a key pair. The **initialize** method initializes a certain key size with a certain degree of randomness. For example, this overload of **initialize** allows you to specify a key size:

```
public void initialize(int keySize)
```

The **generateKeyPair** method generates a new key pair each time it is invoked. Here is its signature:

```
public KeyPair generateKeyPair()
```

For example, the following code creates a **KeyPairGenerator** class and generates a key pair:

```
KeyPairGenerator kpg = KeyPairGenerator.getInstance("DSA");
kpg.initialize(512);
KeyPair kp = kpg.generateKeyPair();
```

The KeyPair Class

This class is a holder for a public/private key pair. It defines these two self-explanatory methods:

```
public PrivateKey getPrivate()
public PublicKey getPublic()
```

The PrivateKey and PublicKey Interfaces

Both **PrivateKey** and **PublicKey** are subinterfaces of the **Key** interface. **Key** does not define any method and serves to group all public key interfaces. The **PrivateKey** interface has several subinterfaces, most notably **DSAPrivateKey** and **RSAPrivateKey**. The **PublicKey** interface also has several descendants, including **DSAPublicKey** and **RSAPublicKey**.

Both **PrivateKey** and **PublicKey** define the following methods.

```
java.lang.String getAlgorithm()
```
　　　Returns the algorithm name for this key.

```
java.lang.String getFormat()
```
　　　Returns the encoding format of this key.

```
byte[] getEncoded()
```
　　　Returns a byte array containing the key.

For example, the following code snippet shows how to construct a DSA **KeyPair** and invokes the methods on both keys.

```
try {
    KeyPairGenerator kpg = KeyPairGenerator.getInstance("DSA");
    kpg.initialize(512);
    KeyPair keyPair = kpg.generateKeyPair();
    PrivateKey privateKey = keyPair.getPrivate();
    PublicKey publicKey = keyPair.getPublic();
    System.out.println(privateKey.getAlgorithm());//prints DSA
    System.out.println(privateKey.getFormat());// prints PKCS#8
    System.out.println(publicKey.getAlgorithm());//prints DSA
    System.out.println(publicKey.getFormat());// prints X.509
} catch (NoSuchAlgorithmException e) {
}
```

As you will witness in the next sections, you most often use instances of **PrivateKey** and **PublicKey** as arguments to methods of other objects.

XML Signature Overview

When exchanging files, it is often necessary to guarantee the data integrity of the files. To get assurance that a digital document (whether it is a Word file or a PDF or an XML document) received has not been changed after it was sent by the document creator. You can guarantee the data integrity of a document by creating an XML signature of the document. You do this by creating a digest of the document, placing the resulting digest value in an XML element, and then digesting that element and digitally signing it. You use your private key to sign it, and the recipient must have your public key (enclosed in a digital certificate) to verify the integrity of the document. Your recipient must use the same method to digest the digest of the received document and compare the result with the signature that is decrypted using your public key.

Different ways exist to distribute a document and its corresponding signature.

1. The document and its signature can be combined into an XML document and the document becomes a child element of the signature. This is the case for enveloping signatures.
2. The document and its signature are combined together in an XML document and the signature is a child element of the element that represents the document. In this case, the signature is called the enveloped signature.
3. The document and its signature can be distributed separately. The relationship between the document and the signature will be described by an XML document, in which the XML element representing the document will be a sibling of that representing the signature. Such signatures are called detached signatures.

The standard for XML signature syntax and processing is defined by W3C and the recommendation can be downloaded from here:

```
http://www.w3.org/TR/xmldsig-core/
```

This section provides a brief tutorial on XML digital signatures so that you can understand the JSR 105 API easily.

The syntax of an XML signature is as follows:

```
<Signature ID?>
    <SignedInfo>
        <CanonicalizationMethod/>
        <SignatureMethod/>
        (<Reference URI? >
            (<Transforms>)?
            <DigestMethod>
                <DigestValue>
        </Reference>)+
    </SignedInfo>
    <SignatureValue>
    (<KeyInfo>)?
    (<Object ID?>)*
```

```
</Signature>
```

Here a question mark (?) denotes an optional element that can only occur once at maximum. The plus sign (+) indicates one or more occurrences, and an asterisk (*) means zero or more occurrences.

The **Signature** element represents the XML signature and the **SignedInfo** element is the information signed. The **CanonicalizationMethod** element under **SignedInfo** refers to the algorithm used to canonicalize the signed information before the latter is digested.

As the name implies, the **SignatureMethod** element contains the name of the algorithm used to convert the signed information into the **SignatureValue** element's value. The signature method is a combination of a digest algorithm and a key dependent algorithm. RSA-SHA1 is an example of a signature method.

The **Signature** element can contain one or more **Reference** elements, each of which includes the digest method and the resulting digest value calculated over the identified data object. An optional **Transforms** element may be present to encapsulate transformations that generated the input to the digest operation.

Last but not least, the **KeyInfo** element contains the key to be used to validate a signature.

Here is an example of an XML signature

```
<Signature xmlns="http://www.w3.org/2000/09/xmldsig#">
  <SignedInfo>
    <CanonicalizationMethod
      Algorithm="http://www.w3.org/TR/2001/REC-xml-c14n-20010315
#WithComments" />
    <SignatureMethod
      Algorithm="http://www.w3.org/2000/09/xmldsig#dsa-sha1" />
    <Reference URI="">
      <Transforms>
        <Transform
          Algorithm="http://www.w3.org/2000/09/xmldsig#enveloped-
signature" />
      </Transforms>
      <DigestMethod
        Algorithm="http://www.w3.org/2000/09/xmldsig#sha1" />
        <DigestValue>dwRmnTsVQ+71pmi0e7tXzqwVl2I=</DigestValue>
    </Reference>
```

```
    </SignedInfo>
    <SignatureValue>
       a82kt+hJQwt3t1AulJwRIzvXxThhd41Et24pYYjg0LaPQLBq0zbsEA==
    </SignatureValue>
    <KeyInfo>
      <KeyValue>
        <DSAKeyValue>
          <P>5t9jQTxeEu0ImbzRMqzVDZkVG9xD7nN1kuFw==</P>
          <Q>li7dzDacuo67Jg7mtqEm2TRuOMU=</Q>
          <G>4pNWMOHCBiNU0NogpsQW5QvnlMpA==</G>
          <Y>784dwOCNPxV++0b31FWjnbyyNnhhmw7uEdg==</Y>
        </DSAKeyValue>
      </KeyValue>
    </KeyInfo>
</Signature>
```

JSR 105 API Overview

This API consists of interfaces and classes in six packages:

- **javax.xml.crypto**
- **javax.xml.crypto.dom**
- **javax.xml.crypto.dsig**
- **javax.xml.crypto.dsig.dom**
- **javax.xml.crypto.dsig.keyinfo**
- **javax.xml.crypto.dsig.spec**

The most important interface in the Java XML cryptography is **javax.xml.crypto.dsign.XMLSignature**, which, of course, represents an XML signature. Other interfaces in the same package represent various elements found in an XML signature, including **SignedInfo**, **CanonicalizationMethod**, **SignatureMethod**, **Transform**, and **Reference**.

The **XMLSignature** interface is crucial because it contains methods for signing XML documents and validating XML signatures. To sign a document, use its **sign** method:

```
void sign(XMLSignContext signContext)
    throws javax.xml.crypto.MarshalException, XMLSignatureException
```

To the **sign** method you pass an **XMLSignContext** object that contains context information for generating XML signatures. **XMLSignContext** is an interface that comes with an implementation, the **DOMSignContext** class in the **javax.xml.crypto.dsig.dom** package. An **XMLSignContext** instance contains two important components: the XML element or node that needs signing and the key to sign it. Look at this constructor of **DOMSignContext**:

```
public DOMSignContext(java.security.Key key, org.w3c.dom.Node node)
```

We'll have an example later to show how to sign an XML document, but now, before we start, how do you obtain an instance of **XMLSignature**? You do this by using a factory class named **XMLSignatureFactory**, again part of **javax.xml.crypto.dsig**. You can obtain an instance of this abstract class by invoking its **getInstance** method:

```
XMLSignatureFactory factory = XMLSignatureFactory.getInstance();
```

And, to create an XML Signature from an **XMLSignatureFactory**, you simply call its **newXMLSignature** method. The simplest of this method's signatures, however, gives the impression that creating an **XMLSignature** instance is not very straightforward. Here it is.

```
public abstract XMLSignature newXMLSignature(SignedInfo signInfo,
        javax.xml.crypto.dsig.keyinfo.KeyInfo keyInfo)
```

That's right, you need a **SignedInfo** object and a **KeyInfo** object before you can obtain an **XMLSignature**. Recall that an XML signature element has various subelements. Here is the syntax again:

```
<Signature ID?>
    <SignedInfo>
        <CanonicalizationMethod/>
        <SignatureMethod/>
        (<Reference URI? >
            (<Transforms>)?
            <DigestMethod>
                <DigestValue>
        </Reference>)+
    </SignedInfo>
    <SignatureValue>
    (<KeyInfo>)?
    (<Object ID?>)*
</Signature>
```

The **KeyInfo** element is optional, therefore you can pass null as the second argument to **newXMLSignature**. Having said that, you still need to know how to create **SignedInfo** and **KeyInfo** instances, and here is how.

The **XMLSignatureFactory** class provides a **newSignedInfo** method for creating an instance of **SignedInfo**. Here is the signature of the method.

```
public abstract SignedInfo newSignedInfo(CanonicalizationMethod cm,
        SignatureMethod sm, java.util.List references)
```

We'll talk about creating the argument objects later.

To create a **KeyInfo** object, you use the **KeyInfoFactory** class, but you need an instance of **java.security.PublicKey**, which you learned about in the section "Java Cryptography" above.

Here is how you can construct a **KeyInfo** object. Note that **KeyInfoFactory** is a member of the **javax.xml.crypto.dsig.keyinfo** package.

```
KeyInfoFactory keyInfoFactory =
        xmlSignatureFactory.getKeyInfoFactory();
KeyValue keyValue = keyInfoFactory.newKeyValue(publicKey);
// Create KeyInfo and add KeyValue
List keyValues = Arrays.asList(keyValue);
KeyInfo keyInfo = keyInfoFactory.newKeyInfo(keyValues);
```

You start by calling **XMLSignatureFactory.getKeyInfoFactory** and invoking **KeyInfoFactory.newKeyValue** to get a **KeyValue** object. Notice that you pass a public key to the **newKeyValue** method. Once you have a **KeyValue** object or **KeyValue** objects, you must put them in a **List** and pass the list as the argument to **KeyInfoFactory.newKeyInfo**.

Now, having a **SignedInfo** object and a **KeyInfo** instance, you can create an XMLSignature object by using this code:

```
XMLSignature signature =
        xmlSignatureFactory.newXMLSignature(signedInfo, keyInfo);
```

There is another piece of the puzzle we have not worked out, though. We need to create a **CanonicalizationMethod**, a **SignatureMethod**, and a list of **References** before we can compose a **SignedInfo**. Recall that this is the signature of the **newSignedInfo** method of the **XMLSignatureFactory** class.

```
public abstract SignedInfo newSignedInfo(CanonicalizationMethod cm,
        SignatureMethod sm, java.util.List references)
```

You use the **XMLSignatureFactory** class's **newCanonicalizationMethod** method to create a **CanonicalizationMethod**. The signature of this method is as follows.

```
public abstract CanonicalizationMethod newCanonicalizationMethod(
        java.lang.String algorithm,
        javax.xml.crypto.XMLStructure params) throws
        java.security.NoSuchAlgorithmException,
        java.security.InvalidAlgorithmParameterException
```

For the first argument, you can choose one of these fields in the CanonicalizationMethod interface:

```
static final java.lang.String INCLUSIVE
static final java.lang.String INCLUSIVE_WITH_COMMENTS
static final java.lang.String EXCLUSIVE
static final java.lang.String EXCLUSIVE_WITH_COMMENTS
```

For the second argument, you can pass any implementation of the javax.xml.crypto.XMLStructure interface. Or, you can pass null.

Again, XMLSignatureFactory comes to rescue when it's time to create a SignatureMethod instance because it provides this xmlSignatureMethod method:

```
public abstract SignatureMethod newSignatureMethod(
        java.lang.String algorithm,
        javax.xml.crypto.spec.SignatureMethodParameterSpec params
        throws java.security.NoSuchAlgorithmException,
        java.security.InvalidAlgorithmParameterException
```

The **SignatureMethod** interface provides a number of fields that specify the algorithms. You can use any of these as the algorithm.

```
static final java.lang.String DSA_SHA1
static final java.lang.String RSA_SHA1
static final java.lang.String HMAC_SHA1
```

The **SignatureMethodParameterSpec** interface represents algorithm parameters for a **SignatureMethod** algorithm. The only implementation so far is **HMACParameterSpec**. For other algorithms, pass null as the second argument to the **newSignatureMethod** method.

Finally, you create a **Reference** object by using the **newReference** method of **XMLSignatureFactory**:

```
public abstract Reference newReference(java.lang.String uri,
        DigestMethod dm)
```

Now, let's review an example that puts together what we've learned so far. The objective of this example is to sign an XML document in Listing 9.1. Of course, you can sign any well-formed XML document.

Listing 9.1: The document to be signed (TransactionDocument.xml)

```
<?xml version="1.0" encoding="UTF-8"?>
<transaction>
        <id>12345</id>
        <date>2006-04-05</date>
        <description>Payment</description>
        <biller-id>102</biller-id>
        <amount>100000</amount>
</transaction>
```

Listing 9.2 presents an **XMLSigner** class that opens the **TransactionDocument.xml** file, signs it, and write the signed version to a new file named **SignedDocument.xml**.

Listing 9.2: The XMLSigner class

```
import java.io.FileInputStream;
import java.io.FileOutputStream;
import java.io.InputStream;
import java.io.OutputStream;
import java.security.KeyPair;
import java.security.KeyPairGenerator;
import java.security.PrivateKey;
import java.security.PublicKey;
import java.util.Arrays;
import java.util.List;
import javax.xml.crypto.dsig.CanonicalizationMethod;
import javax.xml.crypto.dsig.DigestMethod;
import javax.xml.crypto.dsig.Reference;
import javax.xml.crypto.dsig.SignatureMethod;
import javax.xml.crypto.dsig.SignedInfo;
import javax.xml.crypto.dsig.Transform;
import javax.xml.crypto.dsig.XMLSignature;
import javax.xml.crypto.dsig.XMLSignatureFactory;
import javax.xml.crypto.dsig.dom.DOMSignContext;
import javax.xml.crypto.dsig.keyinfo.KeyInfo;
import javax.xml.crypto.dsig.keyinfo.KeyInfoFactory;
import javax.xml.crypto.dsig.keyinfo.KeyValue;
```

```java
import javax.xml.crypto.dsig.spec.C14NMethodParameterSpec;
import javax.xml.crypto.dsig.spec.DigestMethodParameterSpec;
import javax.xml.crypto.dsig.spec.SignatureMethodParameterSpec;
import javax.xml.crypto.dsig.spec.TransformParameterSpec;
import javax.xml.parsers.DocumentBuilder;
import javax.xml.parsers.DocumentBuilderFactory;
import javax.xml.transform.Result;
import javax.xml.transform.Source;
import javax.xml.transform.Transformer;
import javax.xml.transform.TransformerFactory;
import javax.xml.transform.dom.DOMSource;
import javax.xml.transform.stream.StreamResult;
import org.w3c.dom.Document;
import org.w3c.dom.Node;

public class XMLSigner {
    public static void main(String[] args) throws Exception {
        // STEP 1: Create an XMLSignatureFactory
        XMLSignatureFactory xmlSignatureFactory =
                XMLSignatureFactory.getInstance();

        // STEP 2: Create key for signing
        // Create DSA KeyPair
        KeyPairGenerator keyPairGenerator = KeyPairGenerator.
                getInstance("DSA");
        keyPairGenerator.initialize(512);
        KeyPair keyPair = keyPairGenerator.generateKeyPair();

        // Create private key
        PrivateKey privateKey = keyPair.getPrivate();

        // Create KeyValue containing our DSA PublicKey
        PublicKey publicKey = keyPair.getPublic();
        KeyInfoFactory keyInfoFactory = xmlSignatureFactory.
                getKeyInfoFactory();
        KeyValue keyValue = keyInfoFactory.
                newKeyValue(publicKey);

        // Create buat KeyInfo and add KeyValue
        List keyValues = Arrays.asList(keyValue);
        KeyInfo keyInfo = keyInfoFactory.
                newKeyInfo(keyValues);

        // STEP 3: Read the XML document to be signed
        // and prepare the Node
```

```java
String inputFilename = "TransactionDocument.xml";
InputStream inputStream = new
        FileInputStream(inputFilename);
DocumentBuilderFactory documentBuilderFactory =
        DocumentBuilderFactory
        .newInstance();
DocumentBuilder builder = documentBuilderFactory.
        newDocumentBuilder();
Document document = builder.parse(inputStream);
Node node = document.getDocumentElement();


// STEP 4: Prepare the XMLSignatureFactory
// Create DigestMethod
String digestAlgorithm = DigestMethod.SHA1;
DigestMethodParameterSpec digestParams = null;
DigestMethod digestMethod = xmlSignatureFactory.
        newDigestMethod(
        digestAlgorithm, digestParams);

// Create Transform
String transformAlgorithm = Transform.ENVELOPED;
TransformParameterSpec transformParams = null;
Transform transform = xmlSignatureFactory.
        newTransform(
        transformAlgorithm, transformParams);

// Create Reference
String uri = "";
List transforms = Arrays.asList(transform);
String type = null;
String id = null;
Reference reference = xmlSignatureFactory.
        newReference(uri, digestMethod,
        transforms, type, id);

// Create CanonicalizationMethod
String canonAlgorithm = CanonicalizationMethod
        .INCLUSIVE_WITH_COMMENTS;
C14NMethodParameterSpec canonParams = null;
CanonicalizationMethod canonicalizationMethod =
        xmlSignatureFactory.
        newCanonicalizationMethod(
        canonAlgorithm, canonParams);
```

```
            // Create SignatureMethod
            String signatureAlgorithm = SignatureMethod.DSA_SHA1;
            SignatureMethodParameterSpec signatureParams = null;
            SignatureMethod signatureMethod =
                    xmlSignatureFactory.newSignatureMethod(
                    signatureAlgorithm, signatureParams);

            // Create SignedInfo
            List references = Arrays.asList(reference);
            SignedInfo signedInfo = xmlSignatureFactory.
                    newSignedInfo(canonicalizationMethod,
                    signatureMethod, references);


            // STEP 5: Create DOMSignContext and XMLSignature
            DOMSignContext signContext = new
                    DOMSignContext(privateKey, node);
            // Create XML signature
            XMLSignature signature = xmlSignatureFactory.
                    newXMLSignature(signedInfo, keyInfo);


            // STEP 6: Sign the DOMSignContext
            signature.sign(signContext);


            // STEP 7: Write the signed XML to file
            String outputFilename = "SignedDocument.xml";
            OutputStream outputStream = new
                    FileOutputStream(outputFilename);
            Source xmlSource = new DOMSource(document);
            Result outputTarget = new StreamResult(outputStream);
            TransformerFactory transformerFactory =
                    TransformerFactory.newInstance();
            Transformer transformer =
                    transformerFactory.newTransformer();
            transformer.transform(xmlSource, outputTarget);
        }
}
```

If you run the **XMLSigner** class in Listing 9.2 you'll get a **SignedDocument.xml** file identical to the one here.

```
<?xml version="1.0" encoding="UTF-8"?>
<transaction>
  <id>12345</id>
```

```xml
<date>2006-04-05</date>
<description>Payment</description>
<biller-id>102</biller-id>
<amount>100000</amount>
<Signature xmlns="http://www.w3.org/2000/09/xmldsig#">
  <SignedInfo>
    <CanonicalizationMethod
     Algorithm="http://www.w3.org/TR/2001/REC-xml-c14n-20010315
#WithComments" />
    <SignatureMethod
        Algorithm="http://www.w3.org/2000/09/xmldsig#dsa-sha1" />
    <Reference URI="">
      <Transforms>
        <Transform
          Algorithm="http://www.w3.org/2000/09/xmldsig#enveloped-
signature" />
      </Transforms>
      <DigestMethod
        Algorithm="http://www.w3.org/2000/09/xmldsig#sha1" />
        <DigestValue>dwRmnTsVQ+71pmi0e7tXzqwVl2I=</DigestValue>
    </Reference>
  </SignedInfo>
  <SignatureValue>
    a82kt+hJQwt3t1AulJwRIzvXxThhd41Et24pYYjg0LaPQLBq0zbsEA==
  </SignatureValue>
  <KeyInfo>
    <KeyValue>
      <DSAKeyValue>
        <P>
         /KaCzo4Syrom78z3EQ5SbbB4sF7ey80etKII864WF64B81uRpH5
t9jQTxeEu0ImbzRMqzVDZkVG9xD7nN1kuFw==
        </P>
        <Q>li7dzDacuo67Jg7mtqEm2TRuOMU=</Q>
        <G>
         Z4Rxsnqc9E7pGknFFH2xqaryRPBaQ01khpMdLRQnG541Awtx
/XPaF5Bpsy4pNWMOHCBiNU0NogpsQW5QvnlMpA==
        </G>
        <Y>
          KnTYXE96VNQvngdQm1wcxUKNE/ZvVJ7GUpVRRDB8mLri3pviJng784dwO
CNPxV++0b31FWjnbyyNnhhmw7uEdg==
        </Y>
      </DSAKeyValue>
    </KeyValue>
  </KeyInfo>
</Signature>
```

```
</transaction>
```

Signature Validation

The second major task in the XML document signing topic is signature validation. The W3C defines this task to include the following steps:

1. Reference validation
2. Signature validation.

Reference validation is essentially the verification of the digest in each **Reference** element. Here are the steps to perform reference validation.

1. Canonicalize the **SignedInfo** element based on the value of the **CanonicalizationMethod** sub-element.
2. For each **Reference** element, do:
   a. Obtain the data object to be digested.
   b. Digest the resulting data object using its **DigestMethod**.
   c. Compare the generated digest value against the value of **<DigestValue>**. Validation passes if the digested value matches the value of **<DigestValue>**

Here are steps in signature validation:

1. Get the key information from **<KeyInfo>** or from an external source.
2. Get the canonical form of the **SignatureMethod** element and use the result to confirm the **SignatureValue**.

To validate an XML signature in Java you use the **validate** method of the **javax.xml.crypto.dsig.XMLSignature** interface. Here is the signature of the method:

```
boolean validate(XMLValidateContext validateContext)
        throws XMLSignatureException
```

This method returns **true** if the validation passed and returns **false** if it failed. If an unexpected error occurs during validation, an **XMLSignatureException** is thrown.

Yes, of course, you now need to learn about the **XMLValidateContext** interface, an instance of which contains context information for validating

XML signatures. This interface has one implementation, the
DOMValidateContext class. There are two constructors provided by this
class. The first one is this.

```
public DOMValidateContext(java.security.Key validatingKey,
        org.w3c.dom.Node node)
```

The *validatingKey* argument is the public key needed to validate the signature
and the *node* argument is the **Signature** element. Recall that an XML signature
contains a **KeyInfo** element that in turn contains the public key that
corresponds to the private key used to sign the document. In the **XMLSigner**
class in Listing 9.2 you used this code to produce a **KeyInfo** object:

```
// Create KeyValue containing our DSA PublicKey
PublicKey publicKey = keyPair.getPublic();
KeyInfoFactory keyInfoFactory = xmlSignatureFactory.
        getKeyInfoFactory();
KeyValue keyValue = keyInfoFactory. newKeyValue(publicKey);

// Create KeyInfo and add KeyValue
List keyValues = Arrays.asList(keyValue);
KeyInfo keyInfo = keyInfoFactory.newKeyInfo(keyValues);
```

Currently, there is no easy way to retrieve a public key directly from a
Signature element in an XML document. The good news is there is a second
constructor of **DOMValidateContext**, as follows.

```
public DOMValidateContext(javax.xml.crypto.KeySelector ks,
        org.w3c.dom.Node node)
```

The difference between this constructor and the first is that this constructor
accepts a **KeySelector** object as the first argument. You need to get yourself
familiar with this abstract class now.

A **KeySelector** is used to find and return a key using the data contained in
a **KeyInfo** object. Since **KeySelector** is an abstract class, you need to create a
subclass and override its **select** method. This method returns a
KeySelectorResult object, on which you can call the **getKey** method that
returns a **java.security.Key** object. This **Key** object is the public key needed
to validate the signature.

Here is the select method of the **KeySelector** class.

```
public abstract KeySelectorResult select(
```

```
javax.xml.crypto.dsig.keyinfo.KeyInfo keyInfo,
KeySelector.Purpose purpose, AlgorithmMethod method,
XMLCryptoContext context)
throws KeySelectorException.
```

This method is called by the second **DOMValidateContext** class's constructor.

As an example, the code in Listing 9.3 presents an XML validator.

Listing 9.3: XMLSignatureValidator class

```java
import java.io.FileInputStream;
import java.security.Key;
import java.security.KeyException;
import java.security.PublicKey;
import java.util.Collections;
import java.util.Iterator;
import java.util.List;
import javax.xml.crypto.KeySelector;
import javax.xml.crypto.KeySelectorException;
import javax.xml.crypto.KeySelectorResult;
import javax.xml.crypto.KeySelector.Purpose;
import javax.xml.crypto.AlgorithmMethod;
import javax.xml.crypto.XMLCryptoContext;
import javax.xml.crypto.XMLStructure;
import javax.xml.crypto.dsig.SignatureMethod;
import javax.xml.crypto.dsig.XMLSignature;
import javax.xml.crypto.dsig.XMLSignatureFactory;
import javax.xml.crypto.dsig.dom.DOMValidateContext;
import javax.xml.crypto.dsig.keyinfo.KeyInfo;
import javax.xml.crypto.dsig.keyinfo.KeyValue;
import javax.xml.parsers.DocumentBuilderFactory;
import org.w3c.dom.Document;
import org.w3c.dom.NodeList;

public class XMLSignatureValidator {
    private static class MyKeySelector extends KeySelector {
        public KeySelectorResult select(KeyInfo keyInfo,
                KeySelector.Purpose purpose,
                AlgorithmMethod method,
                XMLCryptoContext context)
                throws KeySelectorException {
            if (keyInfo == null) {
                throw new KeySelectorException(
                        "Null KeyInfo object!");
            }
```

```java
        SignatureMethod signatureMethod =
                (SignatureMethod) method;
        List list = keyInfo.getContent();
        String signatureMethodAlgorithm =
                signatureMethod.getAlgorithm();
        // Currently we support DSA_SHA1 and
        // RSA_SHA1 only, but other algorithms are
        // not impossible
        if (signatureMethodAlgorithm.
                equalsIgnoreCase(SignatureMethod.DSA_SHA1) ||
                signatureMethodAlgorithm.
                equalsIgnoreCase(SignatureMethod.RSA_SHA1)) {

            for (int i = 0; i < list.size(); i++) {
                XMLStructure xmlStructure =
                        (XMLStructure) list.get(i);
                if (xmlStructure instanceof KeyValue) {
                    PublicKey publicKey = null;
                    try {
                        publicKey = ((KeyValue)xmlStructure).
                                getPublicKey();
                    } catch (KeyException e) {
                        throw new KeySelectorException(e);
                    }

                    // make sure the algorithm is correct
                    String publicKeyAlgorithm =
                            publicKey.getAlgorithm();
                    if (publicKeyAlgorithm.
                            equalsIgnoreCase("DSA") ||
                            publicKeyAlgorithm.
                            equalsIgnoreCase("RSA")) {
                        return new
                                MyKeySelectorResult(publicKey);
                    }
                }
            }
        }
        throw new KeySelectorException(
                "KeyValue not found!");
    }
}

private static class MyKeySelectorResult implements
    KeySelectorResult {
```

```
        private PublicKey publicKey;
        public MyKeySelectorResult(PublicKey publicKey) {
            this.publicKey = publicKey;
        }
        public Key getKey() {
            return publicKey;
        }
    }

    public static void main(String[] args) {

        // Instantiate the SignedDocument.xml to be validated
        String inputFileName = "SignedDocument.xml";
        DocumentBuilderFactory documentBuilderFactory =
                DocumentBuilderFactory.newInstance();
        documentBuilderFactory.setNamespaceAware(true);
        NodeList nodeList = null;
        try {
            Document document = documentBuilderFactory.
                    newDocumentBuilder().
                    parse(new FileInputStream(inputFileName));
            // Find Signature element
            nodeList = document.getElementsByTagNameNS
                    (XMLSignature.XMLNS, "Signature");
            if (nodeList.getLength() == 0) {
                System.err.println("Signature not found");
                System.exit(1);
            }
        } catch (Exception e) {
            System.err.println(e);
        }

        // Create a DOM XMLSignatureFactory
        XMLSignatureFactory xmlSignatureFactory =
                XMLSignatureFactory.getInstance();

        // Create a DOMValidateContext, passing an instance
        // of MyKeySelector
        DOMValidateContext domValidateContext =
                new DOMValidateContext
                (new MyKeySelector(), nodeList.item(0));

        // unmarshal the XMLSignature
        try {
```

```
        XMLSignature signature =
xmlSignatureFactory.unmarshalXMLSignature(domValidateContext)
;
        // Validate the signature
        if (signature.validate(domValidateContext)) {
            System.out.println("Signature valid.");
        } else {
            System.err.println("Signature failed core
validation");
        }
    } catch (Exception e) {
        System.err.println(e);
    }
  }
}
```

This class reads the **SignedDocument.xml** file produced by the **XMLSigner** class. On a successful validation, it will print this on the console:

```
Signature valid.
```

Now, try tampering with the **SignedDocument.xml** file, maybe by changing the key value, and run the **XMLSignatureValidator** class again. This time, an exception will be thrown, its message explaining why it failed.

Summary

This chapter dealt with the XML Digital Signature API that defines a standard Java API for digitally signing XML documents. Two major tasks you perform using this API are signing a document and validating XML signatures. The chapter provided two examples for these major tasks.

Chapter 10
Streaming API for XML

Prior to the Streaming API for XML (StAX), defined in JSR 173 (http://jcp.org/en/jsr/detail?id=173), to handle XML Java programmers had to work with the two main APIs for XML processing, DOM and SAX. DOM is easy to use and provides you with the ability to convert XML into a tree of objects. The downside is, however, the fact that DOM is inefficient for large XML documents since the whole object tree must be loaded into memory. The event-based SAX is more efficient in terms of memory usage as it does not have to load the whole XML document into memory. In fact, SAX, though harder to program, is fast and can work well with any size of documents. SAX is based on the Observer design pattern, it calls the appropriate listener as it encounters various elements of an XML document. This is a push technology in action. The problem with SAX is that data pushing is not always the perfect solution with all clients. Sometimes, the client, rather than the parser, needs to control the parsing process. In addition, SAX can only be used to read, not write.

Then came StAX. It is a technology similar to SAX, except that StAX is based on a pull technology. It is the client that queries the StAX parser for more elements. It allows you to iterate over the elements being read, similar to having a ResultSet in a JDBC application.

The classes and interfaces that make up the StAX framework belong to the **javax.xml.stream** package and its two subpackages, **javax.xml.stream.events** and **javax.xml.stream.util**. The four most prominent interfaces are **XMLStreamReader**, **XMLEventReader**, **XMLStreamWriter**, and **XMLEventWriter**, all of which are part of **javax.xml.stream**. As the names imply, the first two interfaces are used for reading XML documents and the last two for creating or writing ones.

Reading XML

The **XMLStreamReader** and **XMLEventReader** interfaces can be used for reading XML documents. You get the most speed and efficiency using **XMLStreamReader**, however **XMLEventReader** provides configuration information through the property interface.

XMLStreamReader and **XMLEventReader** have similar functionality. So, you say hopefully, you just need to learn to use the former (the faster one), and not worry about the latter, right? Yes, if **XMLEventReader** did not have a **peek** method that checks the next **XMLEvent** without reading it from the stream. If you ever need such a feature, **XMLEventReader** is your answer.

Using XMLStreamReader

XMLStreamReader allows forward-only, read-only access to XML. You iterate over elements using its **hasNext** and **next** methods. **hasNext** returns **true** if there are more parsing events and returns **false** if it is already at the end of the document. The signature of **hasNext** is as follows.

```
boolean hasNext() throws XMLStreamException
```

Once you're sure there is a next parsing event, you can call the **XMLStreamReader**'s **next** method:

```
int next() throws XMLStreamException
```

This method returns an integer indicating the type of the event. Its value can be one of the following fields:

- ATTRIBUTE
- CDATA
- CHARACTERS
- COMMENT
- DTD
- END_DOCUMENT
- END_ELEMENT
- ENTITY_REFERENCE
- NAMESPACE

- PROCESSING_INSTRUCTION
- SPACE
- START_DOCUMENT
- START_ELEMENT

Depending on the event type returned, you can call the various methods in
XMLStreamReader. For example, upon an **ATTRIBUTE** event, you can
call **next, nextTag getAttributeCount, getAttributeLocalName,
getAttributeName, getAttributeNamespace, getAttributePrefix,
getAttributeType, getAttributeValue**, and **isAttributeSpecified**. Table 10.1
lists the methods that you can call after each event.

Event Type	Valid Methods
ATTRIBUTE	next, nextTag, getAttributeCount, getAttributeLocalName, getAttributeName, getAttributeNamespace, getAttributePrefix, getAttributeType, getAttributeValue, isAttributeSpecified
CDATA	next, getText, getTextCharacters, getTextLength, getTextStart, nextTag
CHARACTERS	next, getText, getTextCharacters, getTextLength, getTextStart, nextTag
COMMENT	next, getText, getTextCharacters, getTextLength, getTextStart, nextTag
DTD	next, getText, nextTag
END_DOCUMENT	close
END_ELEMENT	next, getName, getLocalName, hasName, getPrefix, getNamespaceContext, getNamespaceCount, getNamespacePrefix, getNamespaceURI, nextTag
ENTITY_REFERENCE	next, getLocalName, getText, nextTag
NAMESPACE	next, nextTag getNamespaceContext, getNamespaceCount, getNamespacePrefix, getNamespaceURI
PROCESSING_INSTRUCTION	next, getPITarget, getPIData, nextTag
SPACE	next, getText, getTextCharacters, getTextLength, getTextStart, nextTag
START_DOCUMENT	next, getEncoding, getVersion, isStandalone, standaloneSet, getCharacterEncodingScheme, nextTag

START_ELEMENT	next, getName, getLocalName, hasName, getPrefix, getAttributeCount, getAttributeLocalName, getAttributeName, getAttributeNamespace, getAttributePrefix, getAttributeType, getAttributeValue, isAttributeSpecified, getNamespaceContext, getNamespaceCount, getNamespacePrefix, getNamespaceURI, getElementText, nextTag
All states	getProperty, hasNext, require, close, getNamespaceURI, isStartElement, isEndElement, isCharacters, isWhiteSpace, getNamespaceContext, getEventType, getLocation, hasText, hasName

Table 10.1: The valid methods for each event

You can create an instance of **XMLStreamReader** using one of the methods in the **XMLInputFactory** abstract class. You can base your **XMLStreamReader** on an **InputStream**, a **Reader**, or a **javax.xml.transform.Source**. Here are the factory methods:

```
public abstract XMLStreamReader createXMLStreamReader(
        java.io.InputStream stream) throws XMLStreamException

public abstract XMLStreamReader createXMLStreamReader(
        java.lang.String systemId, java.io.InputStream stream)
        throws XMLStreamException

public abstract XMLStreamReader createXMLStreamReader(
        java.io.InputStream stream, java.lang.String encoding)
        throws XMLStreamException

public abstract XMLStreamReader createXMLStreamReader(
        java.io.Reader reader) throws XMLStreamException

public abstract XMLStreamReader createXMLStreamReader(
        java.lang.String systemId, java.io.Reader reader)
        throws XMLStreamException

public abstract XMLStreamReader createXMLStreamReader(
        javax.xml.transform.Source source) throws XMLStreamException
```

There are two examples in this section. The first one demonstrates the use of **XMLStreamReader** to read XML. The second uses **XMLEventReader**. Both will read XML from the **Source.xml** file in Listing 10.1. The **Source.xml** file describes two products with codes, names, and prices.

Listing 10.1: The Source.xml file

```xml
<?xml version="1.0" encoding="UTF-8"?>
<products>
    <product id="1">
        <code>I001</code>
        <name>Todotodo Chocolate Milk</name>
        <price>$10.95</price>
    </product>
    <product id="2">
        <code>I002</code>
        <name>Bangbang Chocolate Bar</name>
        <price>$2.35</price>
    </product>
</products>
```

The **XMLStreamReaderDemo** class in Listing 10.2 demonstrates the use of **XMLStreamReader**.

Listing 10.2: XMLStreamReaderDemo class

```java
import java.io.FileReader;
import java.io.Reader;
import javax.xml.stream.XMLInputFactory;
import javax.xml.stream.XMLStreamConstants;
import javax.xml.stream.XMLStreamException;
import javax.xml.stream.XMLStreamReader;

public class XMLStreamReaderDemo {
    public static void main(String[] args) {
        try {
            // Create an XMLInputFactory
            XMLInputFactory factory = XMLInputFactory.newInstance();

            // Create a FileReader of source.xml
            Reader fileReader = new FileReader("source.xml");
            XMLStreamReader reader =
                    factory.createXMLStreamReader(fileReader);

            // Iterate over the XML
            while (reader.hasNext()) {
                process(reader);
                reader.next();
            }
        } catch (Exception e) {
            e.printStackTrace();
```

```
        }
    }

    private static void process(XMLStreamReader reader)
            throws XMLStreamException {

        // Event type
        int eventType = reader.getEventType();

        // Check event type
        switch (eventType) {
            case XMLStreamConstants.START_ELEMENT:
                // Display the element's local name
                System.out.println("Start element: " +
                        reader.getLocalName());

                // Display all attributes of the element
                int count = reader.getAttributeCount();
                for (int i = 0; i < count; i++) {
                    String name = reader.getAttributeLocalName(i);
                    String value = reader.getAttributeValue(i);
                    System.out.println("\tAttribute name/value: " +
                            name + "/" + value);
                }
                break;

            case XMLStreamConstants.END_ELEMENT:
                System.out.println("End element: " +
                        reader.getLocalName());
                break;

            case XMLStreamConstants.CHARACTERS:
                System.out.println("Text: " + reader.getText());
                break;
            default:
                break;
        }
    }
}
```

If you run the class in Listing 10.2 you will see this as on your console:

```
Start element: products
Text:

Start element: product
```

```
          Attribute name/value: id/1
Text:

Start element: code
Text: I001
End element: code
Text:

Start element: name
Text: Todotodo Chocolate Milk
End element: name
Text:

Start element: price
Text: $10.95
End element: price
Text:

End element: product
Text:

Start element: product
          Attribute name/value: id/2
Text:

Start element: code
Text: I002
End element: code
Text:

Start element: name
Text: Bangbang Chocolate Bar
End element: name
Text:

Start element: price
Text: $2.35
End element: price
Text:

End element: product
Text:

End element: products
```

Using XMLEventReader

Like **XMLStreamReader**, **XMLEventReader** has a **next** method that returns **true** if there are more events. Once you get an OK from **next**, you can call its **hasNext** method that returns a **javax.xml.stream.events.XMLEvent** object. Alternatively, you can call the **peek** method that checks the next **XMLEvent** without reading it from the stream.

```
javax.xml.stream.events.XMLEvent peek() throws XMLStreamException
```

Note
There is no **peek** method or an equivalent in the faster **XMLStreamReader** interface.

Once you have an **XMLEvent** object, either from **nextEvent** or **peek**, you can enquire the type of the event by calling the **getEventType** method that returns an integer indicating the type of the event. The possible values are identical to the values from **XMLStreamReader.next()**. Alternatively, you can call one of the following methods to find out if the event type is what you're looking for: **isAttribute, isCharacters, isEndDocument, isEndElement, isEntityReference, isNamespace, isProcessingInstruction, isStartDocument,** and **isStartElement**.

You can create an instance of **XMLEventReader** using one of the methods in the **XMLInputFactory** abstract class. There are seven ways of creating an **XMLEventReader,** as you can witness from the following overloads.

```
public abstract XMLEventReader createXMLEventReader(
        java.io.InputStream stream) throws XMLStreamException

public abstract XMLEventReader createXMLEventReader(
        java.io.InputStream stream, java.lang.String encoding)
        throws XMLStreamException

public abstract XMLEventReader createXMLEventReader(
        java.lang.String systemId, java.io.InputStream stream)
        throws XMLStreamException

public abstract XMLEventReader createXMLEventReader(
        java.io.Reader reader) throws XMLStreamException

public abstract XMLEventReader createXMLEventReader(
        java.lang.String systemId, java.io.Reader reader)
        throws XMLStreamException
```

```
public abstract XMLEventReader createXMLEventReader(
        javax.xml.transform.Source source) throws XMLStreamException

public abstract XMLEventReader createXMLEventReader(
        XMLStreamReader reader) throws XMLStreamException
```

As an example, consider the **XMLEventReaderDemo** class in Listing 10.3.

Listing 10.3: XMLEventReaderDemo class

```java
import java.io.FileReader;
import java.io.Reader;
import java.util.Iterator;
import javax.xml.namespace.QName;
import javax.xml.stream.XMLEventReader;
import javax.xml.stream.XMLInputFactory;
import javax.xml.stream.XMLStreamException;
import javax.xml.stream.events.Attribute;
import javax.xml.stream.events.Characters;
import javax.xml.stream.events.EndElement;
import javax.xml.stream.events.StartElement;
import javax.xml.stream.events.XMLEvent;

public class XMLEventReaderDemo {
    public static void main(String[] args) {
        try {
            // Create XMLInputFactory
            XMLInputFactory factory = XMLInputFactory.newInstance();
            // Create FileReader for source.xml
            Reader fileReader = new FileReader("Source.xml");
            XMLEventReader reader =
                    factory.createXMLEventReader(fileReader);

            // Iterate over the XMLStreamReader
            while (reader.hasNext()) {
                XMLEvent event = reader.nextEvent();
                process(event);
            }
        } catch (Exception e) {
            e.printStackTrace();
        }
    }

    // Process events
    private static void process(XMLEvent event)
```

```
            throws XMLStreamException {

    if (event.isStartElement()) {
        StartElement element = (StartElement) event;
        System.out.println("Start Element: " +
                element.getName());

        // Display all attributes
        Iterator iterator = element.getAttributes();
        while (iterator.hasNext()) {
            Attribute attribute = (Attribute) iterator.next();
            QName name = attribute.getName();
            String value = attribute.getValue();
            System.out.println("Attribute name/value: " +
                    name + "/" + value);
        }
    }

    if (event.isEndElement()) {
        EndElement element = (EndElement) event;
        System.out.println("End element:" + element.getName());
    }

    if (event.isCharacters()) {
        Characters characters = (Characters) event;
        System.out.println("Text: " + characters.getData());
    }
    }
}
```

The **XMLEventReaderDemo** class creates an **XMLEventReader** object and then calls its **hasNext** method in a **while** loop. For each **XMLEvent** it retrieves from **nextEvent**, it passes it to the **process** method. The **process** method is interested in the **START_ELEMENT**, **END_ELEMENT**, and **CHARACTERS** events, and will print messages if an event is one of the three.

Running the **XMLEventReaderDemo** class will give you the following messages on your console.

```
Start Element: products
Text:

Start Element: product
Attribute name/value: id/1
```

```
Text:

Start Element: code
Text: I001
End element:code
Text:

Start Element: name
Text: Todotodo Chocolate Milk
End element:name
Text:

Start Element: price
Text: $10.95
End element:price
Text:

End element:product
Text:

Start Element: product
Attribute name/value: id/2
Text:

Start Element: code
Text: I002
End element:code
Text:

Start Element: name
Text: Bangbang Chocolate Bar
End element:name
Text:

Start Element: price
Text: $2.35
End element:price
Text:

End element:product
Text:

End element:products
```

Writing to XML

There are two interfaces in the **javax.xml.stream** package that you can use to write to XML, **XMLStreamWriter** and **XMLEventWriter**. With the first, you add elements through its various **write*XXX*** methods, such as **writeStartDocument**, **writeStartElement**, **writeAttribute**, **writeEndElement**, **writeEndDocument**, and so forth. With **XMLEventWriter**, you add elements with the aid of its **add** methods. Implementations of both interfaces do not need to guarantee the well-formedness of the XML document.

This section features an example that uses **XMLStreamWriter** and an example that employs **XMLEventWriter**.

Using XMLStreamWriter

An instance of **XMLStreamWriter** is used to create and write XML. You create an instance of **XMLStreamWriter** by calling one of the **createXMLStreamWriter** method overloads of the **XMLOutputFactory** class. As you can see in its signatures below, you can pass a **Writer**, an **OutputStream**, or a **javax.xml.transform.Result**.

```
public abstract XMLStreamWriter createXMLStreamWriter(
        java.io.OutputStream stream) throws XMLStreamException

public abstract XMLStreamWriter createXMLStreamWriter(
        java.io.OutputStream stream, java.lang.String encoding)
        throws XMLStreamException

public abstract XMLStreamWriter createXMLStreamWriter(
        java.io.Writer writer) throws XMLStreamException

public abstract XMLStreamWriter createXMLStreamWriter(
        javax.xml.transform.Result result) throws XMLStreamException
```

As for **XMLOutputFactory**, it is an abstract class with **newInstance** methods that return an instance of a subclass.

```
public static XMLOutputFactory newInstace()
        throws FactoryConfigurationError

public static XMLOutputFactory newInstance(
        java.lang.String factoryId, java.lang.ClassLoader loader)
```

```
        throws FactoryConfigurationError
```

Now back to the **XMLStreamWriter** interface, here are some of the methods defined in the interface.

```
void writeStartDocument(java.lang.String version)
        throws XMLStreamException
```
Writes the XML declaration. Currently, the only valid version is 1.0.

```
void writeStartElement(java.lang.String localName)
```
Writes a start tag.

```
void writeCharacters(java.lang.String text)
        throws XMLStreamException
```
Writes text to the output.

```
void writeAttribute(java.lang.String localName,
        java.lang.String value) throws XMLStreamException
```
Writes an attribute without a prefix.

```
void setDefaultNamespace(java.lang.String uri)
        throws XMLStreamException
```
Binds a URI to the default namespace.

```
void flush() throws XMLStreamException
```
Writes cached data to the output.

```
void close() throws XMLStreamException
```
Closes this writer.

For example, the code in Listing 10.4 uses **XMLStreamWriter** to write XML to the console.

Listing 10.4: XMLStreamWriterDemo class

```
import javax.xml.stream.XMLOutputFactory;
import javax.xml.stream.XMLStreamWriter;

public class XMLStreamWriterDemo {
    public static void main(String[] args) throws Exception {

        // Create XMLOutputFactory
        XMLOutputFactory factory = XMLOutputFactory.newInstance();

        // Create XMLStreamWriter to System.out
        XMLStreamWriter writer =
                factory.createXMLStreamWriter(System.out);
```

```
            // Write the start document (XML version 1.0)
            writer.writeStartDocument("1.0");

            // Write root element catalog
            writer.writeStartElement("catalog");

            // Write element book under catalog
            writer.writeStartElement("book");
            // Write the id attribute for <book>
            writer.writeAttribute("id", "1");

            // write element code with value I001
            writer.writeStartElement("code");
            writer.writeCharacters("I001");
            writer.writeEndElement();

            // Write element title under <book>
            writer.writeStartElement("title");
            writer.writeCharacters("German-English Dictionary");
            writer.writeEndElement();

            // Write element price under <book>
            writer.writeStartElement("price");
            writer.writeCharacters("$22.95");
            writer.writeEndElement();

            // write end element
            writer.writeEndDocument();

            // flush and close
            writer.flush();
            writer.close();
        }
}
```

If you compile and run the **XMLStreamWriterDemo** class, you will see the following on the console.

```
<?xml version="1.0"?>
<catalog>
    <book id="1">
        <code>I001</code>
        <title>German-English Dictionary</title>
        <price>$22.95</price>
    </book>
```

```
</catalog>
```

Using XMLEventWriter

The **XMLEventWriter** interface provides two **add** methods to write to XML.

```
void add(XMLEvent event) throws XMLStreamException
```

```
void add(XMLEventReader reader) throws XMLStreamException
```

You create an **XMLEventWriter** with the help of, again, **XMLOutputFactory**. Notice that these four methods are very similar to the **createXMLStreamWriter** methods. You can use any of them to construct an instance of **XMLEventWriter**.

```
public abstract XMLEventWriter createXMLEventWriter(
        java.io.OutputStream stream) throws XMLStreamException
```

```
public abstract XMLEventWriter createXMLEventWriter(
        java.io.OutputStream stream, java.lang.String encoding)
        throws XMLStreamException
```

```
public abstract XMLEventWriter createXMLEventWriter(
        java.io.Writer writer) throws XMLStreamException
```

```
public abstract XMLEventWriter createXMLEventWriter(
        javax.xml.transform.Result result) throws XMLStreamException
```

As an example, the code in Listing 10.5 demonstrates how to use **XMLEventWriter** write to XML.

Listing 10.5: The XMLEventWriterDemo class

```
import java.util.Arrays;
import java.util.List;
import javax.xml.stream.XMLEventFactory;
import javax.xml.stream.XMLEventWriter;
import javax.xml.stream.XMLOutputFactory;
import javax.xml.stream.events.Attribute;
import javax.xml.stream.events.Characters;
import javax.xml.stream.events.EndDocument;
import javax.xml.stream.events.EndElement;
import javax.xml.stream.events.StartDocument;
import javax.xml.stream.events.StartElement;

public class XMLEventWriterDemo {
```

```java
public static void main(String[] args) throws Exception {
    // Create XMLOutputFactory
    XMLOutputFactory outputFactory =
            XMLOutputFactory.newInstance();

    // Create XMLEventWriter
    XMLEventWriter writer =
            outputFactory.createXMLEventWriter(System.out);

    // Create XMLEventFactory
    XMLEventFactory xmlEventFactory =
            XMLEventFactory.newInstance();

    // Create document
    StartDocument startDocument = xmlEventFactory.
            createStartDocument("UTF-8", "1.0");
    writer.add(startDocument);

    // Write root element customer-list
    StartElement startElement = xmlEventFactory.
            createStartElement("", "", "customer-list");
    writer.add(startElement);

    // Create attribute
    Attribute attribute = xmlEventFactory.
            createAttribute("version", "1");
    List attributeList = Arrays.asList(attribute);
    List nsList = Arrays.asList();
    StartElement startElement2 = xmlEventFactory.
            createStartElement("", "", "customer",
            attributeList.iterator(), nsList.iterator());
    writer.add(startElement2);

    // Write code element with value I001
    StartElement codeSE = xmlEventFactory.
            createStartElement("", "", "code");
    writer.add(codeSE);
    Characters codeChars = xmlEventFactory.
            createCharacters("I001");
    writer.add(codeChars);
    EndElement codeEE = xmlEventFactory.
            createEndElement("", "", "code");
    writer.add(codeEE);

    // Write element name with value "ABC Printing"
    StartElement nameSE = xmlEventFactory.createStartElement("",
```

```
                "", "name");
        writer.add(nameSE);
        Characters nameChars = xmlEventFactory.createCharacters(
                "ABC Printing");
        writer.add(nameChars);
        EndElement nameEE = xmlEventFactory.createEndElement("", "",
                "name");
        writer.add(nameEE);

        // Write element contact
        StartElement contactSE = xmlEventFactory.
                createStartElement("", "", "contact");
        writer.add(contactSE);
        Characters contactChars = xmlEventFactory.
                createCharacters("Sean Novell");
        writer.add(contactChars);
        EndElement contactEE = xmlEventFactory.
                createEndElement("", "", "contact");
        writer.add(contactEE);

        // Write end document
        EndDocument ed = xmlEventFactory.createEndDocument();
        writer.add(ed);

        // Flush and close
        writer.flush();
        writer.close();
    }
}
```

This is the outcome (after formatting) of the **XMLEventWriterDemo** class:

```
<?xml version="1.0" encoding="UTF-8"?>
<customer-list>
    <customer version="1">
        <code>I001</code>
        <name>ABC Printing</name>
        <contact>Sean Novell</contact>
    </customer>
</customer-list>
```

Summary

The Streaming API for XML (StAX) is a new technology for efficient access and manipulation of XML documents. Unlike SAX that employs a push technology, StAX is entirely based on a pull technology. Therefore, the client of the parser controls the parsing process. There are four main interfaces in this API, all of which are members of the **javax.xml.stream** package: **XMLStreamReader**, **XMLEventReader**, **XMLStreamWriter**, and **XMLEventWriter**. The first two interfaces are used for reading XML documents and the last two for creating or writing ones. This chapter presented examples that used these interfaces.

Chapter 11
Java Architecture for
XML Binding

Java 6 includes the reference implementation for Java Architecture for XML Binding (JAXB) 2.0, which is defined in JSR 222 (http://jcp.org/en/jsr/detail?id=222). The API can be found in the **javax.xml.bind** package and its subpackages. JAXB 2.0 offers support for binding Java to XML, with the help of the annotation types in the **javax.xml.bind.annotation** package. Unlike JAXB 1.0 that can only convert XML to Java, JAXB 2.0 supports Java-to-schema binding as well.

This chapter presents a brief tutorial on JAXB for the uninitiated and provides an example on the new features in JAXB 2.0

Introduction to JAXB

You need to understand these two terms in JAXB jargon before you start: *marshall* and *unmarshalling*. Marshalling refers to the process of converting or serializing Java objects to XML. Unmarshalling does the reverse, converting or deserializing an instance XML document into Java objects.

You use a **javax.xml.bind.Marshaller** object to marshall Java objects, and a **javax.xml.bind.Unmarshaller** instance to perform unmarshalling. Both **Marshaller** and **Unmarshaller** instances can be created by using the **JAXBContext** class, which is also a member of **javax.xml.bind**. The **JAXBContext** class's **createMarshaller** method creates a **Marshaller** and the **createUnmarshaller** method creates an **Unmarshaller**. Here are the signatures of both methods.

```
public abstract Marshaller createMarshaller() throws JAXBException
public abstract Unmarshaller createUnmarshaller()
```

```
throws JAXBException
```

The **JAXBContext** class itself is abstract, however it comes with two static **newInstance** methods for creating an instance of a subclass. We'll see how to use these methods in the sections to come.

Marshalling Java Objects

You use a **Marshaller** object to marshall Java objects into XML. The main method in the **Marshaller** interface is **marshall**. To make it easy to stream the generated XML into various sinks, there are seven overloads of this method.

```
void marshall(java.lang.Object jaxbElement,
        org.xml.sax.ContentHandler handler) throws JAXBException
```

```
void marshall(java.lang.Object jaxbElement,
        org.w3c.dom.Node node) throws JAXBException
```

```
void marshall(java.lang.Object jaxbElement,
        java.io.OutputStream stream) throws JAXBException
```

```
void marshall(java.lang.Object jaxbElement,
        javax.xml.transform.Result result) throws JAXBException
```

```
void marshall(java.lang.Object jaxbElement,
        java.io.Writer writer) throws JAXBException
```

```
void marshall(java.lang.Object jaxbElement,
        javax.xml.stream.XMLStreamWriter writer)
        throws JAXBException
```

```
void marshall(java.lang.Object jaxbElement,
        javax.xml.stream.XMLEventWriter writer) throws JAXBException
```

The following example shows how you can marshall a Java object. We instantiate the **Country** class in Listing 11.1 and use the **JavaToXML** class in Listing 11.2 to do the action. The output is printed on the console as well as saved to a **result.xml** file.

Listing 11.1: The Country class

```
package marshalling;
import javax.xml.bind.annotation.XmlRootElement;

@XmlRootElement
public class Country {
```

```
    private String code;
    private String name;
    private int population;

    public String getCode() {
        return code;
    }
    public void setCode(String code) {
        this.code = code;
    }
    public String getName() {
        return name;
    }
    public void setName(String name) {
        this.name = name;
    }
    public int getPopulation() {
        return population;
    }
    public void setPopulation(int population) {
        this.population = population;
    }
}
```

One thing to note is the use of the **XmlRootElement** annotation type to decorate the **Country** class. Belonging to the **javax.xml.bind.annotation** package, **XmlRootElement** is used to annotate a top level class or an enum type. Decorating with **@XmlRootElement** indicates that the instance of the class or enum will be mapped to the root element in the XML representation of the object.

Listing 11.2: The JavaToXMLDemo class

```
package marshalling;
import java.io.FileOutputStream;
import java.io.IOException;
import javax.xml.bind.JAXBContext;
import javax.xml.bind.JAXBException;
import javax.xml.bind.Marshaller;

public class JavaToXMLDemo {
    public static void main(String[] args) {
        try {
            // Create a JAXBContext that can handle
            // the Country class
```

```
JAXBContext context = JAXBContext.newInstance(
        Country.class);

// Create a Marshaller
Marshaller m = context.createMarshaller();
m.setProperty(Marshaller.JAXB_FORMATTED_OUTPUT,
        true);

// Create a Country object to be marshalled
Country object = new Country();
object.setCode("CA");
object.setName("Canada");
object.setPopulation(30000000);
// Print the XML to System.out
m.marshal(object, System.out);
m.marshal(object, new FileOutputStream("result.xml"));
} catch (JAXBException e) {
    e.printStackTrace();
} catch (IOException e) {
    e.printStackTrace();
}
}
}
```

The **JavaToXML** class obtains a **JAXBContext** instance by calling **newInstance**, passing the **Country** class.

```
JAXBContext context = JAXBContext.newInstance(
        Country.class);
```

A **JAXBContext** object instantiated this way can be used to create a **Marshaller** capable of serializing instances of the class passed as the argument.

```
// Create a Marshaller
Marshaller m = context.createMarshaller();
m.setProperty(Marshaller.JAXB_FORMATTED_OUTPUT, true);
```

Setting the marshaller's **JAXB_FORMATTED_OUTPUT** to **true** indicates to the marshaller that any resulting XML should be formatted. Failure to set this property will cause the resulting XML elements to be written in a single line.

Next, the **JavaToXML** class creates and populates a **Country** object.

```
Country object = new Country();
```

```
object.setCode("CA");
object.setName("Canada");
object.setPopulation(30000000);
```

Then, it passes the **Country** object to the **marshal** methods of the **Marshaller**.

```
m.marshal(object, System.out);
m.marshal(object, new FileOutputStream("result.xml"));
```

As a result, you can see the XML representation of the **Country** object in **System.out** as well as in the **result.xml** file. Here it is.

```
<?xml version="1.0" encoding="UTF-8" standalone="yes"?>
<country>
    <code>CA</code>
    <name>Canada</name>
    <population>30000000</population>
</country>
```

Unmarshalling

Unmarshalling is trickier than marshalling. For one, you cannot create Java objects out of thin air. You must first generate Java sources for your classes. In other words, you cannot use the generated **result.xml** file in the previous example to reverse the process and obtain an object or two. Fortunately, JAXB brings with it a tool called the XML Binding Compiler (xjb), which you can use to generate Java sources from an XML schema.

Once you have all the source files in place, you can use an **Unmarshaller** object to deserialize XML to Java objects. This section first looks at the xjc tool, which has been there since JAXB 1.0, and then presents an example of unmarshalling.

XML Binding Compiler

The XML Binding Compiler (xjc) can be used to generate Java classes from one or more XML schemas. You can start xjc by using the xjc script provided with your JDK in the **bin** directory of your JDK installation folder.

The usage syntax is this.

```
xjc [-options ...] <schemas>
```

Here are some of the more popular options:

```
-d <dir>
```
> The location of the generated files. If this option is missing, Java source files will be generated in the current directory.

```
-p <pkg>
```
> The package for the generated files.

```
-classpath <arg>
```
> The location of the user's classpath.

```
-readOnly
```
> Sets the generated files to read-only.

```
-version
```
> displays the version information.

For details, check this URL out:

```
http://java.sun.com/webservices/docs/1.6/jaxb/xjc.html
```

If you use the compiler very often, you can also download the ANT task for this from this location:

```
http://java.sun.com/webservices/docs/1.6/jaxb/ant.html
```

The Unmarshaller Interface

With an instance of **Unmarshaller**, you can unmarshall XML from the following data sources: **java.io.File, java.io.Reader, java.io.InputStream, org.xml.sax.InputSource, org.w3c.dom.Node, java.net.URL, javax.xml.transform.Source, javax.xml.stream.XMLStreamReader**, and **javax.xml.stream.XMLEventReader**.

As an example, let's use xjc to generate Java classes out of the **item.xsd** schema in Listing 11.3 and then unmarshall the schema to Java.

Listing 11.3: The item.xsd schema

```
<xsd:schema xmlns:xsd="http://www.w3.org/2001/XMLSchema">
<xsd:element name="item" type="Item"/>
<xsd:complexType name="Item">
```

```
    <xsd:sequence>
        <xsd:element name="code" type="xsd:string"/>
        <xsd:element name="name" type="xsd:string"/>
        <xsd:element name="price" type="xsd:double"/>
    </xsd:sequence>
</xsd:complexType>
</xsd:schema>
```

You generate Java sources from the schema file by issuing this command from the same directory as the **item.xsd** file:

```
xjc item.xsd
```

the xjc program will create two files, **Item.java** and **ObjectFactory.java**, both members of the **generated** package. This package is the default package if xjc is invoked without specifying a package name for the Java sources. Listing 11.4 shows the **Item** class and Listing 11.5 shows the **ObjectFactory** class.

Listing 11.4: The Item.java generated class

```
//
// This file was generated by the JavaTM Architecture for XML
// Binding(JAXB) Reference Implementation, vJAXB 2.0 in JDK 1.6
// See <a
// href="http://java.sun.com/xml/jaxb">http://java.sun.com/xml
// jaxb</a>
// Any modifications to this file will be lost upon recompilation of
// the source schema.
// Generated on: 2006.09.21 at 09:06:52 PM ICT
//
package generated;

import javax.xml.bind.annotation.AccessType;
import javax.xml.bind.annotation.XmlAccessorType;
import javax.xml.bind.annotation.XmlElement;
import javax.xml.bind.annotation.XmlType;
import generated.Item;


/**
 * <p>Java class for Item complex type.
 *
 * <p>The following schema fragment specifies the expected content
 * contained within this class.
 *
```

```
 * <pre>
 * &lt;complexType name="Item">
 *    &lt;complexContent>
 *      &lt;restriction
 *        base="{http://www.w3.org/2001/XMLSchema}anyType">
 *        &lt;sequence>
 *          &lt;element name="code"
 *            type="{http://www.w3.org/2001/XMLSchema}string"/>
 *          &lt;element name="name"
 *            type="{http://www.w3.org/2001/XMLSchema}string"/>
 *          &lt;element name="price"
 *            type="{http://www.w3.org/2001/XMLSchema}double"/>
 *        &lt;/sequence>
 *      &lt;/restriction>
 *    &lt;/complexContent>
 * &lt;/complexType>
 * </pre>
 *
 *
 */
@XmlAccessorType(AccessType.FIELD)
@XmlType(name = "Item", propOrder = {
    "code",
    "name",
    "price"
})
public class Item {

    protected String code;
    protected String name;
    @XmlElement(type = Double.class)
    protected double price;

    /**
     * Gets the value of the code property.
     *
     * @return
     *     possible object is
     *     {@link String }
     *
     */
    public String getCode() {
        return code;
    }

    /**
```

```
 * Sets the value of the code property.
 *
 * @param value
 *     allowed object is
 *     {@link String }
 *
 */
public void setCode(String value) {
    this.code = value;
}

/**
 * Gets the value of the name property.
 *
 * @return
 *     possible object is
 *     {@link String }
 *
 */
public String getName() {
    return name;
}

/**
 * Sets the value of the name property.
 *
 * @param value
 *     allowed object is
 *     {@link String }
 *
 */
public void setName(String value) {
    this.name = value;
}

/**
 * Gets the value of the price property.
 *
 */
public double getPrice() {
    return price;
}

/**
 * Sets the value of the price property.
```

```
     *
     */
    public void setPrice(double value) {
        this.price = value;
    }

}
```

Listing 11.5: The ObjectFactory generated class

```
//
// This file was generated by the JavaTM Architecture for XML
// Binding(JAXB) Reference Implementation, vJAXB 2.0 in JDK 1.6
// See <a
// href="http://java.sun.com/xml/jaxb">http://java.sun.com/xml/
// jaxb</a>
// Any modifications to this file will be lost upon recompilation of
// the source schema.
// Generated on: 2006.02.21 at 09:06:52 PM ICT
//

package generated;

import javax.xml.bind.JAXBElement;
import javax.xml.bind.annotation.XmlElementDecl;
import javax.xml.bind.annotation.XmlRegistry;
import javax.xml.namespace.QName;
import generated.Item;
import generated.ObjectFactory;


/**
 * This object contains factory methods for each
 * Java content interface and Java element interface
 * generated in the generated package.
 * <p>An ObjectFactory allows you to programatically
 * construct new instances of the Java representation
 * for XML content. The Java representation of XML
 * content can consist of schema derived interfaces
 * and classes representing the binding of schema
 * type definitions, element declarations and model
 * groups.  Factory methods for each of these are
 * provided in this class.
 *
 */
@XmlRegistry
public class ObjectFactory {
```

```
private final static QName _Item_QNAME = new QName("", "item");

/**
 * Create a new ObjectFactory that can be used to create new
 * instances of schema derived classes for package: generated
 *
 */
public ObjectFactory() {
}

/**
 * Create an instance of {@link Item }
 *
 */
public Item createItem() {
    return new Item();
}

/**
 * Create an instance of {@link JAXBElement }{@code <}{@link
 * Item }{@code >}}
 *
 */
@XmlElementDecl(namespace = "", name = "item")
public JAXBElement<Item> createItem(Item value) {
    return new JAXBElement<Item>(_Item_QNAME, Item.class, null,
  value);
}

}
```

Now that we have the source files for the **item.xsd** schema, we can unmarshall an XML instance document to Java objects. Listing 11.6 shows the document to be used to generate Java objects.

Listing 11.6: An XML instance document

```
<?xml version="1.0"?>
<item>
        <code>I001</code>
        <name>First item</name>
        <price>100000</price>
</item>
```

Listing 11.7 presents the **UnmarshallingDemo** class that will perform the unmarshalling.

Listing 11.7: The UnmarshallingDemo class

```
import generated.Item;
import java.io.File;
import javax.xml.bind.JAXBContext;
import javax.xml.bind.JAXBElement;
import javax.xml.bind.JAXBException;
import javax.xml.bind.Unmarshaller;

public class UnmarshallingDemo {

    public static void main(String[] args) {
        try {
            // Create a JAXBContext that can handle classes in
            // package generated
            JAXBContext jc = JAXBContext.newInstance("generated");

            // Create Unmarshaller
            Unmarshaller u = jc.createUnmarshaller();

            // Unmarshall the elements in item.xml to Java objects
            File f = new File("item.xml");
            JAXBElement element = (JAXBElement) u.unmarshal(f);

            // Display the values of the new object
            Item item = (Item) element.getValue();
            System.out.println(item.getCode());
            System.out.println(item.getName());
            System.out.println(item.getPrice());
        } catch (JAXBException e) {
            e.printStackTrace();
        }
    }
}
```

The **UnmarshallingDemo** class starts off by creating a **JAXBContext** instance, this time by passing a context path to the **newInstance** method.

```
// Create a JAXBContext that can handle classes in
// package generated
JAXBContext jc = JAXBContext.newInstance("generated");
```

Such a **JAXBContext** object is capable of producing an **Unmarshaller** object to unmarshall a schema to instances of the classes in the package specified as the context path argument.

```
// Create Unmarshaller
Unmarshaller u = jc.createUnmarshaller();
```

The following lines of code shows how you unmarshall an XML instance document residing in a file.

```
// Unmarshall the elements in item.xml to Java objects
File f = new File("item.xml");
JAXBElement element = (JAXBElement) u.unmarshal(f);
```

The result of the **unmarshal** method can then be downcast to **JAXBElement**, and calling **getValue** on the **JAXBElement** return the root of the XML instance document as a Java object.

```
Item item = (Item) element.getValue();
```

Summary

JAXB 2.0 is the most recent release of the Java-XML binding technology. Unlike it predecessor, version 2.0 is capable of Java-to-schema binding, as demonstrated by the sample applications in this chapter.

Chapter 12
Web Services

Mustang includes the reference implementations for web services-related APIs, particularly Java API for XML-based Web Services (JAX-WS) 2.0, which is specified in JSR 224 (http://jcp.org/en/jsr/detail?id-224), and Web Services Metadata for the Java Platform (JSR 181, http://jcp.org/en/jsr/detail?id-181). Together the two APIs define the web services stack that makes developing Java Web Services easier than ever.

JAX-WS 2.0 is the next version of JAX-RPC 1.0 (JAX-RPC 2.0 was renamed JAX-WS 2.0) with the former a conspicuously much better technology than the latter. JAX-RPC 1.0 was overly complex a technology to build Java web services, If you've done web service programming using this API, you must still remember how painful the process was, like riding bareback. It's not surprising that JAX-RPC 1.0 was less appealing than competing alternatives such as Apache Axis. Meanwhile JAX-WS 2.0 easily wins approval among Java programmers and is a welcome upgrade to JAX-RPC 1.0.

While JAX-WS 2.0 defines the Java to XML/WSDL mapping (it employs JAXB 2.0 for its data binding operations), ease of development comes from the annotations defined in JSR 181. In truth, these annotations are what make JAX-WS 2.0 much simpler and more powerful than its predecessor. In addition, JAX-WS 2.0 supports both SOAP 1.1 and SOAP 1.2, as opposed to JAX-RPC 1.0's support for SOAP 1.1 alone. Publishing, too, can never be easier with JAX-WS 2.0, thanks to a light-weight HTTP server to which you can publish your web services and make them available in less than a minute.

This chapter shows you how to build a web service with these web services technologies included in Mustang.

Web Service Annotations

The web service annotation types defined in JSR 181 are members of the **javax.jws** and **javax.jws.soap** packages. The most important of these annotations are **WebService**, **WebMethod**, **WebParam**, and **WebResult**.

WebService

The **WebService** annotation type can be used to annotate an interface or a class. Used with an interface, it indicates that the interface defines a web service interface. Decorating a Java class **@WebService** signifies that the class is an implementation of a web service. Table 12.1 shows the elements of **WebService**.

Element	Description
name	The name of the web service.
targetNamespace	On a service endpoint interface, it is used for the namespace for the wsdl:portType element. On a service implementation bean that does not reference a service endpoint interface, it is used for both the wsdl:portType and the wsdl:service elements. Used with a service implementation bean that references a service endpoint interface, it is used for only the wsdl:service element.
serviceName	The service name of the Web Service.
portName	The name of the wsdl:port when mapped to WSDL 1.1
wsdlLocation	The location of the WSDL describing the service.
endpointInterface	The complete name of the service endpoint interface.

Table 12.1: The WebService annotation type elements

WebMethod

The WebMethod annotation type decorates a web service method. Table 12.2 lists all elements that can be used with @WebMethod.

Element	Description
operationName	The name of the wsdl:operation mapped to this method
action	The action for this operation.
exclude	Used to exclude a method so that it will not be exposed as a Web method.

Table 12.2: The WebMethod annotation type elements

WebParam

This annotation type is used to describe the mapping of a parameter of a web service message part and XML element. The elements of this annotation type are presented in Table 12.3.

Element	Description
name	The name of the parameter
partName	The name of the wsdl:part of this parameter.
targetNamespace	Specifies the namespace for this parameter.
mode	The direction in which the parameter is flowing. The value can be **IN, OUT**, or **INOUT**.
header	Indicates whether or not the parameter is retrieved from a message header and not from the message body.

Table 12.3: The WebParam annotation type elements

WebResult

You use this annotation type to describe the mapping of the return value to a WSDL part and XML element. Table 12.4 shows all elements that come with this annotation type.

Element	Description
name	The name of the return value.
partName	The name of the wsdl:part of this return value.
targetNamespace	The XML namespace for the return value.
header	Indicates if the parameter is retrieved from a message header and not from the message body.

Table 12.4: The WebResult annotation type elements

A Web Service Example

This example shows off how easy it is to develop a web service. The sample application includes a simple web service that returns the string "Hello" followed by the user name, a publisher that publishes the service instantly, and a web service client for you to test the service.

The **Hello** interface in Listing 12.1 provides the functionality of the web service. There is only one method, **sayHello**. The **HelloImpl** class in Listing 12.2 is the implementation class for the **Hello** interface.

Listing 12.1: The Hello interface

```
package server;
import javax.jws.WebService;
import javax.jws.soap.SOAPBinding;

@WebService
@SOAPBinding(style=SOAPBinding.Style.RPC)
public interface Hello {

    String sayHello(String name);
}
```

Listing 12.2: The implementation: the HelloImpl class

```
package server;
import javax.jws.WebService;
import javax.jws.soap.SOAPBinding;

@WebService(endpointInterface="server.Hello")
@SOAPBinding(style=SOAPBinding.Style.RPC)
public class HelloImpl implements Hello {

    public String sayHello(String name) {
```

```
        return "Hello, " + name + " !";
    }

}
```

The Hello interface is no different than ordinary Java interfaces, except for the presence of the **WebService** and **SOAPBinding** annotations. The same annotation types are also used to decorate the **HelloImpl** class.

Compile the interface and the class and you're done developing your web service.

Next, you need to publish your web service so that other people can access it. Typically, you need to build related artifacts and deploy it in a web server, such as Apache or IIS. However, since Mustang has its own HTTP server, you can deploy your web service by using the **javax.xml.ws.EndPoint** class, as demonstrated in the **Publisher** class in Listing 12.3. All you need to do is instantiate your service and pass it to the **publish** method of the **EndPoint** class. The first argument to the **publish** method specifies the location of the service. This simple process is again a major win for Java web service developers. I'd be amazed if you're not amazed by how simple things are.

Listing 12.3: Publisher

```
package server;
import javax.xml.ws.Endpoint;

public class Publisher {
    public static void main(String[] args) {

        HelloImpl impl = new HelloImpl();

        // Creat an EndPoint
        Endpoint endpoint = Endpoint.
                publish("http://localhost:8080/hello", impl);

        boolean status = endpoint.isPublished();
        System.out.println("Web service status = " + status);
    }
}
```

Be warned though, there is no scalability warranty in this type of deployment. If scalability is a requirement, deploy your web service in a Java EE environment.

Once you run the class in Listing 12.3 you can obtain the automatically generated WSDL and use the service. To get the WSDL, direct your web browser here:

```
http://localhost:8080/hello?wsdl
```

Here is the WSDL:

```
<?xml version="1.0" encoding="UTF-8"?><definitions
      xmlns="http://schemas.xmlsoap.org/wsdl/"
      xmlns:tns="http://server/"
      xmlns:xsd="http://www.w3.org/2001/XMLSchema"
      xmlns:soap="http://schemas.xmlsoap.org/wsdl/soap/"
      targetNamespace="http://server/" name="HelloImplService">
  <types></types>
  <message name="sayHello">
    <part name="arg0" type="xsd:string"></part>
  </message>
  <message name="sayHelloResponse">
    <part name="return" type="xsd:string"></part>
  </message>
  <portType name="Hello">
    <operation name="sayHello" parameterOrder="arg0">
      <input message="tns:sayHello"></input>
      <output message="tns:sayHelloResponse"></output>
    </operation>
  </portType>
  <binding name="HelloImplPortBinding" type="tns:Hello">
    <soap:binding style="rpc"
        transport="http://schemas.xmlsoap.org/soap/http">
    </soap:binding>
    <operation name="sayHello">
      <soap:operation soapAction=""></soap:operation>
      <input>
        <soap:body use="literal"
       namespace="http://server/"></soap:body>
      </input>
      <output>
        <soap:body use="literal"
       namespace="http://server/"></soap:body>
      </output>
    </operation>
  </binding>
  <service name="HelloImplService">
    <port name="HelloImplPort" binding="tns:HelloImplPortBinding">
```

```
      <soap:address
       location="http://localhost:8080/hello"></soap:address>
    </port>
  </service>
</definitions>
```

To use the service, you need a client. One has been prepared for you in Listing 12.4.

Listing 12.4: The web service client

```java
package client;
import java.net.MalformedURLException;
import java.net.URL;
import java.util.Iterator;
import javax.xml.namespace.QName;
import javax.xml.ws.Service;
import server.Hello;

public class WSClient {

    public static void main(String[] args)
            throws MalformedURLException {

        // Create a Service instance based on
        // the location of the WSDL
        URL wsdlLocation = new
                URL("http://localhost:8080/hello?wsdl");
        QName serviceName = new
                QName("HelloImplService");
        Service service = Service.
                create(wsdlLocation, serviceName);

        // Return a list of QNames from service endpoints
        System.out.println("List of QNames of service endpoints:");
        Iterator it = service.getPorts();
        while (it.hasNext()) {
            System.out.println("  " + it.next());
        }

        // Get the Hello stub
        Hello hello = service.getPort(Hello.class);
        String result = hello.sayHello("Mustang");
        System.out.println("\nResponse from web service: ");
        System.out.println("  " + result);
```

```
    }
}
```

The core of this class is the **javax.xml.ws.Service** class. With it, you can create a **Service** that serves as a client view of a web service. To obtain an instance of the web service, call its **getPort** method:

```
Hello hello = service.getPort(Hello.class);
```

Then, you can call the methods exposed by the web service. In this example, there is only one method, **sayHello**.

```
String result = hello.sayHello("Mustang");
```

You will see "Hello, Mustang" on the console.

Summary

Two APIs, Java API for XML-based Web Services (JAX-WS) 2.0 and Web Services Metadata for the Java Platform, are the bare bones of modern web service development, replacing the JAX-RPC 1.0 that was difficult to use. Ease of development comes from the annotation types defined in the Web Services Metadata for the Java Platform. This chapter showed how to use these new technologies.

Chapter 13
JavaBeans Activation Framework

For the first time ever, the JavaBeans Activation Framework (JAF) is included in a Java Standard Edition (SE). Traditionally, if you needed JAF services you had to download the reference implementation as a separate JAR or used Java 5 Enterprise Edition. The JAF release that ships with Mustang is version 1.1, the fruit of collaborative work of the JSR 925 committee. The specification is downloadable from http://jcp.org/en/jsr/detail?id=925.

You've probably used the JAF, especially if you've been involved in a Java mail project, without paying much attention to it. This chapter, however, goes the extra mile to explain what JAF really is and how it can be useful in your life as a Java programmer.

Introduction to JAF

Probably the easiest way to understand the JAF is by looking at Windows Explorer. In addition to providing a nice user interface to navigate your Windows file system, Windows Explorer allows you to right-click on a file and select a command from the list associated with the file type. Figure 13.1 shows a list for PDF files and one for MP3 files. Of course, the lists will differ from one computer to another.

When you click a command, Windows Explorer invokes the appropriate application and pass the reference to the right-clicked file.

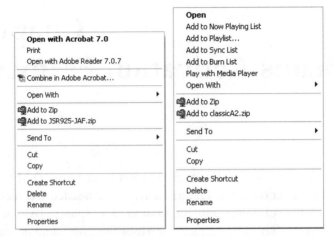

Figure 13.1: Windows Explorer's command list for PDF files (left) and for MP3 files (right)

The JAF is useful if you want to write an application with similar functionality to Windows Explorer's features. For example, you can use the JAF in a Java XML editor so that upon clicking a document (an xml, a dtd, or an xsd), the user will be presented with a command list and be able to select a command that will launch the application to handle the object. Of course, you need to decide the supported types of objects and invoke appropriate JavaBeans that can handle each type of object.

Before you can start, you need to understand some important types in the JAF API.

The DataSource Interface

In the JAF, any data source is modeled by the rightly-named interface in the **javax.activation** package: **DataSource**. The following methods in **DataSource** allow you to enquire about the data and the data type.

`java.lang.String getContentType()`
> Returns the MIME type of the data. If the data type cannot be determined, it should return "application/octet-stream."

`java.lang.String getName()`
> Returns the name of the data source. For instance, if the **DataSource** is a **FileDataSource**, the file name will be returned by this method.

```
java.io.InputStream getInputStream() throws java.io.IOException
```
Returns an **InputStream** representing the data.

```
java.io.OutputStream getOutputStream() throws IOException
```
Returns an **OutputStream** where the data can be written.

Note that each data source is distinguished by a MIME type. Since a data source can be transferred as a file or a URL, there are two implementation classes of **DataSource**, **FileDataSource** and **URLDataSource**. You can therefore create a **DataSource** if you have access to a file or to a URL. Here are the constructors of both implementation classes..

```
public FileDataSource(java.io.File file)

public FileDataSource(java.lang.String filePath)

public URLDataSource(java.net.URL url)
```

The CommandMap Class

The **CommandMap** class acts as a registry of command objects for all supported data types. The map can get its values from different sources depending the implementation. Before you attempt to create an instance of **CommandMap**, be warned though that this is an abstract class. Fortunately, a concrete subclass **MailcapCommandMap** is provided for your convenience. You can configure a **MailcapCommandMap** either programmatically or via configuration files. Configuring a **MailcapCommandMap** means providing it with a list of supported MIME types and a command list for those MIME types). If you do so programmatically, you use the **addMailcap** method of this class:

```
public void addMailcap(java.lang.String mailcap)
```

We'll get to the format of the *mailcap* argument shortly, but let's discuss how you can configure a **MailcapCommandMap** instance through configuration files first.

By default, a **MailcapCommandMap** searches various locations in the following order:

1. Programmatically added entries.
2. The **.mailcap** file in the user's home directory.

3. The **mailcap** file in **JAVA_HOME/lib**.

4. The file or resources named **META-INF/mailcap**

5. The file or resource named **META-INF/mailcap.default**

A mailcap file must conform to RFC 1524, "A User Agent Configuration Mechanism for Multimedia Mail Format Information." (http://www.ietf.org/rfc/rfc1524.txt)

A mailcap entry has the following format:

```
<mime type>; ; <parameter list>
```

A parameter name for **MailcapCommandMap** must start with **x-java-**, followed by the command name. For example, the edit command is **x-java-edit**. The parameter value is the class that can handle that command. For instance, here is a parameter list for MIME type text/plain:

```
text/plain; ; x-java-view=com.brainysoftware.jaf.TextViewer;
x-java-edit=com.brainysoftware.jaf.TextEditor
```

The entry tells the JAF that the MIME type text/plain has two commands, view and edit. It also indicates the class name for each command.

The **CommandMap** class provides a variety of methods to return information a JAF client needs. For instance, the **getMimeTypes** method returns all supported MIME types:

```
public java.lang.String[] getMimeTypes()
```

To get all the commands for a particular MIME type, use **getAllCommands**.

```
public abstract CommandInfo[] getAllCommands(
        java.lang.String mimeType)
```

Note that the **CommandInfo** class will be discussed in the next section.

To retrieve the **CommandInfo** objects for a certain command, use **getComand**:

```
public abstract CommandInfo getCommand(java.lang.String mimeType,
        java.lang.String commandName)
```

Examples of command names include "view," "edit," "print," and so on. For instance, the class in Listing 13.1 shows the **MailcapCommandMap** class in action.

Listing 13.1: The MailcapCommandMapDemo1 class

```java
import javax.activation.CommandInfo;
import javax.activation.MailcapCommandMap;
public class MailcapCommandMapDemo1 {
    public static void main(String[] args) {
        MailcapCommandMap mailcapCommandMap =
                new MailcapCommandMap ();
        // Get all MIME types
        String[] mimeTypes = mailcapCommandMap.getMimeTypes();
        for (String mimeType : mimeTypes) {
            System.out.println(mimeType);
            CommandInfo[] commandInfos = mailcapCommandMap.
                    getAllCommands(mimeType);
            for (CommandInfo commandInfo : commandInfos) {
                System.out.println("     " +
                        commandInfo.getCommandName() +
                        " : " + commandInfo.getCommandClass());
            }
        }
    }
}
```

Running this class prints the following message on your console:

```
image/jpeg
    view : com.sun.activation.viewers.ImageViewer
image/gif
    view : com.sun.activation.viewers.ImageViewer
text/*
    view : com.sun.activation.viewers.TextViewer
    edit : com.sun.activation.viewers.TextEditor
```

By default, the **getMimeTypes** method returns an array of three strings, **image/jpeg**, **image/gif**, and **text/***. The first two MIME types have one command associated with them: view. The command class for viewing a JPEG and GIF is **com.sun.activation.viewers.ImageViewer**. The text/* MIME type has two commands, view and edit. The class name for view is the **TextViewer** class and the class name for edit is **TextEditor**.

If you want you can add more MIME types and commands. For example, the code in Listing 13.2 is similar to the one in Listing 13.1 except for the lines in bold in which we add a new MIME type text/plain with three commands.

Listing 13.2: The MailcapCommandMapDemo2 class

```
import javax.activation.CommandInfo;
import javax.activation.MailcapCommandMap;
public class MailcapCommandMapDemo2 {
    public static void main(String[] args) {
        MailcapCommandMap mailcapCommandMap =
                new MailcapCommandMap();
        String mailcap = "text/plain; ; "
                + "x-java-content-handler=beans.TextHandler;"
                + "x-java-view=beans.TextViewer;"
                + "x-java-edit=beans.TextEditor";
        mailcapCommandMap.addMailcap(mailcap);
        // Get all MIME types
        String[] mimeTypes = mailcapCommandMap.getMimeTypes();
        for (String mimeType : mimeTypes) {
            System.out.println(mimeType);
            CommandInfo[] commandInfos = mailcapCommandMap.
                    getAllCommands(mimeType);
            for (CommandInfo commandInfo : commandInfos) {
                System.out.println("    " +
                        commandInfo.getCommandName() +
                        " : " + commandInfo.getCommandClass());
            }
        }
    }
}
```

Running the class in Listing 13.2 produces this:

```
text/plain
    content-handler : beans.TextHandler
    view : beans.TextViewer
    edit : beans.TextEditor
    view : com.sun.activation.viewers.TextViewer
    edit : com.sun.activation.viewers.TextEditor
image/jpeg
    view : com.sun.activation.viewers.ImageViewer
image/gif
    view : com.sun.activation.viewers.ImageViewer
text/*
    view : com.sun.activation.viewers.TextViewer
    edit : com.sun.activation.viewers.TextEditor
```

As you can see, there's now a new text/plain MIME type.

In addition to adding a MIME type programmatically, you can also do it by storing the mailcap string in a search directory. For example, saving the following mailcap file under the **META-INF** directory adds the MIME type text/plain.

```
text/plain; ; x-java-content-handler=beans.TextHandler; x-java-
view=beans.TextViewer; x-java-edit=beans.TextEditor
```

Note that the file must be named **mailcap** and the **META-INF** directory must be in the same location as the root of the generated class files.

The CommandInfo Class

A **CommandInfo** instance describes the result of a command request. These are the methods in this class.

```
public java.lang.String getCommandName()
```
Returns the command name.

```
public java.lang.String getCommandClass()
```
Returns the command's class name.

```
public java.lang.Object getCommandObject(DataHandler dataHandler,
        java.lang.ClassLoader loader) throws java.io.IOException,
        java.lang.ClassNotFoundException
```
Returns the command object.

We'll review how to use this class in the example to follow.

The CommandObject Interface

A JavaBean that is to be Activation Framework aware should implement this interface. A **CommandObject** instance is capable of handling data sources of a specific MIME type. This interface has only one method, **setCommandContext**, that initializes the **Command** with the verb it is requested to handle and the **DataHandler** that describes the data source:

```
void setCommandContext(java.lang.String verb, DataHandler handler)
        throws java.io.IOException
```

An implementation of **CommandObject** should assign the handler argument to a class level variable so that it can be used from other locations in the class.

The DataHandler Class

Once you have a **DataSource** object, you may want to obtain the application that can handle the data source. The entry point that a JAF client uses to access JAF capabilities is the **DataHandler** class. You can instantiate this class by passing a data source to its constructor:

```
public DataHandler(DataSource dataSource)
```

The following are the more important methods in **DataHandler**.

```
public CommandInfo[] getAllCommands()
```
    Returns all the commands for this type of data.

```
public CommandInfo getCommand(java.lang.String commandName)
```
    Returns the **CommandInfo** object for the specified command name.

```
public java.lang.String getName()
```
    Returns the name of the data object.

```
public java.lang.String getContentType()
```
    Returns the MIME type of this object.

```
public java.lang.Object getContent() throws java.io.IOException
```
    Returns the data.

```
public java.io.InputStream getInputStream()
```
    Returns the **InputStream** for this object.

```
public java.io.OutputStream getOutputStream()
```
    Returns the **OutputStream** for this handler to allow overwriting of the data.

To retrieve the **CommandObject** that can handle a data source, you normally start by obtaining the **CommandInfo** for the required MIME type and command name.

```
CommandInfo commandInfo = mailcapCommandMap.
        getCommand(mimeType, commandName);
```

Then, you can call the **CommandInfo**'s **getCommandObject** to obtain a **CommandObject** instance:

```
Object commandObject = commandInfo.
        getCommandObject(dataHandler, classLoader);
```

A JAF Example

This example shows off an application that provides JavaBeans to handle viewing and editing of text/plain data. A **MailcapCommandMap** is used and is configured using the **mailcap** file in Listing 13.3.

Listing 13.3: The mailcap file to configure MailcapCommandMap

```
text/plain; ; x-java-view=beans.TextViewer; x-java-edit=
beans.TextEditor
```

The command objects in this application implements the **Command** interface in Listing 13.4.

Listing 13.4: The Command interface

```
package beans;
public interface Command {
    void execute();
}
```

Two classes, **TextViewer** and **TextEditor**, implement **Command**. Their instances are used as command objects. **TextViewer** is given in Listing 13.5 and **TextEditor** is presented in Listing 13.6.

Listing 13.5: The TextViewer class

```
package beans;
import java.io.IOException;
import java.io.InputStreamReader;
import javax.activation.CommandObject;
import javax.activation.DataHandler;

public class TextViewer implements CommandObject, Command {

    private DataHandler dataHandler;

    public void setCommandContext(String verb,
            DataHandler dataHandler) throws IOException {
        this.dataHandler = dataHandler;
    }

    public void execute() {
        String name = dataHandler.getName();
```

```
        try {
            Object content = dataHandler.getContent();
            System.out.println("Viewing the content of " +
                    name);
            InputStreamReader reader = new InputStreamReader(
                    dataHandler.getInputStream());
            char[] chars = new char[512];
            int i = reader.read(chars);
            while (i != -1) {
                for (int j = 0; j < i; j++) {
                    System.out.print(chars[j]);
                }
                i = reader.read(chars);
            }
            System.out.println();
        } catch (IOException e) {
            e.printStackTrace();
        }
    }
}
```

Listing 13.6: The TextEditor class

```
package beans;
import java.io.IOException;
import javax.activation.CommandObject;
import javax.activation.DataHandler;

public class TextEditor implements CommandObject, Command {
    private DataHandler dataHandler;

    public void setCommandContext(String verb,
            DataHandler dataHandler)
            throws IOException {
        this.dataHandler = dataHandler;
    }

    public void execute() {
        String name = dataHandler.getName();
        System.out.println("The editor is ready to edit " +
                name);
    }
}
```

The **JAFDemo** class in Listing 13.7 puts everything together and demonstrates the power of JAF:

Listing 13.7: The JAFDemo class

```java
import javax.activation.CommandInfo;
import javax.activation.DataHandler;
import javax.activation.DataSource;
import javax.activation.FileDataSource;
import javax.activation.MailcapCommandMap;
import beans.Command;

public class JAFDemo {
    private MailcapCommandMap mailcapCommandMap;
    private DataHandler dataHandler;

    public JAFDemo() {
        // Create a MailcapCommandMap configured using
        // the META-INF/mailcap file
        mailcapCommandMap = new MailcapCommandMap();

        // Create a DataHandler
        DataSource dataSource = new
                FileDataSource("readme.txt");
        dataHandler = new DataHandler(dataSource);
    }

    public void testCommand(String commandName) {
        ClassLoader loader = getClass().getClassLoader();

        // Get the CommandInfo for the commandName
        CommandInfo commandInfo = mailcapCommandMap.
                getCommand("text/plain", commandName);
        try {
            // instantiate the command object for the command
            Object commandObject = commandInfo.
                    getCommandObject(dataHandler, loader);
            if (commandObject instanceof Command) {
                Command command = (Command) commandObject;
                command.execute();
            }
        } catch (Exception e) {
            e.printStackTrace();
        }
    }

    public static void main(String[] args) {
        JAFDemo demo = new JAFDemo();
```

```
        demo.testCommand("view");
        demo.testCommand("edit");
    }
}
```

A **readme.txt** is used as the data source. It is a simple text file presented in Listing 13.8.

Listing 13.8: The data source for this application

```
Hello World !
from JAF 1.1
```

If you run the **JAFDemo** class, you will see the following message on your console:

```
Viewing the content of readme.txt
Hello World !
from JAF 1.1
The editor is ready to edit readme.txt
```

Summary

JAF technology can be used to determine the type of a piece of data and discover the JavaBeans that are able to handle it, much like Windows Explorer's ability to pick a list of commands for a right-clicked file. In this chapter you learned how to use the JAF and the more important classes and interfaces in the **javax.activation** package, such as **CommandMap**, **DataSource**, and **DataHandler**. You have also learned how to write an application that can handle the text/plain MIME type.

Chapter 14
User-Defined MXBeans

Mustang ships with the reference implementation for the Java Management Extensions (JMX) 1.4. New to this version of JMX are user-defined MXBeans, even though *standard* MXBeans have actually been part of the Java SE since the Tiger era. This chapter teaches you how to write user-defined MXBeans as well as explains the annotation types **@MXBean** and **@DescriptorKey**. An introduction to JMX and standard MBeans, sisters of MXBeans, are also presented at the beginning of this chapter for those new to the technology.

Java Management Extensions (JMX)

JMX technology is a standard API for managing and monitoring Java objects. In a typical Java application, you instantiate a Java class using the **new** keyword from within the static **main** method of the class or another class. However, once your object is created and loaded into memory, you cannot control the object externally. For instance, you cannot read the values of its properties, neither can you call its methods. A JMX-enabled application, on the other hand, provides access to the objects in the application. The JMX framework can create instances of a class and provide references to the instances so that you can read or change their properties or call their methods. In fact, JMX is often used to gather statistics about an application and notify of state changes. For example, Tomcat, the most popular servlet/JSP container on this planet, is JMX-enabled. JMX allows you to peep at the Tomcat server after it is started, and thanks to JMX, you can figure out the number of **HttpSession** objects inside the server when the server is running. Stopping the server, reading its configuration settings, and changing them are also not hard to do.

A Java object that can be managed through JMX is said to be a JMX manageable resource. For a Java object to be a JMX manageable resource, you must create another object called a Managed Bean or MBean. An MBean, however, can be designed to manage more than one Java object.

Once you have an MBean class, you need to instantiate it and register it with another Java object referred to as the MBean server, which is a central registry for all the MBeans in an application. Applications that need to manage or monitor JMX manageable resources are called management applications and they access MBeans through the MBean server. Drawing an analogy between a JMX-enabled application and a servlet application, the management application is equivalent to a web browser. The MBean server is like a servlet container, providing access to the managed-resources to the client (the management application). The MBeans are servlets or JSP pages. Just as web browsers never touch a servlet/JSP page directly but only through a servlet container, a management application accesses MBeans through the MBean server.

There are five types of MBeans: standard, dynamic, open, model, and MXBeans. Standard MBeans are the easiest to write among the five, but offer the least flexibility. Standard MBeans are discussed in the next section to give you the look and feel of writing an MBean, and also because MXBeans, the main topic of discussion in this chapter, are in fact a variant of standard MBeans. Since this book is only concerned with new features in Java 6, other types of MBeans are not discussed.

Architecturally, the JMX specification is divided into three levels, the instrumentation level, the agent level, and the distributed services level. The MBean server resides in the agent level and the MBeans in the instrumentation level.

The instrumentation level of the specification defines the standard for writing JMX manageable resources, namely how to write MBeans. The agent level provides a specification for creating agents. An agent encapsulates an MBean server and services for handling MBeans. Agents and the MBeans they manage normally reside in the same Java Virtual Machine. Because the JMX specification comes with a reference implementation, you do not need to write an MBean server of your own. The reference implementation provides a way of creating a default MBean server.

Now that you know what JMX can do for you, let's look at the JMX API in clear detail.

The JMX API

The JMX reference implementation consists of a core Java library in the **javax.management** package and subpackages specific to certain areas of JMX programming. This section discusses some of the more important types in the API.

MBeanServer

The **javax.management.MBeanServer** interface represents an MBean server. To create an instance of **MBeanServer**, use the **createMBeanServer** method in the **javax.management.MBeanServerFactory** class.

An **MBeanServer** is responsible for registering MBeans and provides methods for retrieving them. To register an MBean with an **MBeanServer**, call the **registerMBean** method on the **MBeanServer** instance. The following is the signature of the **registerMBean** method.

```
public ObjectInstance registerMBean(java.lang.Object object,
        ObjectName name) throws InstanceAlreadyExistsException,
        MBeanRegistrationException, NotCompliantMBeanException
```

To the **registerMBean** method you pass the MBean instance you want to register and an **ObjectName** instance. An **ObjectName** is like a key in a **HashMap**; it uniquely identifies an MBean. The **registerMBean** method returns an **ObjectInstance** that encapsulates the object name of the registered MBean and its class name.

To retrieve an MBean or a set of MBeans matching a pattern, the **MBeanServer** interface provides two methods: **queryNames** and **queryMBeans**. The **queryNames** method returns a **java.util.Set** containing the object names of the MBeans matching the specified pattern object name. Here is the signature of the **queryName** method:

```
public java.util.Set queryNames(ObjectName name, QueryExp query)
```

Here, the *query* argument specifies the filtering criteria. If the *name* argument is null or no domain and key properties are specified, all the **ObjectName** instances of the registered MBeans will be returned. If *query* is null, no filtering is applied.

The **queryMBeans** method is similar to **queryNames**. However, it returns a **java.util.Set** containing **ObjectInstance** objects for the selected MBeans. The **queryMBeans** method has the following signature:

```
public java.util.Set queryMBeans(ObjectName name, QueryExp query)
```

Once you have the object name of the MBean you want, you can manipulate the property of the managed resource or invoke its methods.

You can call any method of a registered MBeans by calling the **MBeanServer** interface's **invoke** method. The **MBeanServer** interface's **getAttribute** and **setAttribute** methods are used to get and set a property of a registered MBean.

ObjectName

An MBean server is a registry for MBeans. Each of the MBeans in an MBean server is uniquely identified by an object name, just like an entry in a **HashMap** is uniquely identified by a key.

An object name is represented by the **javax.management.ObjectName** class. An object name consists of two parts, a domain and a set of key/value pairs. A domain is a string and can be an empty string. The domain is followed by a colon and one or more key/value pairs. A key is a non-empty string that must not contain any of the following characters: equal sign, comma, colon, asterisk, and question mark. The same key may only occur once in an object name.

A key and its value are separated by the equal sign, and two key/value pairs are separated by a comma. For example, the following is a valid object name with two keys:

```
myDomain:type=Car,color=blue
```

An **ObjectName** instance can also represent a property pattern for searching MBeans in an MBean server. An **ObjectName** that is a pattern uses a wildcard in its domain part or key/value pairs. A pattern **ObjectName** may have zero or more keys.

Standard MBeans

Standard MBeans are the simplest MBeans. Here are what you need to do to manage a Java object using a standard MBean.

- Create an interface named after your Java class plus the suffix **MBean**. For example, if the Java class whose objects you want to manage is called **Car**, the interface must be called **CarMBean**.
- Modify your Java class so that it implements the interface you've created.
- Create an agent. The agent class must contain an MBean server.
- Create an **ObjectName** for your MBean.
- Instantiate the MBean server.
- Register your MBean with the MBean server.

As an example , consider the following **Car** class that will be made JMX-manageable:

```
public class Car {
    private String color = "red";

    public String getColor() {
        return color;
    }
    public void setColor(String color) {
        this.color = color;
    }
    public void drive() {
        System.out.println("Baby you can drive my car.");
    }
}
```

The first step you need to do is make it implement the **CarMBean** interface. The modified **Car** class is given in Listing 14.1:

Listing 14.1: The modified Car class

```
package standard;
public class Car implements CarMBean {
    private String color = "red";
    public String getColor() {
        return color;
    }
```

```
        public void setColor(String color) {
            this.color = color;
        }
        public void drive() {
            System.out.println("Baby you can drive my car.");
        }
    }
```

Now, create the **CarMBean** interface in Listing 14.2

Listing 14.2: The CarMBean interface

```
package standard;
public interface CarMBean {
    public String getColor();
    public void setColor(String color);
    public void drive();
}
```

Basically, in the **MBean** interface you declare all the methods that you want the **Car** class to expose. In this example, the **CarMBean** interface lists all the methods in the **Car** class. If, say, you don't want the **drive** method to be available to the management application, you simply remove its definition from the **CarMBean** interface.

Finally, Listing 14.3 offers the **StandardAgent** class that is used to create a standard MBean and manage **Car** objects.

Listing 14.3: The StandardAgent class

```
package standard;
import javax.management.Attribute;
import javax.management.ObjectName;
import javax.management.MBeanServer;
import javax.management.MBeanServerFactory;

public class StandardAgent {
    private MBeanServer mBeanServer = null;
    public StandardAgent() {
        mBeanServer = MBeanServerFactory.createMBeanServer();
    }
    public MBeanServer getMBeanServer() {
        return mBeanServer;
    }
    public ObjectName createObjectName(String name) {
        ObjectName objectName = null;
        try {
```

```
            objectName = new ObjectName(name);
        } catch (Exception e) {
        }
        return objectName;
    }
    private void createStandardBean(ObjectName objectName,
            String managedResourceClassName) {
        try {
            mBeanServer.createMBean(managedResourceClassName,
                    objectName);
        } catch(Exception e) {
        }
    }
    public static void main(String[] args) {
        StandardAgent agent = new StandardAgent();
        MBeanServer mBeanServer = agent.getMBeanServer();
        String domain = mBeanServer.getDefaultDomain();
        String managedResourceClassName =
            "standard.Car";
        ObjectName objectName = agent.createObjectName(domain +
                ":type=" + managedResourceClassName);
        agent.createStandardBean(objectName,
                managedResourceClassName);
        // manage MBean
        try {
            Attribute colorAttribute = new
                    Attribute("Color", "blue");
            mBeanServer.setAttribute(objectName, colorAttribute);
            System.out.println(mBeanServer.getAttribute(objectName,
                    "Color"));
            mBeanServer.invoke(objectName,"drive",null,null);
        } catch (Exception e) {
                e.printStackTrace();
        }
    }
}
```

The **StandardAgent** class is an agent that instantiates an MBean server and uses it to register a **CarMBean** with. The first thing to note is the **mBeanServer** variable, to which the **StandardAgent** class's constructor assigns an **MBeanServer**. The constructor calls the **createMBeanServer** method of the **MBeanServerFactory** class.

```
public StandardAgent() {
```

```
    mBeanServer = MBeanServerFactory.createMBeanServer();
}
```

The **createMBeanServer** method returns a default **MBeanServer** object implemented by the JMX reference implementation. An advanced JMX programmer may wish to provide his/her own **MBeanServer** implementation. For this book, however, we're not interested in doing so.

The **createObjectName** method in the **StandardAgent** class in Listing 14.3 returns an instance of **ObjectName** based on the **String** argument passed to the method. The **createStandardMBean** method in **StandardAgent** calls the **createMBean** method of **MBeanServer**. The **createMBean** method accepts the class name of the managed resource and the **ObjectName** instance that uniquely identifies the created MBean for the managed resource. The **createMBean** method also registers the created MBean in the **MBeanServer**. Because a standard MBean follows a certain naming convention, you don't need to supply the MBean type name to the **createMBean** method. If the managed resource's class name is **Car**, then its MBean will be **CarMBean**.

The **main** method of **StandardAgent** starts off by creating an instance of **StandardAgent** and calls its **getMBeanServer** method to obtain a reference to the **MBeanServer** instance inside the **StandardAgent**.

```
StandardAgent agent = new StandardAgent();
MBeanServer mBeanServer = agent.getMBeanServer();
```

It then creates an **ObjectName** for the **CarMBean**. The **MBeanServer**'s default domain is used as the domain for the **ObjectName**. A key named **type** is appended to the domain. The value for **type** is the fully qualified name of the managed resource.

```
String domain = mBeanServer.getDefaultDomain();
String managedResourceClassName =
        "standard.Car";
ObjectName objectName = agent.createObjectName(domain + ":type=" +
        managedResourceClassName);
```

The **main** method then calls the **createStandardBean** method, passing the object name and the managed resource class name.

```
agent.createStandardBean(objectName, managedResourceClassName);
```

Next, the **main** method manages the **Car** object through the **CarMBean** instance. It creates an **Attribute** object called **colorAttribute** to represent the **Color** attribute and sets the value to blue. It then invokes the **setAttribute** method passing **objectName** and **colorAttribute**. Afterwards, it invokes the **drive** method using the **invoke** method on the **MBeanServer** object.

```
// manage MBean
try {
    Attribute colorAttribute = new Attribute("Color","blue");
    mBeanServer.setAttribute(objectName, colorAttribute);
    System.out.println(mBeanServer.getAttribute(objectName,
            "Color"));
    mBeanServer.invoke(objectName,"drive",null,null);
}
```

Running **StandardAgent** class produces this output.

```
blue
Baby you can drive my car.
```

Standard MBeans are easy to write, but they require that your classes be modified. While this is okay in some projects, in others (especially when there are many classes involved) this is not acceptable. Fortunately, other types of MBeans allow you to manage objects without modifying classes.

MXBeans

An MXBean is similar to a standard MBean, providing a convenient way to bundle related values together in an MBean without requiring clients to be configured to handle the bundles. To write an MXBean, just as you would a standard MBean, you need to create an interface that exposes methods in the JMX manageable resource. The name of this interface must end with **MXBean** (as opposed to **MBean** with standard MBeans), however the prefix does not have to match the name of the manageable class. This is to say your manageable class may be called **Car** and your **MXBean** interface may be named **TruckMXBean**.

Alternatively, if you don't want to follow the naming convention for MXBeans, i.e. you don't want your interface name to end with **MXBean**, you can simply apply the **@MXBean** annotation to your interface definition.

Java SE 5 already includes a number of **MXBeans** in the **java.lang.management** package, such as **ClassLoadingMXBean** and **MemoryMXBean**. You create instances of these MXBeans by calling static methods in he **ManagementFactory** class, such as **getClassLoadingMXBean** and **getMemoryMXBean**. With Mustang, you can define your own MXBeans, as demonstrated in the following sample application. This example shows how easy it is to create an MXBean and an agent and then demonstrates how you can read and change the value of a property through the JConsole tool.

Listing 14.4 shows the **CounterMXBean** interface that represents a bean with a **count** property. **CounterMXBean** defines the **get** and **set** methods to be exposed to the management application.

Listing 14.4: The CounterMXBean interface

```
package userdefined;
public interface CounterMXBean {
    public int getCount();
    public void setCount(int count);
}
```

The **CounterImpl** class in Listing 14.5 is the implementation class of **CounterMXBean**.

Listing 14.5: The CounterImpl class

```
package userdefined;
public class CounterImpl implements CounterMXBean {
    private int count = 0;
    public int getCount() {
        return ++count;
    }
    public void setCount(int count) {
        this.count = count;
    }
}
```

The **MXBeanDemo** class in Listing 14.6 is an agent that creates an instance of **CounterImpl** and an instance of **MBeanServer** and registers the **MXBean** with the server.

Listing 14.6: The MXBeanDemo class

```
package userdefined;
import java.lang.management.ManagementFactory;
```

```
import javax.management.MBeanServer;
import javax.management.ObjectName;
public class MXBeanDemo {
    public static void main(String[] args) throws Exception {
        // Create a CounterMXBean
        CounterMXBean mxBean = new CounterImpl();
        // Create an ObjectName for mxBean
        ObjectName objectName = new
                ObjectName("mymxbean:name=counter");
        // Get an MBeanServer
        MBeanServer server = ManagementFactory.
                getPlatformMBeanServer();
        // Register mxBean with MBeanServer
        server.registerMBean(mxBean, objectName);
        // Prevent program from exiting
        System.out.println("Press enter to exit ...");
        System.in.read();
    }
}
```

Notice that the last line of the **MXBeanDemo** class prevents the program from exiting so that we can read and manipulate the **count** property value through JConsole. Since we're going to use JConsole to manage the MXBean, you need to run the **MXBeanDemo** class with the -D option.

```
java -Dcom.sun.management.jmxremote userdefined/MXBeanDemo
```

Now, run JConsole by running the **jconsole** program in the **bin** directory of your JDK installation. Figure 14.1 shows the first window that JConsole displays.

JConsole can be used to manage local MBeans or remote MBeans. If you're running JConsole in the same machine as the MXBean, you will see your MXBean (**userdefined/MXBeanDemo**) in the list under Local Process. Select the MXBean and click the **Connect** button. When it's connected, click the **MBeans** tab and you will see a window similar to Figure 14.2.

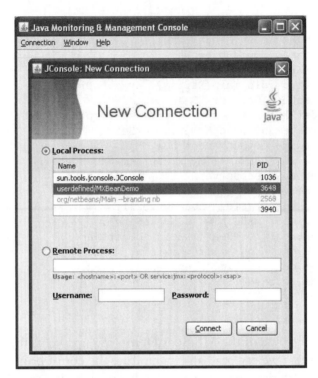

Figure 14.1: The JConsole main window

In the left window you will see your MXBean. Click the **count** attribute and you will see the detailed information about the MXBean. Initially, the **count** property will have the value of 1, as shown on the right pane. Since invoking **getCount** increments the **count** property value, clicking the **Refresh** button changes this value.

Using @MXBean

Mustang introduces the **MXBean** annotation to decorate an MXBean. The advantage of using **@MXBean** is that your MXBean interface does not have to have an **MXBean** suffix on its name. The following example is similar to the previous MXBean example, but uses **@MXBean** to decorate the **Counter** interface in Listing 14.7 to indicate that it is an MXBean.

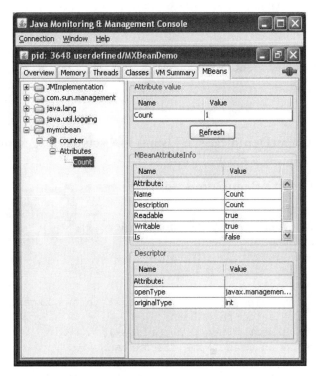

Figure 14.2: Manging the CounterMXBean

Listing 14.7: The Counter interface

```
package withannotation;
import javax.management.MXBean;
@MXBean
public  interface Counter {
    public int getCount();
    public void setCount(int count);
}
```

Note that the **Counter** interface in Listing 14.7 is decorated with **@MXBean**.

The **CounterImpl** class in Listing 14.8 is an implementation of Counter that is identical to the **CounterImpl** class in Listing 14.5.

Listing 14.8: The CounterImpl class

```
package withannotation;
public class CounterImpl implements Counter {
    private int count = 0;
```

```
public int getCount() {
    return ++count;
}

public void setCount(int count) {
    this.count = count;
}
}
```

Finally, the **MXBeanDemo** class in Listing 14.9 acts as an agent for this example.

Listing 14.9: The MXBeanDemo class

```
package withannotation;
import java.lang.management.ManagementFactory;
import javax.management.MBeanServer;
import javax.management.ObjectName;

public class MXBeanDemo {
    public static void main(String[] args) throws Exception {
        // Create a CounterMXBean
        Counter mxBean = new CounterImpl();
        // Create an ObjectName for mxBean
        ObjectName objectName = new
                ObjectName("mymxbean:name=counter");
        // Get an MBeanServer
        MBeanServer server = ManagementFactory.
                getPlatformMBeanServer();
        // Register mxBean with MBeanServer
        server.registerMBean(mxBean, objectName);
        // Prevent program from exiting
        System.out.println("Press enter to exit this demo ...");
        System.in.read();
    }
}
```

You can run the **MXBeanDemo** class and use JConsole to inspect your **MXBean**. It behaves similarly to the MXBean in the preceding example.

Using @DescriptorKey

@DescriptorKey is a meta annotation that has been added to Mustang. It makes it easy to add a descriptor to an MXBean element. At runtime you can retrieve a descriptor by first obtaining the **MBeanInfo** object of the MBean, by calling the **getMBeanInfo** method on the **MBeanServer**.

```
MBeanInfo mbeanInfo = server.getMBeanInfo(objectName);
```

Calling the **getAttributes** method on an **MBeanInfo** instance returns an array of **MBeanAttributeInfo**s. Once you get the appropriate **MBeanAttributeInfo** instance (by first checking its name), you can call its **getDescriptor** method to obtain the **Descriptor** object describing your MBean. Here is a snippet that shows how to retrieve a **Descriptor** object.

```
// Get all attributes
for (MBeanAttributeInfo attributeInfo : mbeanInfo.getAttributes()) {
    String attributeName = attributeInfo.getName();
    if (attributeName.equalsIgnoreCase(attributeName)) {
        Descriptor descriptor = attributeInfo.getDescriptor();
```

Let's now study an example of **@DescriptorKey**.

The methods in the **Note** and **Range** annotation types in Listing 14.10 and Listing 14.11, respectively are emblazoned with **@DescriptorKey**.

Listing 14.10: The Note interface

```
package descriptor;
import java.lang.annotation.Documented;
import java.lang.annotation.ElementType;
import java.lang.annotation.Retention;
import java.lang.annotation.RetentionPolicy;
import java.lang.annotation.Target;
import javax.management.DescriptorKey;

@Documented
@Target(ElementType.METHOD)
@Retention(RetentionPolicy.RUNTIME)
public @interface Note {
    @DescriptorKey("note")
    String value();
}
```

Listing 14.11: The Range interface

```
package descriptor;
import java.lang.annotation.Documented;
import java.lang.annotation.ElementType;
import java.lang.annotation.Retention;
import java.lang.annotation.RetentionPolicy;
import java.lang.annotation.Target;
import javax.management.DescriptorKey;

@Documented
@Target(ElementType.METHOD)
@Retention(RetentionPolicy.RUNTIME)
public @interface Range {

    @DescriptorKey("minValue")
    public int minValue();

    @DescriptorKey("maxValue")
    public int maxValue();
}
```

You can use **@Note** and **@Range** user-defined descriptors to decorate an MBean element. For example, the **Car** interface in Listing 14.12 is an MXBean that defines a method (**getNumberOfDoors**) that is decorated with **@Note** and **@Range**.

Listing 14.12: The Car interface

```
package descriptor;
import javax.management.MXBean;
@MXBean
public interface Car {
    // Use user-defined descriptors
    @Note("Not including the hidden one")
    @Range(minValue=0, maxValue=5)
    public int getNumberOfDoors();
}
```

The **CarImpl** class in Listing 14.13 is an implementation class of the **Car** MXBean.

Listing 14.13: The CarImpl class

```
package descriptor;
```

```
public class CarImpl implements Car {
    private int count = 5;
    public int getNumberOfDoors() {
        return count;
    }

    public void setCount(int count) {
        this.count = count;
    }
}
```

Finally, the **MXBeanDemo** class in Listing 14.14 is the class that puts everything together and shows how you can retrieve the **Descriptor** objects.

Listing 14.14: The MXBeanDemo class

```
package descriptor;
import java.lang.management.ManagementFactory;
import javax.management.Descriptor;
import javax.management.MBeanAttributeInfo;
import javax.management.MBeanInfo;
import javax.management.MBeanServer;
import javax.management.ObjectName;

public class MXBeanDemo {
    public static void main(String[] args) throws Exception {
        // Create an instance of CarMXBean
        CarImpl mxBean = new CarImpl();
        // Create ObjectName for mxBean
        ObjectName objectName = new ObjectName(
                "mymxbean:name=with_descriptor");

        // Get MBeanServer from ManagementFactory
        MBeanServer server = ManagementFactory.
                getPlatformMBeanServer();

        // Register MXBean with MBeanServer
        server.registerMBean(mxBean, objectName);

        // Get MBeanInfo
        MBeanInfo mbeanInfo = server.getMBeanInfo(objectName);

        // Get all attributes
        for (MBeanAttributeInfo attributeInfo :
            mbeanInfo.getAttributes()) {
```

```
              String attributeName = attributeInfo.getName();
              if (attributeName.equalsIgnoreCase("numberOfDoors")) {
                  System.out.println("Attribute " + attributeName);
                  Descriptor descriptor =
                          attributeInfo.getDescriptor();
                  System.out.println("Note = " +
                          descriptor.getFieldValue("note"));
                  System.out.println("minValue = " +
                          descriptor.getFieldValue("minValue"));
                  System.out.println("maxValue = " +
                          descriptor.getFieldValue("maxValue"));
              }
          }
      }
}
```

The output of the demo class is as follows.

```
Attribute NumberOfDoors
Note = Not including the hidden one
minValue = 0
maxValue = 5
```

Summary

JMX is a standard API for managing and monitoring Java objects. The JMX technology enables you to write Java objects called MBeans for exposing properties and methods in a Java object. There are five types of MBeans and one of them is the MXBean.

MXBeans have actually been part of the Java SE since version 5. Tiger includes pre-defined MXBeans in the **java.lang.management** package. Mustang, however, lets you write user-defined MXBeans. This chapter showed you how to achieve that and explained how to use the annotation types **@MXBean** and **@DescriptorKey**.

Chapter 15
Concurrency Updates

The Concurrency Utilities, introduced with the release of Tiger, is comprised of the interfaces and classes in the **java.util.concurrent** package and its subpackages. It reduces programming effort and increases performance. More importantly, it spares you from having to deal with low-level concurrency primitives such as the **wait**, **notify**, and **notifyAll** methods in **java.lang.Object** as well as the **synchronized** and **volatile** keywords. These primitives are notorious for being difficult to use correctly.

The Concurrency Utilities includes concurrent implementations of several members of the Collections Framework. Mustang adds more to the stack by introducing, among others, the **BlockingDeque** interface. This interface is the focus of discussion in this chapter. In addition, this chapter covers the new methods in the **TimeUnit** enum and the new constructor in **ConcurrentHashMap**.

BlockingDeque

A blocking deque, represented by the **java.util.concurrent.BlockingDeque** interface, is a deque that waits to become non-empty before retrieving an element and waits for space to become available before storing an element. A blocking deque is thread-safe and does not permit null elements. **BlockingDeque** is a subinterface of **java.util.concurrent.BlockingQueue** (that was added to JDK 1.5) and **java.util.Deque**, also a new addition to Mustang and was discussed in Chapter 1, "Core Libraries."

The following methods are members of **BlockingDeque**.

```
public boolean offer(E element, long timeout, TimeUnit unit)
```
Inserts the specified element as the last element of the deque. If the deque is full, this method will wait until the specified period of time. It

throws a **java.lang.InterruptedException** if it is interrupted while waiting.

```
public boolean offerFirst(E element, long timeout, TimeUnit unit)
```
Inserts the specified element as the first element of the deque. If the deque is full, this method will wait until the specified period of time. It throws a **java.lang.InterruptedException** if it is interrupted while waiting.

```
public boolean offerLast(E element, long timeout, TimeUnit unit)
```
Inserts the specified element as the last element of the deque. If the deque is full, this method will wait until the specified period of time. It throws a **java.lang.InterruptedException** if it is interrupted while waiting.

```
public E takeFirst()
```
Retrieves and removes the first element of this deque. If the deque is empty, it will wait until an element becomes available. It throws a **java.lang.InterruptedException** if it is interrupted while waiting.

```
public E takeLast()
```
Retrieves and removes the last element of this deque. If the deque is empty, it will wait until an element becomes available. It throws a **java.lang.InterruptedException** if it is interrupted while waiting.

```
public E pollFirst(long timeout, TimeUnit unit)
```
Retrieves and removes the first element of this deque. If the deque is empty, it will wait for the specified wait time until an element becomes available. It throws a **java.lang.InterruptedException** if it is interrupted while waiting.

```
public E pollLast(long timeout, TimeUnit unit)
```
Retrieves and removes the last element of this deque. If the deque is empty, it will wait for the specified wait time until an element becomes available. It throws a **java.lang.InterruptedException** if it is interrupted while waiting.

The **java.util.concurrent.LinkedBlockingDeque** class is the only implementation of the **BlockingDeque** interface that comes with Mustang. You can use one of these constructors to create an instance of **LinkedBlockingDeque**.

```
public LinkedBlockingDeque()
```

```
public LinkedBlockingDeque(java.util.Collection<? extends E> c)
public LinkedBlockingDeque(int capacity)
```

Note that the last constructor allows you to specify a fixed capacity for the **BlockingDeque**.

The following example shows a producer and a consumer that both access the same **BlockingDeque**. The **BlockingDeque** has a capacity of five. The producer adds an Integer to the **BlockingDeque** once every 300 milliseconds. The consumer takes an element from it every 3,000 milliseconds. If the producer runs frequently enough, after 1500 milliseconds or so it will find the **BlockingDeque** full and will have to wait. The example demonstrates this scenario.

The producer is represented by the **Producer** class in Listing 15.1. When creating an instance, you need to pass a name (for logging purpose) and the **BlockingDeque** it will populate.

Listing 15.1: The Producer class

```
package blockingdequedemo;
import java.util.concurrent.BlockingDeque;

public class Producer implements Runnable {
    private String name;
    private BlockingDeque<Integer> deque;
    private int[] numbers = { 1, 2, 3, 4, 5, 6, 7, 8, 9, 10 };

    public Producer(String name, BlockingDeque<Integer> deque) {
        this.name = name;
        this.deque = deque;
    }

    public void run() {
        for (int i = 0; i < 10; i++) {
            try {
                deque.putFirst(numbers[i]);
                System.out.println(name + " puts " + numbers[i]);
                System.out.println(name + " prints data: " + deque +
                        "\n");
                Thread.sleep(300);
            } catch (InterruptedException e) {
                e.printStackTrace();
            }
        }
```

```
        }
    }
}
```

The **Producer** class contains an array of integers named **numbers** and implements the **run** method of **Runnable** to store the elements of **numbers** one at a time each in every 300ms using the **BlockingDeque**'s **putFirst** method.

The **Consumer** class is similar to **Producer**. However, instead of storing data in the **BlockingDeque**, it consumes. The **Consumer** class is given in Listing 15.2.

Listing 15.2: The Consumer class

```
package blockingdequedemo;
import java.util.concurrent.BlockingDeque;

public class Consumer implements Runnable {
    private String name;
    private BlockingDeque<Integer> deque;

    public Consumer(String name, BlockingDeque<Integer> deque) {
        this.name = name;
        this.deque = deque;
    }

    public void run() {
        for (int i = 0; i < 10; i++) {
            try {
                int j= deque.takeLast();
                System.out.println(name + " takes " + j);
                System.out.println(name + " prints data: " + deque +
                        "\n");
                Thread.sleep(3000);
            } catch (InterruptedException e) {
                e.printStackTrace();
            }
        }
    }
}
```

The **Consumer** class calls the **BlockingDeque**'s **takeLast** method to consume the last element in it. It sleeps for 3,000 milliseconds before retrieving the next element in the **BlockingDeque**.

Finally, there is a **Tester** class that puts everything together. It constructs a **Producer** and a **Consumer** and pass the same **BlockingDeque** to both of them. The **Tester** class is shown in Listing 15.3.

Listing 15.3: The Tester class

```
package blockingdequedemo;
import java.util.concurrent.BlockingDeque;
import java.util.concurrent.LinkedBlockingDeque;

public class Tester {

    public static void main(String[] args) {
        // create a blocking deque with a capacity of 5
        BlockingDeque<Integer> deque =
                new LinkedBlockingDeque<Integer>(5);

        // create a producer and a consumer
        Runnable producer = new Producer("Producer", deque);
        Runnable consumer = new Consumer("Consumer", deque);

        // run the producer and consumer
        new Thread(producer).start();
        new Thread(consumer).start();
    }
}
```

The **Tester** class creates a **Producer** object and a **Consumer** object and then runs the producer first before running the consumer. Compiling and running the **Tester** class will gives you the following output.

```
Producer puts 1
Producer prints data: [1]

Consumer takes 1
Consumer prints data: []

Producer puts 2
Producer prints data: [2]

Producer puts 3
Producer prints data: [3, 2]

Producer puts 4
Producer prints data: [4, 3, 2]
```

```
Producer puts 5
Producer prints data: [5, 4, 3, 2]

Producer puts 6
Producer prints data: [6, 5, 4, 3, 2]

Producer puts 7
Consumer takes 2
Consumer prints data: [7, 6, 5, 4, 3]

Producer prints data: [7, 6, 5, 4, 3]

Producer puts 8
Producer prints data: [8, 7, 6, 5, 4]

Consumer takes 3
Consumer prints data: [8, 7, 6, 5, 4]

Consumer takes 4
Consumer prints data: [8, 7, 6, 5]

Producer puts 9
Producer prints data: [9, 8, 7, 6, 5]

Producer puts 10
Producer prints data: [10, 9, 8, 7, 6]

Consumer takes 5
Consumer prints data: [10, 9, 8, 7, 6]

Consumer takes 6
Consumer prints data: [10, 9, 8, 7]

Consumer takes 7
Consumer prints data: [10, 9, 8]

Consumer takes 8
Consumer prints data: [10, 9]

Consumer takes 9
Consumer prints data: [10]

Consumer takes 10
Consumer prints data: []
```

Since the **Producer** started first, the first lines of output were these:

```
Producer puts 1
Producer prints data: [1]
```

After storing the first element, the **Producer** slept for 300 milliseconds. The **Consumer** started almost at the same time and grabbed the only data in the **BlockingDeque**, leaving it empty:

```
Consumer takes 1
Consumer prints data: []
```

Then, the **Consumer** slept for 3,000 milliseconds and the **Producer** woke up. Note that the **Producer** ran 10 times faster than the **Consumer**, so the former could easily fill all the empty spaces in the **BlockingDeque** without distraction from the latter. However, the **BlockingDeque** blocked after it was full, i.e. after there were five elements in it.

```
Producer puts 2
Producer prints data: [2]

Producer puts 3
Producer prints data: [3, 2]

Producer puts 4
Producer prints data: [4, 3, 2]

Producer puts 5
Producer prints data: [5, 4, 3, 2]

Producer puts 6
Producer prints data: [6, 5, 4, 3, 2]
```

At this point, the **BlockingDeque** was filled to capacity. However, the **Producer** had no idea about it and called the **BlockingDeque**'s **putFirst** method again. This time the method did not return right away, until the **Consumer** woke up about 1,500 milliseconds later and consumed an element from the **BlockingDeque**.

Back to the output, the next lines are a bit confusing because it looks as if the **Producer** had managed to store an element to the already full **BlockingDeque**.

```
Producer puts 7
```

```
Consumer takes 2
Consumer prints data: [7, 6, 5, 4, 3]

Producer prints data: [7, 6, 5, 4, 3]
```

How do you explain this? Bear in mind that the following lines in the **Consumer** class are not atomic:

```
int j= deque.takeLast();
System.out.println(name + " takes " + j);
System.out.println(name + " prints data: " + deque + "\n");
```

Since two threads (the producer thread and the consumer thread) were competing to get hold of the **System.out** object, a race condition occurred and the result was unpredictable. In other words, there was no guarantee that the next event after the **takeLast** method was invoked was the execution of the **System.out.println** method printed in bold above. Recall that at that time the **putFirst** method invoked by the **Producer** thread was blocking, and it seems that as soon as a slot was vacant in the **BlockingDeque**, the **putFirst** method returned and the **Producer** thread managed to invoke **System.out.println** before the **Consumer** thread could. Had the three lines above been atomic, the message would have been this.

```
Consumer takes 2
Consumer prints data: [6, 5, 4, 3]

Producer puts 7
Producer prints data: [7, 6, 5, 4, 3]
```

The next lines also explained the occurrence of a race condition:

```
Producer puts 8
Producer prints data: [8, 7, 6, 5, 4]

Consumer takes 3
Consumer prints data: [8, 7, 6, 5, 4]
```

If only each thread had had its own **System.out**, the message would have been this:

```
Consumer takes 3
Consumer prints data: [7, 6, 5, 4]

Producer puts 8
Producer prints data: [8, 7, 6, 5, 4]
```

Nevertheless, the example above has proven that a **BlockingDeque** may block on **putFirst** when it's full.

TimeUnit enum

Java 5 added the **java.util.concurrent.TimeUnit** enum that is useful in concurrent operations. This enum represents time durations at a given unit of granularity. In addition, there are also methods for converting across units and performing timing and delay operations in these units. In Java 6 this enum has the following new methods: **toDays**, **toHours**, and **toMinutes**.

As an example, the code in Listing 15.4 shows how to use the **toMinutes**, **toHours**, and **toDays** methods in **TimeUnit**.

Listing 15.4: Using new methods in TimeUnit

```
import java.util.concurrent.TimeUnit;
public class TimeUnitDemo {

    public static void main(String[] args) {
        TimeUnit tu = TimeUnit.DAYS;
        StringBuilder sb = new StringBuilder();
        sb.append(tu.toDays(1) + " days = ");
        sb.append(tu.toHours(1) + " hours = ");
        sb.append(tu.toMinutes(1) + " minutes");
        System.out.println(sb);
    }
}
```

Running the **TimeUnitDemo** class prints the following message on your console.

```
1 days = 24 hours = 1440 minutes
```

ConcurrentHashMap

The **java.util.concurrent.ConcurrentHashMap** class was a new class in Java 5. It is similar to the **java.util.Hashtable** minus the locking for data retrieval

methods that make **Hashtable** not recommended for use. In Java 6
ConcurrentHashMap adds a new constructor:

```
public ConcurrentHashMap(int initialCapacity, float loadFactor)
```

The **ConcurrentHashMapDemo** class in Listing 15.5 demonstrates the use
of the new constructor.

Listing 15.5: Using ConcurrentHashMap

```
import java.util.concurrent.ConcurrentHashMap;
public class ConcurrentHashMapDemo {
    public static void main(String[] args) {
        ConcurrentHashMap map = new ConcurrentHashMap(10, 0.8f);
    }
}
```

Summary

Mustang brings with it several useful updates to the Concurrency Utilities,
most notably the **BlockingDeque** interface and its implementation the
LinkedBlockingDeque class. In this chapter you learned how to use
BlockingDeque to solve the classic producer-consumer problem that, prior
to Concurrency Utilities, required careful and intricate use of low-level
concurrency primitives to resolve.

Appendix A
Enums

Java 5 added a new type, enum, for enumerating values. With this new type, you can say goodbye to static final fields that so far have been used as constants. However, enum is much more than a substitute for static finals and this appendix presents this new type in detail.

Introduction to enum

You use enum to create a set of valid values for a field or a method. For example, in a typical application, the only possible values for the **customerType** are **Individual** or **Organization**. For the **State** field, valid values may be all the states in the US plus Canadian provinces, and some others. With **enum**, you can easily restrict your program to take only one of the valid values.

An enum type can stand alone or can be part of a class. You make it stand alone if it needs to be referenced from multiple places in your application. If it is only used from inside a class, enum is better made part of the class.

For example, consider the **CustomerType** enum definition in Listing A.1.

Listing A.1: The CustomerType enum

```
public enum CustomerType {
    INDIVIDUAL,
    ORGANIZATION
}
```

The **CustomerType** enum has two enumerated values: **INDIVIDUAL** and **ORGANIZATION**. Enum values are case sensitive and by convention are capitalized. Two enum values are separated by a comma and values can be written on a single line or multiple lines. The enum in Listing A.1 is written in multiple lines to improve readability.

Having an enum is like having another type. For example, the **Customer** class in Listing A.2 has three fields, one of which (the **customerField**) is of type **CustomerType**.

Listing A.2: The Customer class that uses CustomerType

```
public class Customer {
    public String customerName;
    public CustomerType customerType;
    public String address;
}
```

You can use a value in an enum just like you would a class's static final member. For example, this code illustrates the use of **CustomerType**.

```
Customer customer = new Customer();
customer.customerType = CustomerType.INDIVIDUAL;
```

Notice how the **customerType** field of the **Customer** object is assigned the enumerated value **INDIVIDUAL** of the **CustomerType** enum? Because the **customerType** field is of type **CustomerType**, it can only be assigned a value of the **CustomerType** enum.

The use of enum at first glance is no difference than the use of static finals. However, there are some basic differences between enums and classes incorporating static finals.

Static finals are not a perfect solution for something that should accept only predefined values. For example, consider the **CustomerTypeStaticFinals** class in Listing A.3.

Listing A.3: Using static finals

```
public class CustomerTypeStaticFinals {
    public static final int INDIVIDUAL = 1;
    public static final int ORGANIZATION = 2;
}
```

Suppose you have a class named **OldFashionedCustomer** that resembles the **Customer** class in Listing A.2, but uses **int** for its **customerType** field.

The following code creates an instance of **OldFashionedCustomer** and assigns a value to its **customerType** field:

```
OldFashionedCustomer ofCustomer = new OldFashionedCustomer();
ofCustomer.customerType = 5;
```

Notice that there is nothing preventing you from assigning any value of integer, including one that is not valid. This shows that using static finals does not restrict the value of the **customerType** field. In guaranteeing that a variable is assigned only a valid value, enums are better than static finals.

Another difference is that an enumerated value is an object. Therefore, it behaves like an object. For example, you can use it as a **Map** key. The section, "The Enum Class" discusses enums as objects in further detail.

Enums in a Class

You can use enums as members of a class. You use this approach if the enum is only used internally inside the class. For example, the **Shape** class in Listing A.4 defines a **ShapeType** enum.

Listing A.4: Using an enum as a class member

```
public class Shape {
    private enum ShapeType {
        RECTANGLE, TRIANGLE, OVAL
    };
    private ShapeType type = ShapeType.RECTANGLE;
    public String toString() {
        if (this.type == ShapeType.RECTANGLE) {
            return "Shape is rectangle";
        }
        if (this.type == ShapeType.TRIANGLE) {
            return "Shape is triangle";
        }
        return "Shape is oval";
    }
}
```

The java.lang.Enum Class

When you define an enum, the compiler creates a class definition that extends the **java.lang.Enum** class. This class is a direct descendant of **java.lang.Object**. Unlike ordinary classes, however, an enum has the following properties:

- There is no public constructor, making it impossible to instantiate.
- It is implicitly static
- There is only one instance for each enum constant.
- You can call the method values on an enum in order to iterate over its enumerated values. See the next section "Iterating over Enumerated Values" for more details on this.

Iterating over Enumerated Values

You can iterate over the values in an enum by using the enhanced **for** loop. You first need to call the **values** method that returns an array-like object that contains all values in the specified enum. Using the **CustomerType** enum in Listing A.1, you can use the following code to iterate over it.

```
for (CustomerType customerType : CustomerType.values() ) {
    System.out.println(customerType);
}
```

This prints all values in **CustomerType**, starting from the first value. Here is the result:

```
INDIVIDUAL
ORGANIZATION
```

Switching on Enum

Since Java 5 the **switch** statement can also work on enumerated values of an enum. Here is an example using the **CustomerType** enum in Listing A.1 and the **Customer** class in Listing A.2:

```
Customer customer = new Customer();
customer.customerType = CustomerType.INDIVIDUAL;

switch (customer.customerType) {
case INDIVIDUAL:
    System.out.println("Customer Type: Individual");
    break;
case ORGANIZATION:
    System.out.println("Customer Type: Organization");
    break;
}
```

Note that you must *not* prefix each case with the enum type. The following would raise a compile error:

```
case CustomerType.INDIVIDUAL:
    //
case CustomerType.ORGANIZATION:
    //
```

Appendix B
Generics

Generics are the most important feature in Java 5. They enable you to write a type (a class or an interface) and create an instance of it by passing a reference type or reference types. The instance will then be restricted to only working with the type(s). For instance, the **java.util.List** interface has been made generic in Java 5. When creating a **List** object, you pass a Java type to it and produce a **List** instance that can only work with objects of that type. That is, if you pass **java.lang.String**, the **List** instance can only hold **String** objects; if you pass **java.lang.Integer**, the instance can only store **Integer** objects. In addition to parameterized types, you can create parameterized methods too.

The first benefit of generics is stricter type checking at compile time . This is most apparent in the Collections Framework. In addition, generics eliminate most type castings you had to perform when working with the Collections Framework in pre-5 Java releases.

This appendix teaches you how to use and write generic types. It starts with the section "Life without Generics", which reminds us what we missed in earlier versions of JDK's. Then, it presents some examples of generic types. After the discussions of the syntax and the use of generic types with bounds, this chapter concludes with a section that explains how to write generic types.

Life without Generics

All Java classes derive from **java.lang.Object**, which means all Java objects can be cast to **Object**. Because of this, in pre-Tiger JDK's many methods in the Collections Framework accept an **Object** argument. This way, the collections become general-purpose utility types that can hold objects of any type. This imposes unpleasant consequences.

For example, the **add** method of **List** in pre-5 JDK's accepts an **Object** argument:

```
public boolean add(java.lang.Object element)
```

As a result, you can pass an object of any type to **add**. The use of **Object** is by design. Otherwise, it could only work with a specific type of objects and there would then have to be different **List** types, e.g. **StringList**, **EmployeeList**, **AddressList**, etc.

The use of **Object** in **add** is fine, but consider the **get** method, that returns a member element of a **List** instance. Here is its signature prior to Java 5.

```
public java.lang.Object get(int index)
        throws IndexOutOfBoundsException
```

get returns an **Object**. Here is where the unpleasant consequences start to kick in. Suppose you have stored two **String** objects in a **List** named **stringList1**:

```
List stringList1 = new ArrayList();
stringList1.add("Java 5");
stringList1.add("with generics");
```

When retrieving a member from **stringList1**, you get an instance of **java.lang.Object**. In order to work with the original type of the member element, you must first downcast it to **String**.

```
String s1 = (String) stringList1.get(0);
```

With generic types, you can forget about type casting when retrieving objects from a **List**. And, there is more. Using the generic **List** interface in Java 5 and Java 6, you can create **List** instances with special purposes. For example, you can create a **List** instance that only accepts **String** objects, another that only accepts **Employee** objects, and so on.

Introducing Generic Types

Like a method, a generic type can accept parameters too. This is why a generic type is often called a parameterized type. Instead of passing primitives or object references in parentheses as with methods, you pass reference types in angle brackets to generic types.

Declaring a generic type is like declaring a non-generic one, except that you use angle brackets to enclose the list of type variables for the generic type.

```
MyType<typeVar1, typeVar2, ...>
```

For example, to declare a **java.util.List** in Java 5 and Java 6, you write

```
List<E> myList;
```

E is called a type variable, namely a variable that will be replaced by a type. The value substituting for a type variable will then be used as the argument type or the return type of a method or methods in the generic type. For the **List** interface, when an instance is created, E will be used as the argument type of **add** and other methods. E will also be used as the return type of **get** and other methods. Here are the signatures of **add** and **get**.

```
public boolean add<E o>
public E get(int index)
```

Note

A generic type that uses a type variable E allows you to pass E when declaring or instantiating the generic type. Additionally, if E is a class, you may also pass a subclass of E; if E is an interface, you may also pass a class that implements E.

If you pass **String** to a declaration of **List**, as in

```
List<String> myList;
```

the **add** method of the **List** instance referenced by **myList** will expect a **String** object as its argument and its **get** method will return a **String**. Because **get** returns a specific type of object, no downcasting is required.

Note

By convention, you use a single uppercase letter for type variable names.

To instantiate a generic type, you pass the same list of parameters as when declaring it. For instance, to create an **ArrayList** that works with **String**, you pass **String** in angle brackets.

```
List<String> myList = new ArrayList<String>();
```

As another example, **java.util.Map** is defined as

```
public interface Map<K, V>
```

K is used to denote the type of map keys and *V* the type of map values. The
put and **values** methods have the following signatures:

```
public V put(K key, V value)
public Collection<V> values()
```

Note

A generic type must not be a direct or indirect child class of
java.lang.Throwable because exceptions are thrown at runtime, and
therefore it is not possible to check what type of exception that might
be thrown at compile time.

As an example, Listing B.1 compares **List** in JDK 1.4 and in Tiger/Mustang.

Listing B.1: Working with generic List

```
import java.util.List;
import java.util.ArrayList;

public class GenericListTest {
    public static void main(String[] args) {
        // in JDK 1.4
        List stringList1 = new ArrayList();
        stringList1.add("Java 6");
        stringList1.add("with generics");
        // cast to java.lang.String
        String s1 = (String) stringList1.get(0);
        System.out.println(s1.toUpperCase());

        // now with generics in JDK 5 and JDK 6
        List<String> stringList2 = new ArrayList<String>();
        stringList2.add("Java 6");
        stringList2.add("with generics");
        // no need for type casting
        String s2 = stringList2.get(0);
        System.out.println(s2.toUpperCase());
    }
}
```

In Listing B.1, **stringList2** is a generic **List**. The declaration **List<String>** tells the compiler that this instance of **List** can only hold **String** objects. Of course, in other occasions, you can create instances of **List** that work with other types of objects. Note, though, that when retrieving member elements of the **List** instance, no downcasting is necessary because its **get** method returns the intended type, namely **String**.

Note

With generic types, type checking is done at compile time.

What's interesting here is the fact that a generic type is itself a type and can be used as a type variable. For example, if you want your **List** to store lists of strings, you can declare the **List** by passing **List<String>** as its type variable, as in

```
List<List<String>> myListOfListsOfStrings;
```

To retrieve the first string from the first list in **myList,** you would use:

```
String s = myListOfListsOfStrings.get(0).get(0);
```

Listing B.2 presents the **ListOfListsTest** class that demonstrates a **List** (named **listOfLists**) that accepts a **List** of **String** objects.

Listing B.2: Working with List of Lists

```
import java.util.ArrayList;
import java.util.List;
public class ListOfListsTest {
    public static void main(String[] args) {
        List<String> listOfStrings = new ArrayList<String>();
        listOfStrings.add("Hello again");
        List<List<String>> listOfLists =
                new ArrayList<List<String>>();
        listOfLists.add(listOfStrings);
        String s = listOfLists.get(0).get(0);
        System.out.println(s); // prints "Hello again"
    }
}
```

Additionally, a generic type can accept more than one type variables. For example, the **java.util.Map** interface has two type variables. The first defines the type of its keys and the second the type of its values. Listing B.3 presents an example of how to use a generic **Map**.

Listing B.3: Using the generic Map

```
import java.util.HashMap;
import java.util.Map;
public class MapTest {
    public static void main(String[] args) {
        Map<String, String> map = new HashMap<String, String>();
        map.put("key1", "value1");
        map.put("key2", "value2");
        String value1 = map.get("key1");
    }
}
```

In Listing B.3, to retrieve a value indicated by **key1**, you do not need to perform type casting.

Using Generic Types without Type Parameters

Now that the collection types in Java 5 and later have been made generic, what about legacy codes that used the same types? Fortunately, they will still work in Tiger and Mustang because you can use generic types without type parameters. For example, you can still use the **List** interface the old way, as demonstrated by the following part of Listing B.1.

```
List stringList1 = new ArrayList();
stringList1.add("Java 6");
stringList1.add("with generics");
String s1 = (String) stringList1.get(0);
```

A generic type used without parameters is called a raw type. This means that code written for JDK 1.4 and earlier versions will continue working in Java 5 and Java 6.

One thing to note, though. The Java 5 and Java 6 compilers expect you to use generic types with parameters. Otherwise, the compilers will issue warnings, thinking that you may have forgotten to define type variables with the generic type. For example, compiling the code in Listing B.1 gave you the following warning because the first **List** was used as a raw type.

```
Note: GenericListTest.java uses
   unchecked or unsafe operations.
Note: Recompile with -Xlint:unchecked for details.
```

You have these options at your disposal if you do not want to get warnings when working with raw types:

- compile with the **−source 1.4** flag.
- use the **@SupressWarnings("unchecked")** annotation (See Appendix C, "Annotations")
- upgrade your code to use **List<Object>**. Instances of **List<Object>** can accept any type of object and behave like a raw type **List**. However, the compiler will not complain.

Warning

Raw types are available for backward compatibility. New development should shun raw types. It is possible that future versions of Java will not allow raw types.

Using the ? Wildcard

I mentioned that if you declare a **List<*aType*>**, the **List** instance works with instances of *aType* and you can store objects of one of these types:

- an instance of *aType*.
- an instance of a subclass of *aType*, if *aType* is a class
- an instance of a class implementing *aType* if *aType* is an interface.

Note, however, that a generic type is a Java type by itself, just like **java.lang.String** or **java.io.File**. Passing different lists of type variables to a generic type result in different types. For example, **list1** and **list2** below reference to different types of objects.

```
List<Object> list1 = new ArrayList<Object>();
List<String> list2 = new ArrayList<String>();
```

list1 references a **List** of **java.lang.Object** instances and **list2** references a **List** of **String** objects. Even though **String** is a subclass of **Object**, **List<String>** has nothing to do with **List<Object>**. Therefore, passing a **List<String>** to a method that expects a **List<Object>** will raise a compile time error. Listing B.4 shows this.

Listing B.4: AllowedTypeTest.java

```java
import java.util.ArrayList;
import java.util.List;

public class AllowedTypeTest {
    public static void doIt(List<Object> l) {
    }
    public static void main(String[] args) {
        List<String> myList = new ArrayList<String>();
        // this will generate a compile error
        doIt(myList);
    }
}
```

Listing B.4 won't compile because you passed the wrong type to the method **doIt. doIt** expects an instance of **List<Object>** and you are passing an instance of **List<String>**.

The solution to this problem is the **?** wildcard. **List<?>** means a list of objects of any type. Therefore, the **doIt** method should be changed to:

```java
public static void doIt(List<?> l) {
}
```

There are circumstances where you want to use the wildcard. For example, if you have a **printList** method that prints the members of a **List**, you may want to make it accept a **List** of any type. Otherwise, you would end up writing many overloads of **printList**. Listing B.5 shows the **printList** method that uses the **?** wildcard.

Listing B.5: Using the ? wildcard

```java
import java.util.ArrayList;
import java.util.List;

public class WildCardTest {
    public static void printList(List<?> list) {
        for (Object element : list) {
            System.out.println(element);
        }
    }
    public static void main(String[] args) {
        List<String> list1 = new ArrayList<String>();
        list1.add("Hello");
        list1.add("World");
```

```
        printList(list1);

        List<Integer> list2 = new ArrayList<Integer>();
        list2.add(100);
        list2.add(200);
        printList(list2);
    }
}
```

The code in Listing B.5 demonstrates that **List<?>** in the **printList** method means a **List** of any type.

Note, however, it is illegal to use the wildcard when declaring or creating a generic type, such as this.

```
List<?> myList = new ArrayList<?>(); // this is illegal
```

If you want to create a **List** that can accept any type of object, use **Object** as the type variable, as in the following line of code:

```
List<Object> myList = new ArrayList<Object>();
```

Using Bounded Wildcards in Methods

In the section "Using the ? Wildcard" above, you learned that passing different type variables to a generic type creates different Java types, despite a parent-child relationship between the type variables. In many cases, you may want a method to accept a **List** of different types. For example, if you have a **getAverage** method that returns the average of numbers in a list, you may want to pass a list of integers or a list of floats or a list of another number type. However, if you write **List<Number>** as the argument type to **getAverage**, you won't be able to pass a **List<Integer>** instance or a **List<Double>** instance because **List<Number>** is a different type from **List<Integer>** or **List<Double>**. You can use **List** as a raw type or use a wildcard, but this is depriving you of type safety checking at compile time because you can also pass a list of anything, such as an instance of **List<String>**. You could use **List<Number>**, but you must always pass a **List<Number>** to the method. This would make your method less useful because you work with **List<Integer>** or **List<Long>** probably more often than with **List<Number>**.

Java 5 adds another rule to circumvent this restriction, i.e. by allowing you to define an upper bound of a type variable. This way, you can pass a type or its subtype. In the case of the **getAverage** method, you may be able to pass a **List<Number>** or a **List** of instances of a **Number** subclass, such as **List<Integer>** or **List<Float>**.

The syntax for using an upper bound is as follows:

```
GenericType<? extends upperBoundType>
```

For example, for the **getAverage** method, you would write:

```
List<? extends Number>
```

Listing B.6 illustrates the use of such a bound.

Listing B.6: Using a bounded wildcard

```java
import java.util.ArrayList;
import java.util.List;
public class BoundedWildcardTest {
    public static double getAverage(
            List<? extends Number> numberList) {
        double total = 0.0;
        for (Number number : numberList) {
            total += number.doubleValue();
        }
        return total/numberList.size();
    }

    public static void main(String[] args) {
        List<Integer> integerList = new ArrayList<Integer>();
        integerList.add(3);
        integerList.add(30);
        integerList.add(300);
        System.out.println(getAverage(integerList)); // 111.0
        List<Double> doubleList = new ArrayList<Double>();
        doubleList.add(3.0);
        doubleList.add(33.0);
        System.out.println(getAverage(doubleList)); // 18.0
    }
}
```

Thanks to the upper bound, the **getAverage** method in Listing B.6 allows you to pass a **List<Number>** or a **List** of instances of any subclass of **java.lang.Number**.

Lower Bounds

The **extends** keyword is used to define an upper bound of a type variable. Though useable in very few applications, it is also possible to define a lower bound of a type variable, by using the **super** keyword. For example, using **List<? super Integer>** as the type to a method argument indicates that you can pass a **List<Integer>** or a **List** of objects whose class is a superclass of **java.lang.Integer**.

Writing Generic Types

The previous sections concentrated on using generic types, notably the ones in the Collections Framework. Now it's time to learn to write your own generic types.

Basically, writing a generic type is not much different from writing other types, except for the fact that you declare a list of type variables that you intend to use somewhere in your class. These type variables come in angle brackets after the type name. For example, the **Point** class in Listing B.7 is a generic class. A **Point** object represents a point in a coordinate system and has the X component (abscissa) and the Y component (ordinate). By making **Point** generic, you can specify the degree of accuracy of a **Point** instance. For example, if a **Point** object needs to be very accurate, you can pass **Double** as the type variable. Otherwise, **Integer** will suffice.

Listing B.7: The Point generic class

```
public class Point<T> {
    T x;
    T y;
    public Point(T x, T y) {
        this.x = x;
        this.y = y;
    }
    public T getX() {
        return x;
    }
    public T getY() {
        return y;
    }
    public void setX(T x) {
```

```
        this.x = x;
    }
    public void setY(T y) {
        this.y = y;
    }
}
```

In Listing B.7, **T** is the type variable for the **Point** class. **T** is used as the return value of both **getX** and **getY** and as the argument type for **setX** and **setY**. In addition, the constructor also accepts two **T** type variables.

Using **Point** is just like using other generic types. For example, the following code creates two **Point** objects, **point1** and **point2**. The former passes **Integer** as the type variable, the latter **Double**.

```
Point<Integer> point1 = new Point<Integer>(4, 2);
point1.setX(7);
Point<Double> point2 = new Point<Double>(1.3, 2.6);
point2.setX(109.91);
```

Appendix C
Annotations

A new feature in Java 5, annotations are notes in Java programs to instruct the Java compiler to do something. You can annotate any program elements, including Java packages, classes, constructors, fields, methods, parameters, and local variables. Java annotations are defined in JSR 175 (http://www.jcp.org/en/jsr/detail?id=175). Java 5 provided three standard annotations and four standard meta-annotations. Java 6 added dozens, discussed throughout this book.

This appendix is for you if you upgraded from JDK 1.4 to Java 6, skipping Tiger. It tells you everything you need to know about annotations and annotation types, so you won't have problems understanding Java 6 new features, which are often embellished with annotations. It starts with an overview of annotations, and then teaches you how to use the standard annotations in Java 5. It concludes with a discussion of custom annotations.

An Overview of Annotations

Annotations are notes for the Java compiler. When you annotate a program element in a source file, you add notes to the Java program elements in that source file. You can annotate Java packages, types (classes, interfaces, enumerated types), constructors, methods, fields, parameters, and local variables. For example, you can annotate a Java class so that any warnings that the **javac** program would otherwise issue be suppressed. Or, you can annotate a method that you want to override to get the compiler to verify that you are really overriding the method, not overloading it. Additionally, you can annotate a Java class with the name of the developer. In a large project, annotating every Java class can be useful for the project manager or architect to measure the productivity of the developers. For example, if all classes are annotated this way, it is easy to find out who is the most or the least productive programmer.

The Java compiler can be instructed to interpret annotations and discard them (so those annotations only live in source files) or include them in resulting Java classes. Those that are included in Java classes may be ignored by the Java virtual machine, or they may be loaded into the virtual machine. The latter type is called runtime-visible and you can use reflection to inquire about them.

Annotations and Annotation Types

When studying annotations, you will come across these two terms very often: annotations and annotation types. To understand their meanings, it is useful to first bear in mind that an annotation type is a special interface type. An annotation is an instance of an annotation type. Just like an interface, an annotation type has a name and members. The information contained in an annotation takes the form of key/value pairs. There can be zero or multiple pairs and each key has a specific type. It can be a **String**, **int**, or other Java types. Annotation types with no key/value pairs are called marker annotation types. Those with one key/value pair are often referred to single-value annotation types.

There are three annotation types in Java 5: **Deprecated**, **Override**, and **SuppressWarnings**. They are part of the **java.lang** package and you will learn to use them in the section "Built-in Annotations." On top of that, there are four other annotation types that are part of the **java.lang.annotation** package: **Documented**, **Inherited**, **Retention**, and **Target**. These four annotation types are used to annotate annotations, and you will learn about them in the section "Custom Annotation Types" later in this chapter. Java 6 adds many annotations of its own, the discussion of which can be found in many chapters in this book.

Annotation Syntax

In your code, you use an annotation differently from using an ordinary interface. You declare an annotation type by using this syntax.

```
@AnnotationType
```

or

```
@AnnotationType(elementValuePairs)
```

The first syntax is for marker annotation types and the second for single-value and multi-value types. It is legal to put white spaces between the at sign (@) and annotation type, but this is not recommended.

For example, here is how you use the marker annotation type **Deprecated**:

```
@Deprecated
```

And, this is how you use the second element for multi-value annotation type Author:

```
@Author(firstName="Ted",lastName="Diong")
```

There is an exception to this rule. If an annotation type has a single key/value pair and the name of the key is **value**, then you can omit the key from the bracket. Therefore, if the fictitious annotation type **Stage** has a single key named **value**, you can write

```
@Stage(value=1)
```

or

```
@Stage(1)
```

The Annotation Interface

Know that an annotation type is a Java interface. All annotation types are subinterfaces of the **java.lang.annotation.Annotation** interface. It has one method, **annotationType**, that returns an **java.lang.Class** object.

```
java.lang.Class<? extends Annotation> annotationType()
```

In addition, any implementation of **Annotation** will override the **equals**, **hashCode**, and **toString** methods from the **java.lang.Object** class. Here are their default implementations.

```
public boolean equals(Object object)
```
> Returns **true** if *object* is an instance of the same annotation type as this one and all members of *object* are equal to the corresponding members of this annotation.

```
public int hashCode()
```

Returns the hash code of this annotation, which is the sum of the hash codes of its members

```
public String toString()
```
    Returns a string representation of this annotation, which typically lists all the key/value pairs of this annotation.

You will use this class when learning custom annotation types later in this chapter.

Standard Annotations

Java 5 comes with three built-in annotations, all of which are in the **java.lang** package: **Override**, **Deprecated**, and **SuppressWarnings**. They are discussed in this section.

Override

Override is a marker annotation type that can be applied to a method to indicate to the compiler that the method overrides a method in a superclass. This annotation type guards the programmer against making a mistake when overriding a method.

For example, consider this class **Parent**:

```
class Parent {
    public float calculate(float a, float b) {
        return a * b;
    }
}
```

Suppose, you want to extend **Parent** and override its **calculate** method. Here is a subclass of **Parent**:

```
public class Child extends Parent {
    public int calculate(int a, int b) {
        return (a + 1) * b;
    }
}
```

The **Child** class compiles. However, the **calculate** method in **Child** does not override the method in **Parent** because it has a different signature, namely it returns and accepts **int**s instead of **float**s. In this example, a programming mistake like this is easy to spot because you can see both the **Parent** and **Child** classes. However, you are not always this lucky. Sometimes the parent class is buried somewhere in another package. This seemingly trivial error could be fatal because when a client class calls the **calculate** method on an **Child** object and passes two floats, the method in the **Parent** class will be invoked and a wrong result will be returned.

Using the **Override** annotation type will prevent this kind of mistake. Whenever you want to override a method, declare the **Override** annotation type before the method:

```
public class Child extends Parent {
    @Override
    public int calculate(int a, int b) {
        return (a + 1) * b;
    }
}
```

This time, the compiler will generate a compile error and you'll be notified that the **calculate** method in **Child** is not overriding the method in the parent class.

It is clear that **@Override** is useful to make sure programmers override a method when they intend to override it, and not overload it.

Deprecated

Deprecated is a marker annotation type that can be applied to a method or a type (class/interface) to indicate that the method or type is deprecated. A deprecated method or type is marked so by the programmer to warn the users of his code that they should not use or override the method or use or extend the type. The reason why a method or a type is marked deprecated is usually because there is a better method or type and the method or type is retained in the current software version for backward compatibility.

For example, the **DeprecatedTest** class in Listing C.1 uses the **Deprecated** annotation type.

Listing C.1: Deprecating a method

```
public class DeprecatedTest {
    @Deprecated
    public void serve() {
    }
}
```

If you use or override a deprecated method, you will get a warning at compile time. For example, Listing C.2 shows the **DeprecatedTest2** class that uses the **serve** method in **DeprecatedTest**.

Listing C.2: Using a deprecated method

```
public class DeprecatedTest2 {
    public static void main(String[] args) {
        DeprecatedTest test = new DeprecatedTest();
        test.serve();
    }
}
```

Compiling **DeprecatedTest2** generates this warning:

```
Note: DeprecatedTest2.java uses or overrides a deprecated API.
Note: Recompile with -Xlint:deprecation for details.
```

On top of that, you can use **@Deprecated** to mark a class or an interface, as shown in Listing C.3.

Listing C.3: Marking a class deprecated

```
@Deprecated
public class DeprecatedTest3 {
    public void serve() {
    }
}
```

SuppressWarnings

SuppressWarnings is used, as you must have guessed, to suppress compiler warnings. You can apply **@SuppressWarnings** to types, constructors, methods, fields, parameters, and local variables.

You use it by passing a **String** array that contains warnings that need to be suppressed. Its syntax is as follows.

```
@SuppressWarnings(value={string-1, …, string-n})
```

where *string-1* to *string-n* indicate the set of warnings to be suppressed. Duplicate and unrecognized warnings will be ignored.

The following are valid parameters to **@SuppressWarnings**:

- **unchecked**. Give more detail for unchecked conversion warnings that are mandated by the Java Language Specification.
- **path**. Warn about nonexistent path (classpath, sourcepath, etc) directories.
- **serial**. Warn about missing serialVersionUID definitions on serializable classes.
- **finally**. Warn about finally clauses that cannot complete normally.
- **fallthrough**. Check switch blocks for fall-through cases, namely cases, other than the last case in the block, whose code does not include a **break** statement, allowing code execution to "fall through" from that case to the next case. As an example, the code following the case 2 label in this **switch** block does not contain a **break** statement:

```
switch (i) {
case 1:
    System.out.println("1");
    break;
case 2:
    System.out.println("2");
    // falling through
case 3:
    System.out.println("3");
}
```

As an example, the **SuppressWarningsTest** class in Listing C.4 uses the **SuppressWarnings** annotation type to prevent the compiler from issuing unchecked and fallthrough warnings.

Listing C.4 Using @SuppressWarnings

```
import java.io.File;
import java.io.Serializable;
import java.util.ArrayList;

@SuppressWarnings(value={"unchecked","serial"})
public class SuppressWarningsTest implements Serializable {
```

```
    public void openFile() {
        ArrayList a = new ArrayList();
        File file = new File("X:/java/doc.txt");
    }
}
```

Standard Meta-Annotations

Meta annotations are annotations that are applied to annotations. There are four meta-annotation types that come standard with Java 5 that are used to annotate annotations; they are **Documented, Inherited, Retention,** and **Target.** All the four are part of the **java.lang.annotation** package. This section discusses these annotation types.

Documented

Documented is a marker annotation type used to annotate the declaration of an annotation type so that instances of the annotation type will be included in the documentation generated using Javadoc or similar tools.

For example, the **Override** annotation type is not annotated using **Documented.** As a result, if you use Javadoc to generate a class whose method is annotated **@Override,** you will not see any trace of **@Override** in the resulting document.

For instance, Listing C.5 shows the **OverrideTest2** class that uses **@Override** to annotate the **toString** method.

Listing C.5: The OverrideTest2 class

```
public class OverrideTest2 {
    @Override
    public String toString() {
        return "OverrideTest2";
    }
}
```

On the other hand, the **Deprecated** annotation type is annotated **@Documented.** Recall that the **serve** method in the **DeprecatedTest** class in Listing C.2 is annotated **@Deprecated.** Now, if you use **Javadoc** to generate the documentation for **OverrideTest2**, the details of the **serve** method in the documentation will also include **@Deprecated**, like this:

```
serve
@Deprecated
public void serve()
```

Inherited

You use **Inherited** to annotate an annotation type so that any instance of the annotation type will be inherited. If you annotate a class using an inherited annotation type, the annotation will be inherited by any subclass of the annotated class. If the user queries the annotation type on a class declaration, and the class declaration has no annotation of this type, then the class's parent class will automatically be queried for the annotation type. This process will be repeated until an annotation of this type is found or the root class is reached.

Check out the section "Custom Annotation Types" on how to query an annotation type.

Retention

@Retention indicates how long annotations whose annotated types are annotated @Retention are to be retained. The value of **@Retention** can be one of the members of the **java.lang.annotation.RetentionPolicy** enum:

- **SOURCE**. Annotations are to be discarded by the Java compiler.
- **CLASS**. Annotations are to be recorded in the class file but not be retained by the JVM. This is the default value.
- **RUNTIME**. Annotations are to be retained by the JVM so you can query them using reflection.

For example, the declaration of the **SuppressWarnings** annotation type is annotated **@Retention** with the value of **SOURCE**.

```
@Retention(value=SOURCE)
public @interface SuppressWarnings
```

Target

Target indicates which program element(s) can be annotated using instances of the annotated annotation type. The value of **Target** is one of the members of the **java.lang.annotation.ElementType** enum:

- **ANNOTATION_TYPE**. The annotated annotation type can be used to annotate annotation type declaration.
- **CONSTRUCTOR**. The annotated annotation type can be used to annotate constructor declaration.
- **FIELD**. The annotated annotation type can be used to annotate field declaration.
- **LOCAL_VARIABLE**. The annotated annotation type can be used to annotate local variable declaration.
- **METHOD**. The annotated annotation type can be used to annotate method declaration.
- **PACKAGE**. The annotated annotation type can be used to annotate package declarations.
- **PARAMETER**. The annotated annotation type can be used to annotate parameter declarations.
- **TYPE**. The annotated annotation type can be used to annotate type declarations.

As an example, the **Override** annotation type declaration is annotated the following **Target** annotation, making **Override** can only be applied to method declarations.

```
@Target(value=METHOD)
```

You can have multiple values in the **Target** annotation. For example, this is from the declaration of **SuppressWarnings**:

```
@Target(value={TYPE,FIELD, METHOD, PARAMETER,CONSTRUCTOR,
LOCAL_VARIABLE})
```

Custom Annotation Types

An annotation type is a Java interface, except that you must add an at sign before the **interface** keyword when declaring it.

```
public @interface CustomAnnotation {
}
```

By default, all annotation types implicitly or explicitly extend the
java.lang.annotation.Annotation interface. In addition, even though you can
extend an annotation type, its subtype is not treated as an annotation type.

A Custom Annotation Type

As an example, Listing C.6 shows a custom annotation type called **Author**.

Listing C.6: The Author annotation type

```
import java.lang.annotation.Documented;
import java.lang.annotation.Retention;
import java.lang.annotation.RetentionPolicy;

@Documented
@Retention(RetentionPolicy.RUNTIME)
public @interface Author {
    String firstName();
    String lastName();
    boolean internalEmployee();
}
```

Using Custom Annotation Type

The **Author** annotation type is like any other Java type. Once you import it
into a class or an interface, you can use it simply by writing

```
@Author(firstName="firstName",lastName="lastName",
internalEmployee=true|false)
```

For example, the **Test1** class in Listing C.7 is annotated **Author**.

Listing C.7: A class annotated Author

```
@Author(firstName="John",lastName="Guddell",internalEmployee=true)
public class Test1 {
}
```

Is that it? Yes, that's it. Very simple, isn't it?

The next subsection "Using Reflection to Query Annotations" shows how the **Author** annotations can be of good use.

Using Reflection to Query Annotations

In Java 5, the **java.lang.Class** has a few methods related to annotations.

```
public <A extends java.lang.annotation.Annotation> A getAnnotation
       (Class<A> annotationClass)
```
Returns this element's annotation for the specified annotation type, if present. Otherwise, returns **null**.

```
public java.lang.annotation.Annotation[] getAnnotations()
```
Returns all annotations present on this class.

```
public boolean isAnnotation()
```
Returns **true** if this class is an annotation type.

```
public boolean isAnnotationPresent(Class<? extends
       java.lang.annotation.Annotation> annotationClass)
```
Indicates whether an annotation for the specified type is present on this class

The **com.brainysoftware.jdk5.app18.custom** package includes three test classes, **Test1**, **Test2**, and **Test3**, that are annotated Author. Listing C.8 shows a test class that employs reflection to query the test classes.

Listing C.8: Using reflection to query annotations

```
public class CustomAnnotationTest {
    public static void printClassInfo(Class c) {
        System.out.print(c.getName() + ". ");
        Author author = (Author) c.getAnnotation(Author.class);
        if (author != null) {
            System.out.println("Author:" + author.firstName()
                    + " " + author.lastName());
        } else {
            System.out.println("Author unknown");
        }
    }

    public static void main(String[] args) {
        CustomAnnotationTest.printClassInfo(Test1.class);
        CustomAnnotationTest.printClassInfo(Test2.class);
        CustomAnnotationTest.printClassInfo(Test3.class);
```

```
        CustomAnnotationTest.printClassInfo(
                CustomAnnotationTest.class);
    }
}
```

When run, you will see the following message in your console:

```
Test1. Author:John Guddell
Test2. Author:John Guddell
Test3. Author:Lesley Nielsen
CustomAnnotationTest. Author unknown
```

Index